The Lesbian Menace

The Lesbian Menace

Ideology, Identity, and the
Representation of Lesbian Life

Sherrie A. Inness

University of Massachusetts Press
Amherst

Copyright © 1997 by
The University of Massachusetts Press
All rights reserved
Printed in the United States of America
LC 96-53173
ISBN 1-55849-090-6 (cloth); 091-4 (pbk.)
Designed by Sally Nichols
Set in Berkeley by Keystone Typesetting, Inc.
Printed and bound by Braun-Brumfield, Inc.
Library of Congress Cataloging-in-Publication Data
Inness, Sherrie A.
    The lesbian menace : ideology, identity, and the representation of
lesbian life / Sherrie A. Inness.
        p.   cm.
    Includes bibliographical references and index.
    ISBN 1-55849-090-6 (cloth : alk. paper). —
ISBN 1-55849-091-4 (pbk. : alk. paper)
    1. American literature—20th century—History and criticism.
2. Lesbians in literature.   3. Lesbians—United States—Identity.
4. Popular culture—United States.   5. Gays in popular culture.
6. Literature and society—United States—History—20th century.
I. Title.
PS228.L47I56   1997
810.9'9206643—dc21   96-53173
                                                              CIP
British Library Cataloguing in Publication data are available.

For my mother and father
and Michele

Contents

Acknowledgments

I would like to thank a number of people who have read drafts of my book or parts of it, including Ruth Ebelke, Valija Evalds, Faye Parker Flavin, Julie Inness, Kate Johnson, Michele Lloyd, Debra Mandel, Diana Royer, Judith Russo, Kathryn Shevelow, Annette Shook, Nicole Tonkovich, and Bonnie Zimmerman. Michele Lloyd deserves special thanks for providing crucial critical support during this project; she not only read the entire work a number of times but also cowrote chapter 8 and provided input to chapter 6.

My thanks go to my friends, among them Alice Adams, Martina Barash, Nikki Barry, Sherry Darling, Cathy Ebelke, Valija Evalds, Kate Johnson, Marcy Knopf, Debra Mandel, Gillian O'Driscoll, Cindy Reuther, Wendy Walters, and my colleagues at Miami University who have helped support me intellectually and emotionally as I wrote this book. Miami University granted me a Summer Research Appointment and an Assigned Research Appointment for one semester, both of which allowed me time to develop this project. I would also like to thank the editorial staff at the University of Massachusetts Press, particularly Barbara Palmer, Bruce G. Wilcox, and Pam Wilkinson, and the library staff at Miami University, who have done much to expedite this project.

It is impossible to name all the scholars who have influenced and enriched my own academic work, but I would like to mention some who have been important: Judith Butler, Claudia Card, Sue-Ellen Case, Terry Castle, Danae Clark, Jill Dolan, Lillian Faderman, Marilyn Frye, Judith Halberstam, Karla Jay, Esther Newton, Shane Phelan, Erica Rand, Judith Roof, Eve Kosofsky Sedgwick, Catharine R. Stimpson, Martha Vicinus, Kath Weston, Bonnie Zimmerman, and Jacquelyn Zita, all of whom have helped to show me the variety and richness of approaches to lesbian studies. Susan J. Douglas, Stuart Ewen, Dick Hebdige, George Lipsitz, Tania Modleski, Janice Radway, Andrew Ross, and Susan Willis have all influenced my approach to cultural studies.

A special thank-you goes to my parents and my sister, who have always supported me. They continue to enrich and encourage my intellectual growth.

For permission to republish altered versions of my earlier work I would like to acknowledge the following journals and book:

"G.I. Joes in Barbie Land: Recontextualizing Butch in Twentieth-Century Lesbian Culture." With Michele E. Lloyd. *NWSA Journal* 7.3 (1995): 1–23.

"G.I. Joes in Barbie Land: Recontextualizing the Meaning of Butch in Twentieth-Century Lesbian Culture." With Michele E. Lloyd. Revised version. In *Queer Studies: A Lesbian, Gay, Bisexual, and Transgender Anthology*. Ed. Brett Beemyn and Mickey Eliason. New York: New York University Press, 1996. 9–34.

"Is Nancy Drew Queer?: Popular Reading Strategies for the Lesbian Reader." *Women's Studies: An Interdisciplinary Journal*. 26.3 (1997).

"Who's Afraid of Stephen Gordon? The Lesbian in the Popular Imagination of the United States." *Perversions: The International Journal of Gay and Lesbian Studies* 4 (1995): 81–111.

"Who's Afraid of Stephen Gordon? The Lesbian in the United

States Popular Imagination of the 1920s." *NWSA Journal* 4.3 (1992): 303–20.

Finally, I wish to express my gratitude to all the writers who, by finding their own voices, have helped to make this book possible: Dorothy Allison, Ann Bannon, Djuna Barnes, Natalie Barney, Alison Bechdel, Elizabeth Bishop, Rita Mae Brown, Willa Cather, Hilda Doolittle, Leslie Feinberg, Radclyffe Hall, Patricia Highsmith, Sarah Orne Jewett, Jenifer Levin, Audre Lorde, Amy Lowell, Edna St. Vincent Millay, Adrienne Rich, Sappho, May Sarton, Sarah Schulman, Gertrude Stein, Vita Sackville-West, Sylvia Townsend Warner, Christa Winsloe, Jeanette Winterson, Monique Wittig, and Virginia Woolf.

The Lesbian Menace

Introduction

Electroshock. Hysterectomy. Lobotomy.[1] These are only three of the many "cures" to which lesbians were subjected in the mid-twentieth century. "The severity of these treatments," historian John D'Emilio writes, "suggests a perception of homosexuality as a disease almost as threatening to society as the sin of Sodom that provoked the destruction of biblical cities" (18). How does a culture evolve to have such a deep-rooted aversion to a particular minority? What persuades otherwise rational people to maltreat and maim those who proclaim their homosexuality? The answers to these questions are tremendously complex and beyond the scope of the present work, but it is thinking about such issues that has led to this book. In the chapters that follow, I examine one means by which American society in the twentieth century has perpetuated cultural stereotypes about lesbians—namely, through their depiction in the popular media, including books, movies, magazines, and music.[2] *The Lesbian Menace* begins with an exploration of the ways that the dominant society has sought to promulgate the idea of a lesbian menace, implying that lesbians are sinister, sexually rapacious, vampirelike women whose only desire is to prey on innocent, unsuspecting heterosexuals.

It would be a mistake, however, to suggest that lesbians are controlled in our society solely through depicting them as evil seductresses. There are various other representational strategies that can limit the threat posed by the lesbian to the hegemonic order, which is why this book also explores seemingly more positive portrayals of lesbianism, such as its depiction in women's magazines from the 1980s and 1990s. I question whether such depictions are as challenging to the status quo as they might appear on the surface, and I show that representing a lesbian as identical or nearly identical to a heterosexual woman can be as reactionary as picturing her as a predatory vampire.

But it would be a one-sided argument if I only pointed out the ways that representational forces construct a vision of lesbians and their lives for heterosexuals. I also wish to examine the ways that lesbians manipulate and subvert texts aimed at a heterosexual audience. How can lesbians interpret mainstream texts, such as *Cosmopolitan* or a Nancy Drew novel, as doing anything other than perpetuating heterosexuality and stereotypical gender roles? Moreover, in what ways do lesbians devise their own texts in order to be active creators of their lives rather than merely spectators? These are questions that I take up in part II of *The Lesbian Menace*.

This book is not focused only on how texts help constitute lesbianism. It is also about how lesbian identities are constructed within the lesbian and gay culture. I am concerned with the ideologies from both within and without lesbian society that have shaped lesbian identities in the last century. In assessing the impact of different ideologies on lesbians, I have chosen not to separate representations and reality, because I feel that it is impossible to draw such a division and undesirable to try to do so. Beyond the texts that have influenced and continue to influence the construction of lesbian identities, I am also interested in the many other forces that affect lesbians, such as geography. Of course, a single book can deal with only a few of these elements, and there are many topics that deserve further attention. For instance, I would like to spend more time thinking about how race and class function in lesbian communities. I would also like to explore many more popular texts, such as lesbian murder mysteries and lesbian romances, than I have examined in this book.

I have trained my attention on popular culture because it is one of the most influential forces shaping lesbian identities and heterosexual perceptions of lesbianism. Many scholars in the 1990s, including Belinda Budge, Paul Burston, Corey K. Creekmur, Alexander Doty, Gabriele Griffin, Diane Hamer, Erica Rand, and Colin Richardson, have studied the intersections of gay/lesbian life and popular culture.[3] Due to the low visibility of lesbians for much of this century, even up to the present, they are particularly susceptible to being "created" by popular representations. In other words, since the dominant culture has marginalized lesbians, representations of them, such as those found in articles in *Cosmopolitan* or juvenile books, can constitute the "reality" of lesbianism for many people, particularly those who have little or no acquaintance with real lesbians. This experience, of course, is not unique to lesbians. Many minority groups, including Asian Americans and African Americans, have been "created" through representations of their lives and cultures. What is unique about lesbians and gay men is that they have an identity that is sometimes not easily visible, and they are also more stigmatized than other minority groups in the United States. Thus, even at the present moment it is possible for a large number of heterosexual Americans to claim that they have never met a "real" lesbian or gay man, whether or not that is actually the case. This real or imagined absence of the lesbian allows representations to take on unusual importance. As critic Erica Rand writes in her book *Barbie's Queer Accessories* (1995)," [C]ultural products need political attention. Political battles are fought over and through the manipulation of cultural symbols. People use them to signal political identities, to effect political coalitions, to disrupt and challenge beliefs and connections that have come to seem natural. People also glean their sense of possibility and self-worth partly from available cultural products—objects, narratives, interpretations" (5). What *Cosmopolitan* does or does not say about lesbian lives has the potential to shape how millions of readers view lesbianism, which is why in a number of my chapters I focus on how representational forms have constituted lesbianism for heterosexuals.

How representation helps to create reality is an issue that I also addressed in my previous book, *Intimate Communities: Representation and Social Transformation in Women's College Fiction, 1895–1910* (1995). Although *Intimate Communities* did not have the same explicit lesbian content that this book does, it was concerned with popular texts and how they help to constitute women's realities, an issue that lies at the heart of the chapters in the first part of *The Lesbian Menace*. Furthermore, *Intimate Communities* focused on how readers have the potential to subvert texts that at first might appear to be geared only to maintain the status quo; in a similar fashion, *The Lesbian Menace*, particularly chapter 4, is concerned with how readers subvert texts such as the Nancy Drew books that are targeted at a heterosexual audience. *Intimate Communities* was also concerned with the complex interactions between texts and the cultures that create them, again an issue that is important in *The Lesbian Menace*.

Although this book shares some of the research interests that I developed in my earlier work, there are important ways that *The Lesbian Menace* explores new territory for me. The book has been profoundly influenced by my moving from San Diego, California (I had previously lived most of my life in the San Francisco bay area, Boston, and near Northampton, Massachusetts), to the uncharted suburbs of Cincinnati, Ohio, a change in location that has made me rethink my relationship to gay/lesbian/queer culture and recognize more fully the differences that separate the many gay/lesbian communities in the United States. Living in the Midwest has made me more cognizant of the geographical specificity of lesbian communities—being a lesbian in the Midwest or on the East Coast or in the South might mean something very different. My geographical shift has forced me to reconsider some unexamined assumptions about the construction of lesbian identities and has helped shape the chapters in the last section of this book.

The Lesbian Menace addresses concerns that range historically from the 1920s to the present, rather than focusing on turn-of-the-century issues, as did *Intimate Communities*. This change reflects my

growing interest in how modern lesbian identities have been constructed and how dominant ideologies about the nature of lesbianism
have become entrenched in the twentieth century. This book, along
with the many excellent works that are being produced in what can
only be called a golden age of lesbian studies, will help readers, I hope,
to understand how lesbians have been constituted as a "menace" in
our society and how lesbians have sought to find their own meanings
in texts. I also hope this book will cause readers to examine their own
location in gay/lesbian society, questioning any assumptions they have
made about what constitutes the norm in that culture.

The first chapter focuses on two texts from the 1920s, Radclyffe
Hall's novel *The Well of Loneliness* and Edouard Bourdet's play *The
Captive*. By examining these works in the context of 1920s popular
writings about lesbianism, I explore the ways that the contemporary
audience might have reacted to the portrayal of lesbianism in Hall's
and Bourdet's works. In particular, I argue that Hall in many ways
created a heroine, Stephen Gordon, who conformed to conventional
thoughts about the masculine character of the lesbian, whereas Bourdet's feminine lesbians posed a greater threat to heterosexuality because of their ability to go unnoticed, even invading the sanctuary of
the heterosexual family. Although I do not question the subversive
possibilities posed by Hall's novel for her lesbian readers in the 1920s
and beyond, in this chapter I am primarily interested in how heterosexual readers could read the text. I examine *The Captive* along with
The Well because I am curious about the relative obscurity of the
former and the prominence of the latter.

Chapter 2 also focuses on depictions of lesbianism in the interwar years. In this chapter, I discuss popular novels written about life at
women's colleges, exploring the many ways that what was referred to
as a "lesbian menace" was depicted as associated with such institutions. I argue that fiction played a crucial role in helping to establish
the presumed linkage between women's colleges and lesbianism, a
linkage, I suggest, that has been used throughout much of this century
to downplay and disparage the unity and strength of women's colleges.
By reinforcing the ideology that suggests lesbianism and single-sex
environments are connected, such novels have been used successfully

to control women and women's colleges and to discourage single-gender bonding. Like the first chapter, the second examines the ways that texts have helped and continue to help constitute lesbianism in the twentieth century, often to perpetuate stereotypes about lesbian behavior, such as the myth that lesbians are predatory vampires who prey on heterosexual women.

Chapter 3 continues to focus on how lesbianism is constituted at least partially through its textual representation. By studying the depiction of lesbians in contemporary women's magazines, such as *Cosmopolitan, Glamour, Mademoiselle, Redbook,* and *Vogue,* I demonstrate the ways that the media construct an image of the lesbian that assures heterosexual readers that lesbians are actually not much different from heterosexual women. Examining the changing depiction of lesbianism in these magazines, as well as others, from the late 1960s to the 1990s, I argue that these magazines helped to inform readers about the socially desirable attitudes to adopt toward lesbianism. Moreover, these magazines, which are read by huge audiences, also have had a role in altering how heterosexual readers perceive lesbianism in the 1990s.

Part I explores how popular texts help constitute an image of the lesbian that is aimed primarily at heterosexual consumers, although homosexual readers can also read these texts and carry away very different messages than those intended. Part II considers the myriad ways that lesbians subvert texts intended for a heterosexual audience or create their own texts to describe lesbian lives and experiences. The focus here is on how a unique lesbian perspective is created. The lesbian perspective, according to Julia Penelope, "demands heterodoxy, deviant and unpopular thinking, requires us to love ourselves for being outcasts, to create for ourselves the grounds of our being" ("The Lesbian" 50). Heterodoxy and deviancy are at the heart of the two chapters in Part II as they explore the diverse ways that lesbians approach texts. Certainly, it might be considered by some "deviant" to analyze the Nancy Drew books as queer, which is the focus of chapter 4. These novels, which have been popular reading for many lesbians, reveal a great deal about how lesbians read texts that, at least on the surface, seem to appeal specifically to the interests of heterosexuals. This chapter argues that lesbian readers redesign the Drew books, looking at them from a distinctly "queer" perspective that emphasizes the homoeroticism of the women's community depicted in the books, understands the relationship between George and Beth as mimicking a lesbian relationship, and notes Nancy's autonomy from men. By interviewing dozens of lesbian readers, I was able to understand better the ways that lesbians redesigned these texts. The relationship between lesbians and apparently heterocentric texts is an important one since lesbians, after all, are submerged in a marketplace where the vast majority of texts are heterocentric. Thus it is as important to understand how lesbians can refashion such texts as it is to explore the ways that lesbians read texts written by and for a lesbian audience.

Chapter 5 addresses the depiction of lesbians in children's literature. Children's books are a particularly intriguing area of study because they, like all books, are not ideologically innocent. In his book *Criticism, Theory, and Children's Literature* (1991), theorist Peter Hunt aptly describes the common assumption that children's books are innocent: "We fail to see not only that we cannot be apolitical, but also that much of the ideology in and around children's books is hidden— and indeed often masquerades as the opposite of what it really is" (142). Children's books have become a battleground for defending adult ideas about the nature of homosexuality, with political conservatives grouped on one side and liberals on the other. Neither is willing to give an inch, and each side is convinced that winning the war is imperative. This chapter explores this battleground because the books being fought over are a fruitful source for studying changing societal attitudes toward lesbianism. In particular, I am interested in examining how the image of lesbianism in children's books has changed in the last two decades and whether that change has been entirely positive. I suggest that many lesbian juvenile books, despite their often positive portrayal of lesbians, are still entrapped in the genre conventions of books aimed at heterosexual readers.

The chapters in Part III scrutinize the ways that lesbians, themselves a marginalized group, have created a society that, in turn, relegates some of its members to the outskirts. One of the most significant ways that lesbians have been marginalized is through their relationship to geography, an issue at the heart of chapter 6. Geography often has been overlooked in queer studies, I argue, and scholars need to examine more closely how lesbians (and gay men) are shaped and influenced by their geographical and spatial locatedness. This chapter also points out the dominance of certain cities and towns (i.e., San Francisco, New York, Northampton, and Fire Island) in constituting what I label "queer geography." I examine what it would mean to question the dominance of these locations and whether such questioning would result in a more equitable understanding of the diversity of gay and lesbian experiences in the United States. This chapter draws on my personal experience because I have been led to reflect on the differences between various geographical locations, having moved from California to the Midwest, a move that took me from what is commonly regarded as the center of lesbian/gay life to what is typically regarded as the margin. The chapter explores what it means for a culture to have a center and a periphery and urges readers to reflect on how geography and space have helped to constitute their own lives.

Chapter 7 was one of the most difficult to write because it caused me to question my earlier thoughts about passing and its significance for lesbians. I had assumed that passing was an unmitigated evil that should be abolished, but when I thought about the issue more closely, I recognized how complex an issue passing actually is. It is not one experience but many. I examine the variety of ways that lesbians pass, arguing that all lesbians pass in one fashion or another, even if only reluctantly. This chapter calls for new attention to the vast number of ways that passing works and questions whether it is desirable to perceive passing as a bipolar term. I also suggest that some forms of passing might be less blameworthy than others and explore the different levels of accessibility people have to passing.

The final chapter, which I cowrote with Michele Lloyd, studies the marginalization of butch identity by theorists and other writers who have shown far more interest in butch-femme identity than in butch identity or butch-butch identity. This elision has created a one-sided portrait of the butch, often assuming that she is only part of the dyadic butch-femme system rather than an autonomous identity. This chapter wrestles with the thorny problem of how a butch should be defined, trying to arrive at a definition that allows for variety in self-expression but still signifies the butch's uniqueness. In many ways the thoughts in chapter 8 are a continuation of those I develop in chapter 1. In the first chapter I discuss the power of the feminine lesbian to subvert the social order, and in the last I show how the masculine lesbian can also be a subversive force. Rather than contradicting one another, these two chapters in tandem reveal the potential for subversion held by lesbians who adopt remarkably different forms of self-presentation.

More than anything else, I hope that this book disturbs my readers. If reading *The Lesbian Menace* makes people think more closely about how lesbian identities have been constructed in the twentieth century and how ideologies both within and without the gay and lesbian communities have shaped and continue to shape lesbian experiences, it will have been successful.

1

Inventing the Lesbian

1
Who's Afraid of Stephen Gordon?

The Lesbian in the United States
Popular Imagination of the 1920s

Radclyffe Hall's novel about lesbianism, *The Well of Loneliness* (1928),
is commonly regarded as a text that scandalized heterosexual readers
when first published. James Douglas, London editor of the *Sunday
Express,* was one of many who considered Hall's work shocking. "I
would rather give a healthy boy or a healthy girl a phial of prussic acid
than this novel," he commented (qtd. in Brittain 57). But was Stephen
Gordon, the heroine of the novel, such a new and disruptive portrayal
of the lesbian? Into what preestablished discourses about lesbianism
did she fit? Other critics have argued that *The Well* marked the start of
public discourse about lesbianism, but I suggest that this literary work
was only one example of many popular representations of the mannish lesbian, a figure that was well established when the text was first
published.[1] By examining *The Well* in the context of popular ideology
about the character of the lesbian and by looking at another 1920s text
about lesbianism, Edouard Bourdet's 1926 play *The Captive (La Prison-*

nière), we can better understand that, far from being radical, Stephen Gordon represented an almost comfortingly conventional lesbian image. In actuality, for the heterosexual audience of the 1920s, the feminine portrayal of the lesbian in *The Captive* was far more disturbing than the mannish Stephen Gordon of *The Well*.[2]

Despite their differing portrayals of lesbians, the two works share some striking similarities. Both appeared in the United States at almost the same time, slightly more than two years apart.[3] *The Captive* was hailed by critics as the first play on the American stage to deal openly with what one reviewer called a "repulsive abnormality" (Carb 82).[4] Similarly, *The Well* was considered by Havelock Ellis to be the first novel to present "in a completely faithful and uncompromising form, one particular aspect of sexual life as it exists among us to-day" (qtd. in Radclyffe Hall, n.p.). Both works were censored.[5] *The Well* triggered one of the most famous British court cases about censorship; it also faced obscenity charges in the United States.[6] *The Captive* met a similar fate; after a run of less than five months, the play was raided and closed down by police.[7]

One glaring difference exists between these texts: Whereas *The Captive* fell into obscurity, *The Well* became the best-selling and best-known lesbian novel of the twentieth century.[8] According to Jeffrey Weeks, Radclyffe Hall "more than anyone else during this period gave lesbianism a name and an image" (117). From 1928 through the 1960s, *The Well* was the one novel most frequently sought out by the lesbian wanting to know more about her sexual orientation. Historian Lillian Faderman states simply, "There was probably no lesbian in the four decades between 1928 and the late 1960's capable of reading English or any of the eleven languages into which the book was translated who was unfamiliar with *The Well of Loneliness*" (*Surpassing* 322).[9] Even lesbians who have not read *The Well* are likely to be familiar with Stephen's role as the prototypical mannish lesbian.

Critics have sought to explain the unquestionable dominance of *The Well* in the literary market by focusing on the relationship between the lesbian reader and this novel. They have tried to account for the book's popularity with lesbians by emphasizing its radical portrayal of the mannish lesbian and her obvious sexuality. For instance,

Jeffrey Weeks explains the appeal of the masculine image of Radclyffe
Hall (and Stephen Gordon): "Only by asserting one's identity so vehe-
mently, as Radclyffe Hall recognized, could you begin to be noticed
and taken seriously" (115). Esther Newton also stresses how the lesbian reader of *The Well* identified with Stephen's mannish image as an
affirmation of lesbian sexuality. It is worthwhile to define some of the
reasons for the popularity of the book with lesbian readers; but to understand *The Well's* popularity more fully, one must consider a broader
readership.[10] The 20,000 copies of this novel that were sold in its first
month probably cannot be explained by 20,000 lesbians descending
upon their local bookstores.[11] Instead of focusing on the lesbian reader
or the small group of elite readers who argued for and against *The Well*
in its court trials, I seek to understand how the large heterosexual
audience of this novel contextualized it in the 1920s, and into what
popular discourses about lesbianism the novel fits.[12] Esther Newton
writes that "Stephen [Gordon] is trapped in history" ("Mythic" 570);
in this chapter I try to re-create some of this history.

It is only with insight into how heterosexuals might have read
this novel that we can fully understand why many lesbians and gay
men in the 1920s and 1930s were critical of the text. For example, in
1934, Henry Gerber called *The Well* "ideal anti-homosexual propa-
ganda" (qtd. in Katz 405). Some gays disliked the novel's stereotyped
lesbians, feeling that the book was what Violet Trefusis called a "loath-
some example" (qtd. in Faderman, *Surpassing* 322). Many lesbians
feared that heterosexuals would understand Stephen Gordon as confirming rather than challenging the lesbian's isolation from "normal"
society. Gays and lesbians perceived *The Well* as portraying a lesbian
who reinforced heterosexual assumptions about the mannish character of the lesbian. Stephen is, as Newton has pointed out, "the most
infamous mannish lesbian" ("Mythic" 559), but actually she is only
the refinement of an image that had existed in popular ideology since
the 1880s and was particularly well defined in the 1920s.

On the other hand, the lesbian that *The Captive* portrayed was
not so familiar to American heterosexuals. Attractive, feminine, and
seductive, she contrasts sharply with handsome, boyish Stephen Gordon and is less easily separated from heterosexual society. The play

dismantles the idea of the lesbian as the easily recognizable Other (i.e., the mannish lesbian) and, instead, portrays a lesbian prototype that, I would suggest, was much more threatening to society than the masculinized Stephen Gordon. This "new" lesbian is a heterosexually desirable woman who can drain a man financially, emotionally, and physically, yet maintain her lesbianism even when given the option of "joining" heterosexual society through marriage. She is a trickster figure, a woman who slyly pretends to be what she is not: a member of the heterosexual community.

To obtain a better understanding of the position of the lesbian in 1920s culture, we must examine social perceptions of the lesbian before this period and analyze why public interest in homosexuals reached a high point in the 1920s. There are records of women adopting masculine garb and behaviors hundreds of years before the 1800s, but such women were not classified as lesbians. Although some early nineteenth-century French writers, such as Théophile Gautier and Balzac, described a linkage between lesbianism and masculine women, it was only in the 1880s and 1890s that a definite pathology began to be constructed by medical professionals to categorize such women as lesbians. Sexologists, including Richard von Krafft-Ebing and Havelock Ellis, described lesbians who could be easily distinguished from heterosexual women because of their masculine carriage, dress, and actions. One might even say that Krafft-Ebing and Ellis not only described the mannish lesbian but also created her by giving "scientific sanction to tradition" (Newton, "Mythic" 565). The sexologists devised a detailed scientific discourse that made the connection between masculinity in women and lesbianism unmistakable.

In Ellis's case histories of lesbians, he writes that the "commonest characteristic of the sexually inverted woman is a certain degree of masculinity or boyishness" (*Studies* 244). The "degree of masculinity" is not always visible to the untrained individual but is readily apparent to the expert. For example, one lesbian's body appears feminine, "But with arms, palms up, extended in front of her with inner sides of hands touching, she cannot bring the inner sides of [her] forearms together, as nearly every woman can, showing that the feminine angle of arm is lost" (229). Ellis justifies society's need for trained medical professionals (such as Ellis himself) who are able to categorize correctly the abnormal. In his taxonomy of the lesbian, even a slight sign of masculinity can be interpreted as signifying a woman's lesbianism.

After Ellis's *Studies in the Psychology of Sex* was published in 1897 and widely read in professional circles, educators, physicians, psychologists, and psychiatrists were provided with a discourse that could be used to categorize women who deviated from feminine norms as potential or actual lesbians. The general public, however, was not so quick to make this connection. For example, in her 1901 article, "Women Who Have Passed as Men," Marian West does not mention the sexual identification of the women she describes, only commenting that they must have wished to pursue masculine opportunities and have had a "lust for martial glory" (274). Evidently she never speculated whether these women were sexually perverse, and the popular periodical *Munsey's* published her article apparently without a qualm.[13] West's article is only one example of society's viewing mannish women as social deviants but not necessarily as sexual deviants.

One reason the general American public did not openly connect mannish women with lesbianism before the early 1920s is relatively simple: The books that provided information about the lesbian were mostly medical books—ponderous, expensive tomes written in medical jargon, which were supposed to be distributed only to physicians and other medical professionals. These books could not have been better designed for a restricted readership. For example, Krafft-Ebing used a scientific title, technical terms, and Latin to make *Psychopathia Sexualis* (1886) virtually inaccessible to a mass audience. Thus the ideas of Krafft-Ebing, Ellis, and other sexologists were disseminated, but mostly to a limited, elite group. (Although small, this group wielded disproportionate influence over the way others would come to perceive lesbianism.)

At the end of the 1910s, a limited network of professionals was informed about the perceived linkage between the masculine woman and lesbianism. By the early 1920s, however, this connection was broadly recognized, as information about lesbians and gay men had become more readily available to the general public. In particular,

Freud's theories, which I shall discuss later, gained a popularity never achieved by the earlier sexologists' ideas (Faderman, *Surpassing* 314). Watered-down versions of his works appeared in countless mass-market periodicals, in pseudoscientific publications, and in self-help literature. As Faderman points out, writers of popular literature "regurgitated" Freud's writings on lesbianism for the general public (*Surpassing* 315). Through popularized versions of Freud such as Dr. Joseph Collins's *The Doctor Looks at Love and Life* (1926) or somewhat more scholarly studies like Wilhelm Stekel's *Homosexual Neurosis* (1922), the information about homosexuality that was available to the public slowly began to grow.[14]

The spread of these popular Freudian texts was only one example of a larger fascination with homosexuality. In the 1920s, lesbianism was understood as a problem that concerned both lesbians *and* the mass heterosexual audience. In 1928, S. D. Schmalhausen commented: "the world has suddenly awakened to the startlingly wide existence among persons of high and low degree of homosexual attachments" (51). Fred Allen similarly describes intellectuals as "all agog over the literature of homosexuality" (234). Although it is an overstatement to say the whole world was aware of lesbianism, it was discussed much more openly and by a far larger audience in the 1920s than even a decade earlier. This increased popular interest in homosexuality can be understood as a logical outcome of the era's fascination with Freud and with sexuality in general; Schmalhausen remarked about the Freudian emphasis on sexuality that it "may almost be said to have created a new psychology of attention" (50). Did this signify more or less tolerance of homosexuality? Sonja Ruehl views this increased interest as "liberal" because it transformed homosexuality from an individual problem into a social problem (28), overlooking the fact that classifying homosexuality as a social problem is one way in which it can be more exactly charted and policed by the social body. More attention was directed toward lesbianism, but it was heterosexual attention, which confirmed a representation of the lesbian that justified her status as an outcast from the community.

The new interest in popular psychology created an apparent boom in lesbianism. In the 1920s and early 1930s, many popular

Freudian works depicted homosexuality as growing rampantly. Maurice Chideckel and Olga Knopf, writing in 1935, each point out the increase in lesbianism:

> Unreserved homosexuality characterized the lives of many ladies of the generations that preceded ours, and it is more prevalent in our own day than ever before. (Chideckel 4)

> It would be far from complete if, in discussing the relationships between women in modern society, we neglected to mention the recent increase in homosexuality, among both men and women. (Knopf 157)

Phyllis Blanchard, writing in 1924, mentions the "increasing role which homosexuality is coming to play in the life of the modern girl" (169). Although it is difficult to know whether lesbianism was actually growing more prevalent in this period, certainly the representation of lesbianism was becoming more overt.[15] Chideckel's, Knopf's, and Blanchard's statements show the growing social unease over the status of women, particularly the young bourgeois women of the 1920s who sought more sexual freedom and personal independence than their mothers had ever dreamed of. In eras such as the 1890s, 1920s, or early 1970s, when women have sought to gain new social powers, they have at the same time been stigmatized by society as lesbians. Similarly, in groups of women agitating for change, lesbianism has often been perceived as increasing. At times of profound social upheaval, popular ideology constructs an image of the lesbian that serves a primarily conservative function, reminding women that they would be operating outside the heterosexual norm if they persisted in their rebellion. Furthermore, the conservative construction of the lesbian always accentuates her mannish character, emphasizing that she has departed from what society perceives as woman's proper femininity.

It is in this environment of heightened scrutiny of homosexuality that *The Well of Loneliness* first appeared. An extensive summary of the novel is unnecessary, but a brief synopsis might be useful to refresh the memory of those who have not read the novel recently. Stephen Gordon is the only daughter of a wealthy English gentleman. When she is still a child, Stephen is recognized to be a congenital invert by her father, Sir Philip Gordon. She has all the telltale signs: a crush on the maid, a boyish appearance, and a love of athletics. Stephen has an affair with a married woman, who rejects her in favor of a man. When Stephen's mother hears of this "disgraceful" affair, she banishes her daughter from Morton, her ancestral home. While an ambulance driver during World War I, Stephen meets and falls in love with Mary Llewellyn, and after the war Mary moves in with Stephen. Mary, however, is not a "true" invert; when she develops a close friendship with Martin (a man who had once asked Stephen to marry him), Stephen pretends to be having a love affair with another woman so that Mary will leave her and seek happiness with Martin. Although Mary at first does not wish to go, Stephen convinces her to leave because Stephen feels that she is unable to provide Mary with the social acceptance that she would gain from a relationship with a man. The novel ends with Stephen's tortured plea to God, "We have not denied You, then rise up and defend us. Acknowledge us, oh God, before the whole world. Give us also the right to our existence!" (437).

To ascertain how the mass heterosexual audience reacted to this novel in the 1920s, we must contextualize the novel within popular ideology about homosexuality. In particular, I shall focus on three recurring ideas about lesbians from popular medical literature of the 1920s and 1930s: (1) They can be identified by their mannish appearance, including their clothing and their low-pitched voices; (2) they can easily recognize one another—even while wearing socially acceptable female clothing; and (3) they are always exceedingly unhappy. After analyzing how *The Well* works to affirm these stereotypical notions, I shall examine Bourdet's play more closely, exploring how *The Captive* projected a more radical and much more frightening image of the lesbian than did *The Well* for the heterosexual audience of the time. In this light the subsequent suppression of *The Captive* and the continued popularity and publication of *The Well* becomes not a fluke but a clear example of how the heterosexual-dominated market supports an image of the lesbian that helps to confirm dominant ideology while firmly suppressing an image of the liminal lesbian.

Stephen Gordon's masculinity is apparent in her name, her physique, and her attire. When Mary investigates Stephen's room, she observes "a long, neat line of suits," "orderly piles of shirts, crêpe de

Chine pyjamas—quite a goodly assortment," hand-knitted silk ties, and "the heavy masculine underwear that for several years now had been worn by Stephen" (*The Well* 322). To Stephen, this wardrobe holds the ritual supplies necessary to maintain her lesbian identity. Her clothing must also be understood in terms of pre–World War II beliefs held by heterosexual readers that the "woman homosexual likes to dress like a man, and makes every effort to appear like one" (Podolsky 373). According to Olga Knopf, "In certain circles a custom has arisen of wearing what might almost be called a homosexual uniform—a severely masculine suit with men's shirts or mannish blouses to match. It was not originally a fashion confined to homosexuals; but nowadays, if one sees a young woman who has previously dressed like everybody else suddenly take to this uniform, one will hardly go wrong if one guesses that she has become a homosexual and is advertising the change" (165). According to Knopf, the lesbian's "severely masculine" and "mannish" attire identifies her as a woman who is aping a man, trying to be what she can never truly be. Her choice of clothing frees Stephen from stereotyped femininity only to imprison her in the stereotyped mannishness of the lesbian. Moreover, from Knopf's point of view, Stephen Gordon's masculine garb advertises her sexual proclivity. It is expected that the heterosexual reader would see Stephen's clothes as a way of making explicit her alienation and self-definition outside the norms of heterosexual society.

But how disturbing was Stephen's action? The lesbian who stood out from the crowd in the 1920s and 1930s because of her masculine attire fit neatly into the established popular discourse about what *all* lesbians wore. Rather than seeking to re-form Stephen Gordon by forcing her to adopt feminine fashions, heterosexual society better served its interests by allowing her to wear mannish clothing, distinguishing her visually from heterosexuals. In this way, a semiotics of lesbianism is created in which the sign "lesbian" functions only if a woman is defined by masculine attire. Thus, Hall helped construct an image of the lesbian that could be contextualized within popular heterosexual ideology. In 1886, Krafft-Ebing wrote, "Uranism may nearly always be suspected in females wearing their hair short, or who dress in the fashion of men" (398); in this later period, Hall simply affirmed the validity of Krafft-Ebing's description. It would have been much more frightening to the heterosexual reader if Stephen Gordon had defied contextualization by *not* wearing masculine clothing.

Even if Stephen altered her clothing style to conform to feminine norms, her deep voice would still mark her as irretrievably outside the heterosexual fold. Other lesbians in *The Well* also have voices that give them away: Dickie's voice is "a little too hearty" (381); Margaret Roland, despite her feminine appearance, is betrayed by a voice that has "something peculiar about it. It [is] like a boy's voice on the verge of breaking" (351). Radclyffe Hall traps the lesbian in her role; even if she chooses to deny or hide her sexual identification, the lesbian's voice acts as a transcendent signifier of her lesbianism. Although this identifying mark, as Esther Newton states, could be useful for a lesbian seeking to make herself visible to another woman ("Mythic" 565), it also conforms to then-current heterosexist ideas about how the homosexual could be identified by her (or his) voice.

Dr. Chideckel goes further than Radclyffe Hall in describing a lesbian who is given away by her voice. He claims that not only the timbre of one's voice but also the manner of speaking is revelatory. In his opinion, the wearing of clothing "appropriate" to one's gender is not sufficient to hide homosexuality; what clothing conceals, speech reveals: "Great care is exercised by many homosexuals in their speech so as not to betray themselves. Some will give themselves away by their talk. Their speech is sexualized. Sexualization of language is an old established fact. This always goes along with sexualization of thinking. The homosexual unconsciously finds a magnetic quality in words, and derives gratification from utterances" (121).[16] Both Hall, with her lesbian characters who give themselves away with something not quite right about their voices, and Chideckel, with his much more detailed construction of "sexualized" speech, succeed in defining the lesbian as a woman who can neither escape nor long conceal her sexual orientation. Chideckel does not cite a particular homosexual vocabulary but, instead, refers to all homosexual speech as sexualized. The lesbian is so completely imbued with her sexuality that it creeps into her speech, pinpointing her more definitely than would a class or foreign accent. Chideckel creates an image of a lesbian who is never acceptable, even if she, like Stephen, possesses an impeccable class background.

If the lesbian can identify another lesbian by her masculine clothing or by her sexualized voice, what happens if a woman is dressed in conventional feminine attire and has laryngitis? Can she still be recognized by other lesbians and gay men? In the first half of the twentieth century, some commentators claimed homosexuals had the uncanny (but enviable) ability to spot each other in crowds. For example, Dr. Collins wrote: "Homosexuals are gifted with something akin to a sixth sense that permits them to detect their like in individuals, groups and crowds in which the normal person sees only his own kind. . . . [T]here is a kind of freemasonry between them" (73). For Collins, the freemasonry that exists among homosexuals and their possession of a sixth sense legitimized their position as social scapegoats. If lesbians have a sixth sense, as Collins suggests, they could pose a potential threat to heterosexual society, since a unified group is more dangerous to the status quo than an isolated individual. His analogy between homosexuals and freemasonry further justifies the persecution of lesbians. The Masonic order, like a group of lesbians, is a secretive organization, which appears sinister to people unfamiliar with the meaning of Masonic rituals. Like lesbianism, Masonry was perceived to be growing in the 1920s, and both were seen as threatening social order.[17] In *The Cause of World Unrest* (1920), Masonry is described as a dangerous secret society, which acts as "a disguise . . . almost impossible to penetrate" (Gwynne 10). Similar words could be used to describe lesbianism. Despite the apparent threat of Masonry and lesbianism, the Freemason's or the lesbian's allegiance to a community of similar individuals also operates to make him or her more easily visible to outsiders. For instance, a person might be identifiable as a Mason only in a gathering with other Masons. Similarly, an individual lesbian might escape detection, but a group of lesbians, such as the circle of women surrounding Djuna Barnes, is easy to recognize. A lesbian's identification with a community of other lesbians makes her appear to be a greater threat to heterosexual order but simultaneously makes her reassuringly easier to identify.

Hall suggests in *The Well* that a homosexual freemasonry might

truly exist. At a train station, Stephen notices "unmistakable figures. . . . [S]he would single them out of the crowd as by instinct"
(271). Here, Stephen has an instinct (or a sixth sense) that helps her to
distinguish other lesbians and potentially form a community with the
women with whom she identifies. Also, Stephen belongs, somewhat
marginally, to the homosexual circle that surrounds Valerie Seymour.
Thus Stephen's affiliation with a group of gays and lesbians raises the
popular specter of homosexual organization and unity.

Despite belonging to a community of similar individuals, the
lesbian was not perceived as a happy individual in the general ideology
of this period. Quite to the contrary, she never escaped her "true"
unhappiness. Chideckel claims homosexuality is "an abnormality, a
perversion, a monstrous craving for the unnatural by phantasy-fed,
mostly frantically unhappy women, with minds run riot" (163). Hall
fails to undermine this assumption explicitly, and the conclusion of
The Well seems to affirm rather than refute Chideckel's statement. The
ending (Barbara dies; Jamie commits suicide; Mary leaves Stephen)
can be interpreted in two very different ways: as a logical dénouement
to a novel dealing with "frantically unhappy women, with minds run
riot," or as a condemnation of a heterosexual society that ostracizes
lesbians. (A similar double meaning can be attributed to the novel's
title.) The lesbian reader most likely would favor reading The Well as a
condemnation of heterosexual society, but we risk ahistoricism if we
assume that the general audience of the 1920s uniformly received this
message from Hall's novel. The image of the miserable lesbian, with its
long history in the works of Krafft-Ebing, Ellis, Freud, and pseudo-
medical texts about homosexuality, was not an unfamiliar one to the
general audience of the 1920s.[18] She was most specifically contextualized, as is apparent in Chideckel's statement, as discontented because
of what was viewed as her pathology. Although condemning society
rather than the lesbian for the lesbian's outcast position might have
been Hall's intention when she wrote The Well, there is another way of
reading her novel, perhaps closer to the contemporary heterosexual
reception, that confirms rather than refutes the character of the lesbian
as pathologically unhappy.

To find a more disturbing interpretation of the 1920s lesbian, we must turn to *The Captive,* a play about two lesbians: Madame d'Aiguines, a sophisticated older woman who, though married, has been an avowed lesbian for many years, and Irene de Montcel, a beautiful, feminine young woman captivated by Madame d'Aiguines.[19] In act 1, the audience is introduced to Irene, whose father wants her to move from Paris to Rome with him. When she refuses, he is enraged and suspects that she has been having an affair with a man. Irene is forced to give him the name of Jacques Virieu, who had asked to marry her a year ago. Since he is still in love with her, Jacques reluctantly agrees to pretend to be her fiancé.

In the next act, Madame d'Aiguines's husband tells Jacques, an old school friend, the true reason Irene wants to stay in Paris. Jacques is upset but considers Irene's infatuation with Madame d'Aiguines less significant than an affair with a man. Although Irene is fascinated with Madame d'Aiguines, she does not succumb immediately to her allure and even pleads with Jacques to save her from lesbianism by marrying her. Although Irene recoils from his ardent embrace, Jacques agrees.

Act 3 takes place a year after Irene's marriage. She assures Jacques that she has not seen Madame d'Aiguines despite the older woman's attempts to get in touch with her, but he doubts her. He accuses her of being sexually cold and of not caring that his former mistress is going to stop by to visit him in the afternoon. Irene casts aside his aspersions as ridiculous. Later that day, however, she appears, looking distraught. She admits having seen Madame d'Aiguines, who was lying in wait for her, and asks Jacques to leave Paris with her. He refuses to have anything more to do with "her kind." The play concludes with Irene leaving to go to Madame d'Aiguines while Jacques leaves to renew his old relationship with his ex-mistress.

Although the audience hears about Madame d'Aiguines's beauty, she never actually appears on stage. Her presence is evoked only by the countless bunches of violets that she sends to Irene, but her absence in no way reduces the threat of what one 1920s critic called her "vivid and malignant character" (John Mason Brown 811). Her power lies in her resistance to classification; she cannot be as neatly defined as Stephen Gordon, who is inscribed by her clothing, her voice, and her "sixth sense."

To understand why the representation of the lesbian in Bourdet's work is more threatening to heterosexuals than that of the lesbian in Hall's novel, one must first understand that the image of the lesbian as a feminine, heterosexually desirable woman was not familiar to Americans, who were less exposed to the French libertine tradition of the lesbian as a beautiful older woman who seduces younger women.[20] Both the unfamiliarity of the French image and its foreign nature operate to increase Anglo-American heterosexual fears. Because the play was French, it was more socially suspect than Hall's novel, but the play's origin alone fails to explain adequately why it was perceived as so threatening. The real danger of Bourdet's lesbians lies in their conformity to stereotypical notions of femininity, giving men a false sense of the women's sexual availability.

We must also take into account the different schools of thought used to define the lesbians in both Hall's novel and Bourdet's play. Whereas Hall used Krafft-Ebing's and Ellis's theories of the congenital lesbian to define Stephen Gordon, Bourdet relied on Freud's theories about lesbianism to identify Irene. As I shall explain, Freud's beliefs about the causes of lesbianism were perceived to be far more threatening to the social order than Krafft-Ebing's and Ellis's understanding of the lesbian as a congenital fluke. Even more frightening to the heterosexual audience, Madame d'Aiguines is undefinable within any system of medical knowledge. She becomes the ultimate symbol of the liminal lesbian who threatens the domestic tranquillity of the bourgeois home.

Bourdet establishes a Freudian reason for Irene's lesbianism: She grew up without a mother. In his essay "The Transformations of Puberty" (1916), Freud wrote that the sexual activity of young girls is "particularly subject to the watchful guardianship of their mother. They thus acquire a hostile relation to their own sex which influences their object-choice decisively in what is regarded as the normal direction" (96). Since Irene has never been under the "watchful guardianship of [a] mother," she has been unable to make a "normal" object choice; yet this is not the only potential reason for her lesbianism. Her father also has a mistress, so "a sexual impression [could have] occurred which left a permanent after-effect in the shape of a tendency to homosexuality" (Freud, "Sexual" 6). Irene's homosexuality might have resulted from multiple causes, which is more unsettling to the heterosexual than the single answer provided in Hall's novel (i.e., one is born homosexual); by accepting Freud's statements about the sources of lesbianism, a woman could never feel completely secure in her sexual orientation. A tendency to homosexuality may surface at any time to challenge the tenuous grasp she has on heterosexuality.

No visual sign provides a clue to Irene's lesbianism. She is attractive, wears feminine finery, and at one point even comes on stage in a negligee to show off her feminine attributes. This is not a woman who can be described as mannish. The heterosexual viewers of this play in the 1920s were probably disturbed to discover that Helen Menken, the actress who played Irene at the Empire Theatre in New York, was costumed in a close-fitting, knee-high dress, high heels, long strands of beads, and wore a cloche. In this attire, she looked very much like a contemporary flapper. Thus lesbianism was linked to the new sexual freedom and the image of the flapper, but, unlike the mannish lesbian, the flapper-lesbian was not easily identified. How could a lesbian be separated from "normal" society if she wore the same attire as millions of young heterosexual women? One can imagine the uneasy stirrings in the audience on September 29, 1926, at the opening of *The Captive* when many women in the audience might have realized that they were dressed very much like Irene.

I have previously pointed out how linking Stephen Gordon with a homosexual community allows the heterosexual audience to single her out more easily. Irene resists being identified in this fashion. She is never portrayed with any lesbian cohorts and is represented as an independent woman who works alone in her art studio. She is not even portrayed on the stage with Madame d'Aiguines. Rather than minimizing the frightening image of the lesbian she projects, her solitary nature only makes her sexual identification more frightening because heterosexual society cannot ascertain her lesbianism by observing her relationship to other lesbians.

Madame d'Aiguines with "all the feminine allurements, every one" (150), emerges as a lesbian far more threatening to the hegemony of heterosexuality than the easily identified Stephen Gordon or the young Irene. Madame d'Aiguines's husband describes her as "the most harmonious being that has ever breathed" (150); although he knows about her lesbianism, he is unable to resist her fascination. The choice of the word "harmonious" to describe Madame d'Aiguines aptly signifies her dangerous potential to appear to be in accord with a largely heterosexual society when, in reality, her lesbianism destroys the harmony of the heterosexual household. Her lesbianism would not be so dangerous if, like Stephen, she stood out from other women as being different.

Unlike Stephen, who is no match for Martin and unable to compete against his "true" maleness, Madame d'Aiguines is more than a match for the men around her; when Jacques is relieved to find out that Irene is involved with a woman rather than a man, Monsieur d'Aiguines tells him that it is a mistake to feel this way:

> If she had a [male] lover I'd say to you: Patience. . . . But in this case I say: Don't wait! There's no use. She'll never return—and if ever your paths should cross again fly from her. . . . Otherwise you are lost! One can never overtake them! They are shadows. They must be left to dwell alone among themselves in the kingdom of shadows! Don't go near them . . . they're a menace! Above all, never try to be anything to them, no matter how little—that's where the danger lies. For, after all, they have some need of us in their lives. . . . [I]t isn't easy for a woman to get along. So if a man offers to help her . . . she accepts. . . . So long as he doesn't exact love, she's not concerned about the rest. (148–49)

The danger that Dr. Collins locates in a lesbian freemasonry Monsieur d'Aiguines finds in a "kingdom of shadows." This organized community of lesbians exists in isolation from the realm of heterosexuals. In contrast to Hall's detailed description of Stephen Gordon as a mannish lesbian, it is difficult to categorize or describe the inhabitants of this shadowy world. If "shadow" signifies both "ghost" and the dark image thrown by a human figure, the lesbian exists only as an absence. The human being whose ghost this is or whose shadow is apparent is never actually visible to men, who glimpse only the trace of a reality they can never completely comprehend.

This shadow-lesbian can be understood metaphorically as a sign of male discomfort with the growing independence and sexual expressiveness of young middle-class women in the 1920s. Critics such as Carroll Smith-Rosenberg have portrayed the flapper as a woman searching for "heterosexual pleasures" ("New Woman" 283), overlooking the apprehension men must have felt about women who bobbed their hair and bound their breasts to minimize their femininity and were disinterested in single sexual attachments to men. As Faderman states, some people feared that the suppression of a woman's secondary sexual characteristics would inevitably lead to lesbianism (*Surpassing* 339). Furthermore, with the rage for flapper fashions, a group of women did emerge whose very similarity suggested an understanding among women about which men could only wonder.

Thus Madame d'Aiguines's success in rousing Irene emotionally was a disturbing suggestion to the male of the 1920s that he was no longer a necessity in a woman's life, even for her sexual satisfaction. Madame d'Aiguines is more capable than Jacques of stirring a woman emotionally and (potentially) sexually. When Irene sees her former friend after a year of married life, Madame d'Aiguines is capable of bringing Irene to "trembling" life. Jacques is furious at Irene's obvious emotion: "Look at yourself! You're breathless—your eyes are dazed—your hands are trembling—because you've seen her again, that's why! For a year I've been living with a statue and that woman had only to reappear for the statue to come to life" (249–50). His words reflect the myth of Pygmalion and Galatea. My reading of this myth differs from that of feminist critic Susan Gubar, who calls it a myth of "male primacy" (244) in which the sculptor, Pygmalion, reveals his ability to create "female life as he would like it to be" (243). Gubar overlooks that it is the goddess Venus, *not* Pygmalion, who gives life to the statue. In both this myth and in *The Captive,* the male is unable to breathe life into a statue. Only a female (Madame d'Aiguines or the goddess) can bring Irene or Galatea to life. Jacques, rather than being able to create "female life as he would like it to be," is unable to mold Irene into the form that he desires; Madame d'Aiguines's ability to bring Irene to emotional life points out Jacques's inability, and he, not the lesbian, is revealed to be the one to fail. (Compare this to the affirmation of Martin's masculine superiority when he, not Stephen, is able to offer Mary greater social acceptance.)

Madame d'Aiguines's position as an insider to heterosexual life allows her to threaten and even possibly to destroy the heterosexual bond between a married couple, something Stephen Gordon never fully achieves. Jacques refuses to take this menace seriously even when Monsieur d'Aiguines warns him of the danger:

> Understand this: they are not for us. They must be shunned, left alone. Don't make my mistake. Don't say ... "Oh, it's nothing but a sort of ardent friendship . . . nothing very serious. . . ." No! We don't know anything about it! We can't begin to know what it is. . . . Under cover of friendship a woman can enter any household, whenever and however she pleases—at any hour of the day—she can poison and pillage everything before the man whose home she destroys is even aware of what's happening to him. When finally he realizes things it's too late—he is alone! Alone in the face of a secret alliance of two beings who understand one another because they're alike, because they're of the same sex, because they're of a different planet than he, the stranger, the enemy! (149–50)

Madame d'Aiguines has a radically different relationship to the heterosexual world than does Stephen, who is easily spotted as "not belonging." In sharp contrast, Madame d'Aiguines's lesbian identity is obscured by the "mask" and "cover" of friendship. Her sexual orientation concealed, she can invade even that site of heterosexual sanctity, the home. This passage implies that female friendships are suspect and, thus, all women are potential lesbians. What is worse, the male is powerless because he cannot easily identify the woman who comes to "poison and pillage" his domain. Identifying the lesbian would be a simple task if she were a mannish lesbian like Stephen Gordon, but Bourdet's invading lesbian is impossible to differentiate from heterosexual women.

We can see that to the heterosexual reader of the 1920s Stephen Gordon, with her masculine attire and physique and sexualized language, was impossible *not* to identify as a lesbian. Although I agree with Esther Newton that creating a masculine persona might have offered a lesbian new opportunities to reveal rather than conceal her sexual identity, this must be understood concurrently with how heterosexuals used these same identifying features to isolate lesbians and to justify their persecution. Furthermore, such a reading strategy suggests that lesbian-feminist theorists studying representations of lesbianism directed at a mass audience should not ignore the heterosexual public while valorizing the lesbian audience. Rather, both the lesbian and heterosexual perceptions of lesbian representation must be studied to understand how a particular cultural work (i.e., *The Well*) may be simultaneously perceived by lesbians as affirming homosexuality and understood by heterosexuals as affirming the social ostracism of gays and lesbians. In effect, considering the heterosexual audience keeps critics of lesbian literature from engaging in a form of myth-making in which the lesbian reader of a text becomes so important as to subsume the heterosexual reader entirely.

While *The Well* depicts a lesbian heroine who is unable to conceal her sexual identification, *The Captive* presents the lesbian as trickster, a beautiful woman who can "pass" when she so desires. More dangerously, she does not wish to change her sexual identification and can outmaneuver a man in the pursuit of a mate. This woman is impossible to distinguish and impossible to isolate. She, unlike Stephen, could not be easily described in the popular psychology books of the 1920s and 1930s aimed at defining the sexual Other for the heterosexual audience. If this feminine, desirable woman could be a lesbian, then many women, not only mannish women, could conceivably be categorized as lesbians.

Today, Bourdet's representation of the lesbian as a feminine woman is largely subsumed in popular heterosexual ideology by the image of the mannish lesbian, which persists as the most common American stereotype. The beautiful, feminine woman who is desired by men yet still persists in her lesbianism is an almost unbelievable creation to many; it is an image that has been selectively censored from the popular imagination because, as I have argued, the image presents a greater threat to heterosexual order than does the mannish lesbian. We must recognize that Madame d'Aiguines was as much a part of the lesbian world in the 1920s as Stephen Gordon, and she still is today.

The suppression of her image in favor of Stephen Gordon's serves a purpose: to legitimize an image of the lesbian as an easily excluded outsider.

I do not wish to suggest, however, that the mannish lesbian has no power to challenge the status quo. In fact, I believe the opposite to be true. What I have pointed out in this chapter is how heterosexual society has used stereotypical images of the mannish lesbian to justify her exclusion. This in no way means that the mannish lesbian has not been a powerful and positive role model in the lesbian community. Chapter 8 discusses in greater depth the considerable importance of the masculine lesbian in lesbian culture.

2

"Malevolent, neurotic, and tainted"

The Lesbian Menace in Popular
Women's College Fiction

> All that feminine atmosphere. I don't believe in [women's] college
> communities. It's the soil where Sapphism flourishes. (Neff 148)

The above quotation from Wanda Neff's novel *We Sing Diana* (1928)
about life at imaginary Petersfield College is an appropriate beginning to a chapter that focuses on the complex interrelation between
women's colleges and lesbianism, examining the widely held cultural
assumption that women's colleges *are* the "soil where Sapphism flour-
ishes." A reviewer for the London *Times* commented in 1928 that
Neff's "revolt against an exclusively feminine society—the society
which creates the Lesbian—is obvious" ("*We Sing*" 738) but failed to
question whether it is also obvious that such a community actually
does cause lesbianism or is only represented in this fashion. Discussions of whether women's colleges encourage lesbianism continue up
to the present.[1] As recently as 1991, the presidents of both Smith
and Wellesley (Mary Maples Dunn and Nan Keohane, respectively)
made statements about their institutions' positions on lesbianism that
seemed designed to refute assumptions that there was any special link

between women's colleges and a high rate of lesbianism. The *Los Angeles Times* published Dunn's remarks, reflecting society's broad curiosity about what the article refers to as "the 'L' word." Although Dunn proclaims "a doctrine of tolerance of all lifestyles," she simultaneously attempts to distance Smith College from its long connection with lesbianism by suggesting that homosexuality only became a word attached to Smith in the late 1960s and early 1970s because "the great men's colleges began to shift to coeducation, and single-sex education began to appear 'abnormal'" (Mehren E14). Dunn overlooks that issues of "abnormal" sexuality have been connected with women's colleges throughout the twentieth century.

This chapter will provide a longer history of the linkage between women's colleges and lesbianism than does Dunn. My analysis focuses in particular on the 1920s and 1930s, a period when the imagined connection between a single-sex education and lesbianism became obvious to a mass audience. We find that a number of factors, including Freud's theories on homosexuality, Edna St. Vincent Millay's turbulent career at Vassar College, and the many women's college novels that were published in these decades emphasizing the lesbianism of students and teachers, worked to increase public awareness of the connection between women's colleges and potential lesbianism. Furthermore, I suggest that twentieth-century society has consistently used the fear of lesbianism to effectively defuse the threat posed by women's single-gender organizations, particularly those openly challenging the status quo, whether family values are involved, or job equality, or gender discrimination.

Since there has already been extensive research on women's homoaffectionate relationships in the nineteenth and early twentieth centuries, I shall provide only a brief synopsis of this historical background.[2] During this period, women's close, even passionate, friendships were generally tolerated and accepted as suitable substitutes for women who could not find or did not desire husbands. Schoolgirl crushes, complete with ardent love letters, kissing, hand holding, and bed sharing, were considered normal relationships for high school and college women and were not regarded as friendships that would hinder a young woman's progression into mature heterosexuality.

Since female friendships were categorized as asexual, they were rarely perceived as a significant threat to the patriarchal social order. Thus the crushes and lifetime relationships that frequently developed at women's colleges were worrisome only because they heightened fears that the "best" women (Anglo-Saxon college graduates) were failing to marry and bear children, but there was little apprehension about the sexuality of these women.[3] Nineteenth-century society typically regarded the women's college as a nonsexual sphere.

At the turn of the century and in the first quarter of the twentieth century, it became increasingly difficult to view women's colleges as free from sexuality. As the views on lesbianism promulgated by sexologists such as Krafft-Ebing, Ellis, and Freud became more broadly available to a general audience,[4] people began to perceive the women's college as "the great breeding ground" of lesbianism, as it was identified in a 1902 periodical article entitled "Dr. Havelock on Sexual Inversion" (qtd. in Faderman, *Odd Girls* 49). Ellis's *Studies in the Psychology of Sex* (1897) with its appendix, "The School-Friendships of Girls," made the link between schoolgirl crushes and lesbianism seem unmistakable. In this appendix, Ellis connected life at a single-sex school to an increased rate of lesbianism, stating that over 60 percent of women's college students had crushes (376), relationships he considered "morbid fetishism[s] [*sic*]" (374). Even women's college students began to question the nature of crushes, causing one student to write a caustic commentary on the common use of the word "crush" at Smith College in 1911:

> I . . . wonder how many of us have ever given any thought whatsoever to the use of "crush." Now I admit that there may be times . . . when this word may be rightfully applied to a demoralizing, sentimental attachment between two girls. But why should we use this odious term in connection with every two girls . . . who seem to have discovered in one another a congenial spirit? We may be so hardened to being told we have a "crush" that it makes absolutely no impression upon us, but surely not everyone has reached that stage. There are girls who are sensitive about such matters, who retire within themselves when the girl across the hall makes suggestive remarks or points the finger of derision. ("Public" 4)

Although rumors about the presumed widespread lesbianism at women's colleges began to spread at the turn of the century, it took a number of years for these suspicions to filter through society. As late as the early 1920s, many people did not link the word "lesbian" with a sexual abnormality. Certainly, the editors of the 1920 Oberlin College yearbook were not aware of any such linkage when they identified pictures of thirty-two women students as members of the Oberlin Lesbian Society—a poetry club (Faderman, *Odd Girls* 52). It is unlikely that even five years later the Oberlin students would have used the word "lesbian" so naively, as the growing interest in psychology entailed an increase in awareness about lesbianism. During the 1920s, as historian Jeffrey Weeks remarks, Freud and Ellis were "openly influential" (142).[5] Likewise, in her book *The Grounding of Modern Feminism* (1987), Nancy Cott argues that lesbianism was a freely used discourse in the 1920s; maladjustment (insufficient heterosexual impulses), she comments, was "a general theme in popular and scientific culture in the 1920s" (159).

We cannot understand this widespread interest in lesbianism unless we recognize that lesbianism presented two different faces to the public of the 1920s. On one hand, as Christina Simmons remarks, "fear of lesbianism constituted . . . a significant problem in the dominant heterosexual ideology of the 1920's and 1930's" (54). Many people worried that, due to changing moral standards and the disturbances in social roles caused by World War I, lesbianism was actually increasing (56). Others blamed the perceived increase in lesbianism on women's social activism. For example, C. G. Jung commented in 1928 that "In Anglo-Saxon countries . . . homosexuality among women appears recently to have acquired more significance than Sapphic lyricism, inasmuch as it seems to serve the ideas of women's social and political organization as an advantageous undercurrent" (329). In the 1920s, lesbianism became a flexible signifier, which did far more than identify those engaged in "abnormal" sexual practices; indeed, lesbianism was hinted at whenever women attempted to change the patriarchal balance of power, whether by pursuing formerly male-dominated jobs, organizing to vote, refusing to marry, living alone, fighting for women's rights, or pursuing higher education. Lesbianism became—and still is—the transcendent signifier that a woman has violated accepted gender roles and needs to be punished.

On the other hand, an influential minority in the 1920s regarded lesbianism as glamorous and alluring. As Lillian Faderman remarks, lesbianism in the 1920s and 1930s was the new "cosmopolitan chic" both in the United States and in France (*Surpassing* 361). Although equating lesbianism with chic never gained mass acceptance, it was a view held by a number of intellectuals and people in artistic and literary circles, some of whom only dallied with homosexual practices while others professed to be lesbians and conducted their lives accordingly. In Europe, Djuna Barnes, Gertrude Stein, and Radclyffe Hall were among the most famous women of this period who wrote about lesbian relationships and reinforced the idea that lesbianism was both sophisticated and a viable option to heterosexuality.

In the United States, Edna St. Vincent Millay was tremendously influential in promoting lesbianism or bisexuality as options for the most avant-garde women. Millay, or "Vincent" as she preferred to be called, often commented that she liked to "live dangerously" and led a highly publicized life while attending Vassar and, later, living in Greenwich Village. Her early sexual adventures with women were a little-concealed secret; she memorialized her affairs in half-hidden allusions in her poetry, such as when she pleads in "Interim," her elegy to her dead friend Dorothy Coleman, "If only God / Had let us love,—and show the world the way!" (*Collected Poems* 18). In Anne Cheney's book *Millay in Greenwich Village* (1975), the author discusses Vincent's lesbian relationships at Vassar and mentions that Millay, like Sappho, surrounded herself with a circle of young women admirers, among them Isobel Simpson, whom Millay called her "own true love" (Macdougall 92). Another implicit reference to Millay's influence is found in Dorothy Bromley and Florence Britten's study *Youth and Sex: A Study of 1300 College Students* (1938), in which the writers discuss the "*éclat*" that "out-and-out homosexuality" enjoyed in the 1920s when "a few campus leaders in several of the larger women's colleges made it something of a fad" (118).[6] Although Bromley and Britten do not mention Millay's name, their implied reference to her is difficult to avoid.

"A nest of perversity": Representing the Women's College

Given American society's widespread interest in Millay in the 1920s and 1930s (she was, after all, the period's best-known woman poet), it is hardly surprising that a number of authors wrote novels about life at women's colleges that were ill-concealed inspections of Millay's own career at Vassar. Mary Lapsley, for instance, wrote *The Parable of the Virgins* (1931), a novel about the wild student life at Walton College (i.e., Vassar) in which the central character, Crosby O'Connor, is modeled after Millay.[7] The similarities are obvious: Both women write prize-winning poetry, both act in college plays, both are older than the other students, both are at school on scholarships, and both dally with lesbianism. Similarly, in Kathleen Millay's novel *Against the Wall* (1929), the writer undoubtedly is focusing on her famous sister's college career when she describes life at Matthew College for Rebecca, a scholarship student from Maine. As I shall show, both of these novels contain scathingly critical portrayals of the lesbianism that was alleged to flourish at actual women's institutions.

Other writers did not focus on Millay's college career but were no less thorough than Mary Lapsley and Kathleen Millay in denigrating the single-sex environment of a women's school. Lillian Hellman's play *The Children's Hour,* Marion Patton's novel *Dance on the Tortoise,* Clemence Dane's novel *Regiment of Women,* Warner Fabian's sensationalist book *Unforbidden Fruit,* Christa Winsloe's play *Girls in Uniform,* Tess Slesinger's short story "The Answer on the Magnolia Tree," Wanda Neff's novel *We Sing Diana,* and Carol Denny Hill's novel about Barnard life, *Wild,* are a few of the texts from the 1920s and 1930s intimating that a single-sex institution leads to lesbianism among both students and faculty members. Although a book reviewer for the *New York Times* was referring to *Against the Wall* when he called the novel "a most bitter and thorough indictment of women's colleges," this definition could be appropriately applied to all of these works, which condemn women's schools as breeding places for "Sapphism" ("*Against*" 14). Moreover, the very prevalence of these texts and the popularity of some of them (Hellman's play, for instance) suggest their importance in helping to construct and to promulgate cultural fantasies about the women's school, fantasies that most likely had a greater influence on how the mass populace conceptualized women's single-sex education than did the actual institutions themselves.

These texts operate to mark the single-gender female environment, wherever it might appear (in schools, convents, or businesses), as abnormal. This is a reversal from the nineteenth century when it was frequently the mixed-sex environment that signified social unacceptability. (For instance, in the late 1800s, women's colleges such as Bryn Mawr, Mount Holyoke, Wellesley, and Vassar were considered less socially suspect for women than coeducational institutions such as Cornell University, Stanford University, and the University of California, where men and women could intermingle with minimal chaperonage.) Perceiving women's single-gender environments as abnormal and as potentially contributing to lesbianism has been an effective strategy throughout the twentieth century to curtail female empowerment. It makes little difference whether a women's organization is entirely composed of lesbians or has no lesbian members; since the belief that single-gender communities lead to an increased prevalence of lesbianism has become an ideological construct, the linkage is impossible to overlook and has had a profound effect on women's organizations. We are all familiar with the ways that the media manipulated the threat of lesbianism to inflate the threat posed by Second Wave feminism. In addition, the perceived presence of lesbianism has been used repeatedly throughout the twentieth century to delegitimize same-sex schools for women. (I doubt that any young woman today can attend a women's college without having to address the fears of family members or friends that such an institution shelters lesbians or that the girl herself is one since she wishes to attend a single-sex school.)

We should not ignore the importance of popular fiction in promoting a view of the women's college as a hotbed of lesbian desire and in encouraging students to police their own sexual expression to ensure that it does not become full-fledged lesbianism. For example, *The Parable of the Virgins* instructs the women's college student to limit homoerotic relationships with other women to mild flirtations that will vanish once she finds the proper man. In this novel, one student,

Crosby O'Connor, who is described as having "lax morals" (Lapsley 14), feels no qualms about asking for a "real kiss" from a woman friend who stops by for a casual visit. The reader, however, is expected to understand the resulting passionate kiss not as a sign of Crosby's innate lesbian tendencies but rather as a display of the "unnatural" tendencies that are, according to the book's logic, inevitably bred by the women's college. The novel even suggests that the best-intentioned administrators and faculty members might inadvertently increase lesbianism. For instance, until she goes to college, Crosby fails to understand why she may not wear male clothing, her typical attire:

> When I came here, I was as innocent as a lamb, and the first thing I did was to parade around the campus in men's clothes—Leslie wanted an escort to some party. Up I went before the President.
>
> "Miss O'Connor," he said, "we can't have such immoral conduct at Walton. . . ."
>
> "But President Madison . . . it isn't as if I were a man."
>
> "That's just the point. . . . I will not have Walton become a nest of perversity." (123–24)

This exchange between Crosby and Walton's president proves to be a criticism not of Crosby's dalliance with activities that might have lesbian connotations but of the way that the institution is operated and of its obfuscation over the issue of lesbianism. Since Crosby does not understand Madison's cryptic warning, she turns to reading "abnormal psych books" to discover his meaning.[8] Thus the novel claims that the women's college with its close scrutiny and policing of students turns even "normal" women like Crosby toward lesbianism, which becomes more attractive and enticing precisely because it is forbidden.

Although she admits receiving a thrill from kissing either a man or a woman, Crosby clearly prefers male companionship when it is available. She is what Freud defined as a contingent invert. For these homosexuals, Freud claimed, "under certain external conditions—of which inaccessibility of any normal sexual object and imitation are the chief—they are capable of taking as their sexual object someone of their own sex and of deriving satisfaction from sexual intercourse with [her]" ("Sexual" 3). For Freud, the contingent invert, such as Crosby, points out the abnormality of a single-sex environment that does not allow a woman to have access to her normal sexual objects: men. Contingency, much more than Krafft-Ebing's and Ellis's earlier theories about the lesbian as a congenital fluke, is an effective strategy to use in policing women's behavior. Since it is easy to trigger lesbianism merely by exposure to certain environmental factors, it follows that a heterosexual woman should avoid a same-sex institution lest her sexual orientation be temporarily or permanently altered.

Sophisticated Crosby, however, avoids becoming entangled in any full-fledged lesbian relationship. Most women, the novel warns, are not so strong, and homoerotic crushes are depicted as an infectious plague at Walton College. An adviser warns one student: "Don't get a crush. You can admire some girls a lot, nice earnest girls, but don't get slushy about it. It makes a girl conspicuous, and the college authorities don't approve. . . . Why, there are some girls in this college who actually hug and kiss each other as if they mean it" (32). Similarly, in *Against the Wall,* Matthew College's student handbook warns students: "*Don't get a crush!* It will make you notorious but you won't be popular" (K. Millay 149). Students are told in hygiene lessons about "friendships at school" that "it [is] all right to be friends, of course—but . . . draw the chalk line at the bedroom door" (341). Lapsley's and Millay's attention to fictional crushes, of course, should not be understood as an accurate or reliable account of the lesbian activities at real women's colleges. I argue, however, that this lack of mimesis does not mitigate the influence these texts had in helping to construct a representation of the women's college as a site of rampant lesbian desire. Indeed, we find that these novels were only one element of a larger cultural discourse about women's single-sex education and its perceived tendency to breed lesbianism, a discourse that involved scholarly as well as popular texts. For instance, in her 1923 work, *The Education of Women: Its Social Background and Its Problems,* Willystine Goodsell was warning educators about crushes: "A flood of light has recently been thrown upon the sex life of girls which tends to show that, although vicious sex practices may be less prevalent in girls' schools than in boys', nevertheless unwholesome gossip about sex is very common. Furthermore, the tendency of girls to develop 'crushes' seems to be far more marked in separate girls' schools than in coeducational institutions. And the potentialities for evil of these sentimental affairs between girls are too well known to need more than passing comment" (137).[9] Although, as I have previously mentioned, it is difficult to demonstrate conclusively whether women's lesbian relationships actually were any more prevalent in the interwar years than in previous eras, many educators thought there was an increase in such relationships.[10]

Administrators of women's colleges implemented new disciplinary rules in order to handle the perceived threat of crushes and lesbianism. For example, women's college students in the 1930s could be expelled not only for staying out at night with a man but also for having an intense relationship with another women (B. Solomon 162). And Dorothy Bromley and Florence Britten in their 1930s study mention that in order to discourage lesbianism "a number of the women's colleges [had to endeavor] to counteract the dangers of segregation" by allowing for more male visiting hours and permitting men from nearby colleges to play the male roles in school dramatics, as well as letting their students "swim with [men] in the college pool" (118). Through such actions, women's colleges attempted to police their students and to reshape the public assumption that the women's colleges sheltered and even encouraged lesbianism.[11]

Inevitably, the women's colleges faced a losing battle in altering public views that single-sex institutions led to lesbianism because so many novels, as well as numerous other texts, informed readers that women's colleges harbored lesbianism and numerous other sexual "abnormalities." Warner Fabian, for example, wrote in the foreword to his novel *Unforbidden Fruit* that he had chosen to present a "peculiar atmosphere of compressed femininity which produces an intellectual and social reaction not unlike the prison psychosis of our penal institutions. There is no doubt but that, in this environment, normal tendencies and appetites, including sex, become at times exaggerated and inflamed" (v). Such sensationalist rhetoric and veiled references to "abnormal" sexuality are typical in the myriad women's school stories of the 1920s and 1930s. For instance, in *We Sing Diana,* the heroine, Nora, attends a women's college, Petersfield, where she is shocked to discover the existence of lesbian attachments. She calls one lesbian relationship a "poison" and a "rank growth" "feeding on rot" (64). This hyperbolic language makes it clear what position on lesbianism the reader is expected to adopt. Even women with "normal tendencies and appetites" are explicitly warned about avoiding the single-sex institution because of the deleterious effect of its "peculiar atmosphere." One can extrapolate from this assumption that any excessive same-gender contact is potentially perverse; in this fashion, women readers are encouraged to consider emotional bonds with males as always superior to and more "normal" than emotional ties with other females.

The only way Nora escapes the rampant lesbianism of Petersfield is by having an affair with a man when she is on leave from school for a year. When he conveniently dies, she prepares to assume the presidency of her college, where she will presumably implement widespread changes to alter the "unnatural" maleless environment. She even adopts a boy "to counteract the feminine influence at Petersfield" (339), reiterating her belief that it is the effect of the single-sex environment on women, not the actions of a few individual lesbians, that makes the school so dangerous. Rather than being appalled at the text's dubious homophobic "logic," some readers expressed satisfaction in the author's revelation of a supposed truth about single-sex institutional life. A London *Times* book reviewer, for instance, praised the novel for its author's "revolt against an exclusively feminine society—the society which creates the Lesbian, the invert and the hysterical weakling" ("*We Sing*" 738). If even a reputable source such as the *Times* could discuss the potential of a women's community to lead to lesbianism, clearly then this was a discourse that was broadly disseminated in both English and American society, since the reviewer felt no need to justify his assertions and seemed to assume that his readers would concur with his beliefs.

Other texts display similar biases about lesbianism in women's schools. For instance, Marion Patton's novel *Dance on the Tortoise,* like Neff's, depicts lesbianism as an abnormality produced by the environment. The novel's heroine, Lydia, who teaches at a girls' boarding school, falls in love with the French teacher, Hélène, although they never go so far as having sexual relations. Despite her own love for another woman, Lydia disapproves of the lesbian relationship between two older teachers, remarking, "I suppose . . . when you don't marry, when neither of you marries, then a friendship like that goes on. It's a substitute" (25). Like Nora, Lydia blames the school's single-sex atmosphere for the lesbianism she notices among faculty members: "These bunches of women living together, falling in love with each other because they haven't anyone else to fall in love with! It's obscene" (266).[12] Despite such condemnatory words, after Hélène dies Lydia feels herself drifting into a relationship with another woman professor. The message of this novel is that the only way a woman can avoid becoming a contingent lesbian is by fleeing the single-sex environment, which Lydia does. Like many similar novels, this one reinforces the cultural stereotype that single-sex environments inevitably produce homosexuals and should be avoided at all costs.

Absolute Inverts: Vampires and Suicidal Women

Thus far this chapter has focused on how the women's college is depicted as an environment where contingent inverts, as Freud called them, flourish. The women's college, however, is also frequently used as a fictional space to examine the lives of "absolute inverts": those homosexuals whom Freud defined as having sexual objects exclusively of their own sex. While contingent lesbians are often portrayed in fiction as victims of their environment, absolute lesbians are perfunctorily condemned as "vampires" who mesmerize and sometimes seduce younger, more naive students. Teachers who have or desire lesbian relationships with their students are depicted as particularly despicable. In Francis Young's novel *White Ladies* (1935), domineering Miss Cash, headmistress of St. Monica's School for Girls, is described as "a vampire who lives on blood" (219). Similarly, a *New York Times* book review of Clemence Dane's *Regiment of Women* (1917) informs the reader that this novel is a "story in which a sort of vampire woman in a girl's school has the temperament and character that enable her to produce a 'crush' upon herself whenever she likes" ("*Regiment*" 33). A great gap exists between the more positively portrayed Crosby O'Connor, who likes to kiss other women but does not pursue her sexual advances any further, and characters like Miss Cash, who are described as hardly human. In the mind of the heterosexual reader of these books, a lesbian hierarchy is established with the contingent invert deserving the most sympathy and the absolute invert deserving the least. In both situations, the single-sex environment of a women's institution is criticized because it is seen as contributing to the development of contingent inverts and provides a safe refuge for vampire-teachers like Miss Cash. In this fashion, lesbianism is depicted to the heterosexual reader as a social evil that can be controlled by curtailing women's intimacy with other women.

In these novels, students who are absolute lesbians are depicted as stereotypically masculine. In *Unforbidden Fruit,* Olga Tremwich, for example, sings second alto in the glee club and is cast only in men's roles in school plays. In *The Parable of the Virgins,* Elizabeth Munroe, described as "a slim athletic-looking girl" (25), is, according to the text's logic, an obvious lesbian. By encouraging the belief that the "true" lesbian can be easily identified, these literary works promote a system of feminine scrutiny. As Nora, a student at Petersfield College, notices, all women observe one another: "Intimacies between two girls [are] watched with keen, distrustful eyes. Among one's classmates, one looked for the bisexual type, the masculine girl searching for a feminine counterpart, and one ridiculed their devotions" (Neff 199). The single-sex community is not seen as offering an escape from heterosexual norms, nor is it seen as conducive to the development of female camaraderie. Instead, women are portrayed as becoming increasingly distrustful of and more alienated from one another because of the omnipresent fear that proffered friendship might mask lesbianism.

When a lesbian is not represented as mannish and athletic, she is depicted as a neurotic, possessive femme fatale, who is doomed to suffer for her "abnormal" love. For example, in *The Parable of the Virgins,* Mary Nugeon and Jessica Raleigh are two lesbians who dance together every night after supper at the student dances and kiss "lingeringly" (95). When Marguerite, a naive freshman, admires Mary and Jessica, a more knowledgeable sophomore warns her about such friendships:

> "They never dance with anyone but each other. . . ." [T]he
> disapproval in her voice was marked and she added, "They ought
> to follow Dr. Royal's advice [to keep] their hearts wrapped in
> cotton batting till the right man comes along."
>
> Marguerite pondered this remark; it seemed very cryptic.
> Some instinct told her that perhaps after she had listened to Dr.
> Royal's freshman lectures on hygiene she would understand it. . . .
> One thing she knew, of course; that remark had something to do
> with "crushes"; the guidebook had warned about them. (41)

Although Mary and Jessica are an attractive couple, admired by their
fellows, their love affair is short-lived and undermined by psychological problems. Mary is pathologically jealous when her lover dances
with another woman at one of the student dances. Later, when the
school physician tells Mary that she is an "immoral influence in the
college" (253) and persuades Jessica to leave her, Mary commits
suicide. Her anger and subsequent suicide fit a stereotype of the
lesbian that was widely described in the 1920s and 1930s. For instance, in her popular study of women's sexuality, *Women on Their
Own* (1935), Olga Knopf lists jealousy and possessiveness among the
ills that, according to her, inevitably accompany a lesbian relationship:
"Any one who has had occasion to observe these unions between two
women cannot have helped noticing that the demands made and the
domination exerted by both partners are infinitely greater than could
take place in a heterosexual union. Jealousy and possessiveness constantly betray the insecurity these women feel over their attractiveness
and their ability to keep the love of another human being" (160).
Similarly, Dorothy Bromley and Florence Britten inform their readers:
"Whether or not homosexual relationships are accompanied by physical manifestations of affection, they frequently tend to encourage
tyrannical possessiveness, incessant demands in the name of love,
recurring states of instability, and an exclusiveness that cuts off the
partners from other interests and friendships" (129–30). The authors
contend that lesbians are subject to jealousy, possessiveness, and mental instability to a far greater degree than heterosexuals. This stereotypical pattern is typified in Lapsley's novel. She does not consider
whether *any* relationship would be stable and exclusive if it existed in

a society that consistently denigrated such a relationship as perverse. Instead, negative personality flaws are depicted as essential attributes of the absolute invert, making it even more crucial for the contingent lesbian to avoid entanglements with such a borderline psychotic personality, entanglements, Lapsley warns, that might even lead to death.

The Parable of the Virgins does suggest that heterosexual society (mainly, the women's college) is at least partly responsible for Mary's death. A professor reflects that the death could have been avoided "If the college only started its campaign against crushes before they got so intense. . . . If the administration didn't talk in hushed whispers and avoid the word homosexual . . . or if they even differentiated between the environmental and the genuine Lesbian, one could hope for some results" (315). But he blames the "abnormal environment," not the prevailing heterosexual bias against homosexuals. If, as the professor assumes, a single-sex atmosphere causes "environmental" lesbianism, it becomes a threatening sphere for any heterosexual woman who seeks to maintain her sexual orientation. The constant fear exists that homosexuality might result as a consequence of even a brief stay at a women's school. Moreover, this argument could be expanded: Too much same-sex contact of any sort could be dangerous.

The supposed linkage between women's schools and suicidal lesbians became even more explicit after the tremendous success of Hellman's *The Children's Hour.* In Hellman's play, it is apparent that the public discourse about the connection between lesbianism and single-sex schools was already well established, since a young girl, Mary Tilford, is knowledgeable enough to accuse her two private-school teachers, Karen Wright and Martha Dobie, of lesbianism. Although Mary's accusation is a lie, it still has a tremendous impact, causing many parents to withdraw their daughters from Wright and Dobie's school. The teachers sue for libel but lose; after the court case, they are forced to stay indoors as pariahs in their small community. In the sensationalist conclusion, Martha announces that Mary was right; Martha is a lesbian and has always loved Karen. Then Martha walks into another room and commits suicide. When Karen hears the shot she does not rush to Martha's assistance, revealing a harsh critique of a society in which a lesbian would be better off dead. But Hellman's play also constructs the women's school as an unsafe environment for heterosexual women, even when there is no apparent evidence of lesbianism, since the potential for it always exists, sometimes scarcely below the surface. It is implied that any unmarried teacher, like Martha, can turn out to be a suicidal lesbian. In this fashion, the play raises doubts about the many teachers at women's colleges who are unmarried. Hellman's play and the other works I have studied suggest that the women's institution is impossible to separate from lesbianism.

The Present

Although this chapter has concentrated on how heightened awareness and representation of lesbianism in the 1920s and 1930s were used to police and control women's colleges, in the second half of the twentieth century, as Mary Maples Dunn points out, the women's school continues to be represented as a breeding ground for lesbianism. Probably we all remember sophisticated Lakey from Mary McCarthy's *The Group* (1954), a novel about a group of students at Vassar before and after their graduation. With her silk-and-lace peignoirs and batiste-and-lace nightgowns, Lakey, like Mary Nugeon, is a clear replication of the lesbian as femme fatale. Unlike Mary, Lakey is not inclined toward suicide and is even admired by her friends; Lakey's friends, however, are haunted by her lesbianism: "It bothered Polly and Helena to think that what was presented to their eyes was mere appearance, and that behind that, underneath it, was something of which they would not approve" (373). Although McCarthy's novel is not as explicit as many earlier twentieth-century texts about the undesirability of lesbianism, it still implies that lesbianism should be kept a secret, as it can never be completely acceptable to heterosexuals.

In other more recent works, lesbianism at women's colleges is openly condemned. For instance, in Sylvia Plath's novel *The Bell Jar* (1971), a Smith lesbian, Joan, is described as horsey and unattractive. When she attempts to proposition Esther, the novel's narrator, Joan is rebuffed by Esther's comment, "[you] make me puke" (180). Esther also recalls a "minor scandal . . . when a fat, matronly-breasted senior, homely as a grandmother and a pious religion major, and a tall, gawky freshman with a history of being deserted at an early hour in all sorts of ingenious ways by her blind dates, started seeing too much of each other" (180). Plath's novel is only one example of the numerous depictions of lesbianism at women's colleges that appear in contemporary fiction and films. But whether the represented lesbian is glamorous and attractive, as is Lakey, or homely and unappealing, as are Joan and the two unnamed lesbians in Plath's novel, her function is the same: to make the women's college (or any women's group) appear less socially tolerable to a mass audience by representing the school as having a connection with lesbianism. Moreover, since in our society associating any group with homosexuality is stigmatic, it follows that intimating that women's communities or educational institutions have a propensity for lesbianism weakens their influence and undermines their prestige.

What I do not wish to suggest is that either in the present or in the past have the actual lesbians at these institutions in any way harmed the schools or negatively affected the schools' performance. Indeed, some of the most renowned women's college presidents (M. Carey Thomas of Bryn Mawr and Mary Woolley of Mount Holyoke), as well as numerous famous faculty members and students, had long-term relationships with other women, yet these women enhanced the reputations of these schools and significantly contributed to their success. I argue, however, that actual lesbians who attend or teach at the schools have little to do with how the heterosexual-dominated press represents lesbianism in women's colleges. A prolific and highly respected scholar such as Thomas, who lived with her lover in the Bryn Mawr president's house for over twenty years, has less to do with promulgating heterosexual fears of lesbianism than do fictional characters such as Miss Cash and Olga Tremwich, stereotyped representations of lesbians that have become so much a part of the dominant ideology that their counterparts signify lesbianism wherever they appear. For much of the twentieth century, the dominant society has effectively used the construct of a "lesbian menace" to police and condemn women's behavior in a variety of contexts. How this ideology is constructed and mapped must be more closely analyzed by theorists and cultural critics if we are to understand how the fear of homosexuality is instilled in the public and manipulated in order to maintain a predominantly hetero-sexual society.

Postscript

"It's germ warfare," said Barbara Reinhold, director of Smith College's career development office and director for planning and administration, when asked in 1991 about the school's and other women's colleges' identification with lesbianism. "And I think it causes institutional consternation because something that is so irrelevant to what we are trying to do here . . . can be used in such a powerfully negative way. It makes us so sad that these noble goals are being tarnished by something that is absolutely irrelevant to the educational process" (qtd. in Mehren E14). Reinhold's words reveal that the representation of lesbianism and the women's college is an issue just as current in the 1990s as it was over fifty years ago, but they also demonstrate the colleges' uneasiness about this issue. On one hand, she expresses the thoughts of many when she suggests that lesbianism is an "irrelevant" aspect of higher education that can be conveniently obscured by a reference to the "noble goals" of women's colleges. On the other hand, former presidents Dunn and Keohane proclaim tolerance of all life-styles, including lesbianism. Nowhere is the presence of divergent viewpoints more evident than in Wellesley's decision in the early 1990s to allow a lesbian and her lover to become dormitory house-parents, but not in freshman dormitories. It is this Janus-faced approach to lesbianism with which the women's colleges must still wrestle, until they recognize that only by acknowledging with pride the long tradition of contributions by lesbians to their institutions can they hope to defuse the threat posed by the "lesbian menace" that has been associated with their schools throughout much of the twentieth century.

The next chapter shows that popular representations of lesbians in women's magazines share the two-faced approach to lesbianism, depicting it, paradoxically, as both inferior and superior to heterosexuality. As in this chapter, the next one addresses how popular texts negotiate lesbianism when representing it for a largely heterosexual audience. Again, we shall discover that such texts ultimately reinforce the notion that lesbianism might be fine as a fleeting fantasy but is not appropriate for a lifetime existence.

3

"They're here, they're flouncy, don't worry about them"

Depicting Lesbians in Popular Women's Magazines, 1965–1995

> Are gay women happy? Sexually satisfied? What about their professional and social success? This comprehensive report *tells*—in full, uncensored detail—what it is to love not men but others of your own sex. (Lyle 233)

When it comes to discussing lesbianism, women's magazines have often favored the scandalous, voyeuristic, tell-all tone found in the above quotation from *Cosmopolitan,* but increasingly in recent years they have adopted the attitude suggested by Alisa Solomon's tongue-in-cheek comment, "They're here, they're flouncy, don't worry about them" ("*Cosmo*" 24). Repeatedly, they have promoted an image of lesbians who act, dress, and look very much like the models in the magazines. Why have so many contemporary women's magazines chosen in the last decade to depict lesbians as clones of the other stylish women (presumably heterosexual) who fill their pages? How has the representation of lesbians changed in these magazines in the decades since the late 1960s, when many of them first brought up the "L" word? How have these changes represented and even helped to mold cultural mores about lesbianism? What are the reasons for the magazines' long-lasting fascination with lesbians? These are a few of the questions that

this chapter seeks to answer as it explores the changing characterization of lesbianism in women's magazines, notably *Cosmopolitan, Essence, Glamour, Mademoiselle, Redbook,* and *Vogue,* six of the most
popular fashion and lifestyle magazines for women. This chapter
focuses on how women's magazines operate to "normalize" lesbians by
assuring heterosexual readers that lesbians are, indeed, very much like
heterosexuals, partially stripping lesbians of their identities. Also,
however, these magazines, particularly in the 1980s and 1990s, frequently appear to advance lesbian rights, insisting that lesbians should
be able to design their lives in any way they desire. How are we to
interpret these two different images of lesbianism?

Mass-market women's magazines are a fascinating source for
studying society's struggle with lesbianism and other feminist issues
because of their textual ambiguity, which a number of scholars have
noted in previous studies.[1] In her essay "Women's Magazines: Slouching towards Feminism" (1993), Kalia Doner comments that women's
magazines "serve up a confusing hodge-podge of self-loathing attitudes and empowering opinion" (37). But she also has praise for
the magazines: "for all their sloppy thinking and destructive images
and attitudes, women's magazines do not consistently undermine
women—not by a long shot. In fact, many feminist ideas have become
part of popular culture thanks to the constant play they receive in the
magazines" (38). Janet Lee, talking specifically about *Cosmopolitan,*
argues that the magazine "is not itself monolithic. There are levels of
co-option, but also of genuine consonance with feminism. . . . [F]or
many readers, it may map out a route, however unsophisticated and
stereotypical, towards feminine independence" (170). In spite of the
widespread feminist horror at these "tools of the patriarchy," women's
magazines, with their combination of fluff and feminism, *have* spread
feminist ideas far and wide, from Poughkeepsie to Peoria, from San
Francisco to San Antonio, from Anchorage to Atlanta. These magazines, with their circulations often in the millions, have reached many
women who would never have learned about feminist ideas from other
sources, such as a college women's studies course or a consciousness-
raising group. The broad influence of these magazines becomes even
more interesting when one considers the still taboo subject of lesbian-

ism. Since this issue is even today rarely discussed freely in many circles, women's magazines might present the only forum about lesbianism that some women will be exposed to over an entire lifetime. For numerous readers who do not know a lesbian—or think they do not know one—women's magazines could provide the only in-depth discussion of lesbianism that they ever read. Thus, since women's magazines are playing a role in constituting lesbianism for millions of people, what these magazines do or do not suggest is very important.

I am interested, however, not only in the perceptions of heterosexual readers but also in those of homosexual ones. I, myself, can remember when I was an undergraduate and Candace Lyle's article "Lesbian Life Styles" (1982) appeared. My friends and I gathered around to read it in my roommate's copy of *Cosmopolitan,* and we laughed uproariously at the photograph of two long-haired, feminine pseudolesbians in silk teddies, finding it difficult, if not impossible, to imagine ourselves in such attire. We also found it difficult to imagine that *we* were the women who were being discussed in the article. The image of lesbianism *Cosmo* presented was distant and foreign, but we read avidly because we were all curious about how the mass media constituted our identities. And, ultimately, that article did present us with possible ideas, although somewhat far-fetched ones, about what it meant to be a lesbian. Some of those images are probably still lurking in our subconscious minds and, just as important, lurking in the collective subconscious of all the heterosexuals who read that edition of *Cosmo,* potentially influencing their thoughts about lesbians. I do not wish to imply that this one magazine single-handedly shaped its audience's perceptions of lesbianism. But that magazine, along with myriad other depictions of lesbians, helped to constitute lesbian identity for its readers.

Lyle's article was only the first of many about lesbianism that I have read in other women's magazines through the years. Pam Black's "When a Friend Tells You She's Gay" (1983), Martha Barrett's "Double Lives: What It's Like to Be a Lesbian Today" (1989), Renita Weems's "Just Friends" (1989), Valerie Louis's "What It's Like to be a Gay Woman Now" (1989), S. Catherine Eaton's "A Matter of Pride: Being a Gay Woman in the Nineties" (1993)—I read these articles and others, not because I was bewildered about what to do if a friend told me she was gay or because I wanted information about being gay in the nineties, but because I wanted to discover how lesbian identities were being shaped, constructed, and coded by these magazines. Others shared my interest; whenever one of these articles appeared, I always found lesbians discussing it and criticizing or praising the magazine's representation of lesbianism. A similar reaction occurs when the rare television show or movie appears that depicts lesbianism, and there emerges a debate from coast to coast about what *Personal Best, Entre Nous, Desert Hearts,* or *Go Fish* did or did not achieve in its depiction of lesbianism. Because mainstream images of lesbianism are still extremely rare, the few that do emerge can be extremely influential.

The critics who have studied lesbian representation in women's magazines have different responses about what those depictions signify. For instance, in her essay "Lesbian Journalism: Mainstream and Alternative Press" (1994), Veronica Groocock, using an article from *Cosmopolitan* as an example, praises some women's magazines, commenting, "there have always been mainstream publications which treated lesbian issues in a positive and non-sensationalist manner" (104). Continuing her discussion of contemporary mainstream women's magazines, she writes, "There is a sense in which lesbianism is a given, an accepted part of mainstream culture, not confined to the closet but bursting out of it, not marginalized out of existence but integrated and absorbed into the social fabric" (105). Contrasting sharply with Groocock, Janice Winship adopts a more negative perspective on lesbian imagery in women's magazines: "When the rare article about lesbianism appears, it is addressed, somewhat voyeuristically, to heterosexual women and expresses and urges a liberal tolerance rather than a feminist understanding" (116). The author continues: "for all *Cosmo's* explorations of 'choice' within heterosexuality the identity itself is never questioned" (117). Groocock's and Winship's different viewpoints show how multivalent the depictions of lesbianism in women's magazines are. Only by studying the magazines themselves can we become aware of the ambiguity that characterizes most articles on lesbianism in women's magazines.

This chapter analyzes the representation of lesbianism not in just one particular magazine, such as *Cosmopolitan,* but, instead, as it has been represented in a number of magazines, including *Essence, Glamour, Mademoiselle, Redbook,* and *Vogue.* I selected these magazines because they discuss lesbianism fairly frequently and are all successful, well-established magazines with large circulations. For instance, in 1993, *Redbook* had a circulation of 3.3 million, *Glamour* had a subscription of 2.1 million, *Vogue's* was 1.2 million, and *Cosmopolitan's* figure was 2.7 million (Doner 39). *Essence* had a circulation of 950,000 in 1993. (These numbers would be significantly higher if one considered that a number of people most likely read each magazine.) Although these numbers do not even come close to *Better Homes and Gardens'* 8 million circulation figure, they still represent a sizable share of the reading market (Doner 39). Also, due to different marketing, these fashion and lifestyle magazines are more likely to contain articles about lesbianism than more conservative magazines, such as *Better Homes and Gardens, Good Housekeeping, Family Circle,* and *Woman's Day.* I chose to look at more mainstream magazines rather than *Ms.,* even though *Ms.* had by far the greatest number of articles about lesbianism of any of the popular magazines that I inspected, because *Ms.* is targeted toward feminists or women with feminist sympathies and presents a far more sympathetic view of lesbianism than most popular women's magazines. Thus I decided to leave it out of my study, since I was more curious about how magazines were constructing lesbianism for the broader public.

Analyzing these women's magazines and their peculiar combination of "feminist ideas with stunningly superficial stories" (Doner 39) can offer critics a better understanding of how the popular media help to constitute and contain lesbians. For many people, it might be difficult, if not impossible, to separate the representation of the lesbian from the reality; the very realism of the magazines encourages the collapse of representation and reality, as Ellen McCracken explains in her study *Decoding Women's Magazines: From "Mademoiselle" to "Ms."* (1993): "The ostensibly authoritative grand narrative of reality developed month after month in these texts appears to be a women-centered articulation of the world. Rendering thousands of aspects of everyday life as knowable, controllable entities, women's magazines suggest, much as nineteenth-century realist narrative did, that an apparently comprehensive and straightforward detailing of the everyday can capture reality discursively for readers" (2). In other words, even the design and style of the magazines encourage readers to consider such material as factual and true. The magazines never suggest that their accounts about lesbians might be inaccurate or even false; with the notable exception of *Essence,* a magazine targeted at African American women, they give hardly any attention to the many issues, such as racial, ethnic, age, or socioeconomic differences, that divide lesbian communities and make it impossible to posit one monolithic lesbian identity. In the *Cosmo* world, the lesbian is white, beautiful, financially successful, young, and well dressed. This fantasy of what lesbian life is like has the power to become more "real" than the world that exists outside the magazine's fictional universe.

Why scholars and theorists need to study such popular representations is explained by Annamarie Jagose in her book *Lesbian Utopics* (1994): "the most efficacious task for lesbian theorists is not to secure a body or a sexuality beyond networks of power but to understand that body, that sexuality, as incoherently constituted through discourse" (4–5). This incoherent image of the lesbian body is at the center of the frequent discussions of lesbianism in women's magazines, as they struggle to find ways in which to describe lesbians and lesbian lives in such a way as not to damage the heterosexual status quo, since these magazines' survival in their present form is based on a highly structured system of differences between the genders. The lesbian body, I would argue, is particularly susceptible to appropriation by the mainstream because it is a hidden body, a secret body, a taboo body. Such a concealed body can easily be appropriated by the media to sell everything from clothing to magazine subscriptions. Because of its taboo nature, showing the lesbian body can be an effective way to connect the product being sold with images of the forbidden or avant-garde. In this fashion, the lesbian body becomes a sign that can be manipulated in many different ways, not all of them benevolent.

The process of coopting the lesbian body is described in Cathy Griggers's essay "Lesbian Bodies in the Age of (Post)mechanical Reproduction" (1993), in which the writer describes the position of lesbian bodies in contemporary society. "While all social bodies are plied by multiple regimes of signs," Griggers writes, "lesbian bodies in the age of (post)mechanical reproduction are particularly paradigmatic of a radical semiotic multiplicity" (183). She continues: "Lesbians in the public culture of postmodernity are subjects-in-the-making whose body of signs and bodies as sign are up for reappropriation and revision" (183). Nowhere are Griggers's words more accurate than in the postmodern landscape of women's magazines, where the lesbian body frequently loses all association with real lesbians. The following analysis will examine how this appropriated lesbian body functions, and how it operates to uphold and reinforce dominant stereotypes about lesbian lives.

From Perversion to High Fashion: The History of Lesbian Images in Women's Magazines

In her best-selling critique of modern beauty standards, *The Beauty Myth: How Images of Beauty Are Used against Women* (1991), Naomi Wolf points out that "Women's magazines for over a century have been one of the most powerful agents for changing women's roles" (64). Along with altering women's roles, for the last thirty years women's magazines have been engaged in changing society's attitudes about homosexuality. During this period, women's magazines have simultaneously reflected and helped to create society's perceptions about gay men and lesbians, both of whom have received a fair amount of attention from the magazines.[2] As early as 1965, the *Ladies' Home Journal* ran a scathingly negative article about male homosexuality, in which a physician called homosexuality a "sexual perversion" and an "illness" (Lathbury 43). This article, however, was a rare exception; most women's magazines ignored this controversial subject in the early and mid 1960s. Only in the late 1960s, when the Stonewall riots and the burgeoning women's movement were making it more acceptable to talk about sexuality, did articles about lesbians and gay men start to appear with some frequency. In October of 1968, the *Ladies' Home Journal,* for instance, ran an article about homosexuality in the column, "Can This Marriage Be Saved?" The article focuses on a husband, Thad, who is a homosexual. Thad is far from accepting of his sexual orientation. He despises himself and condemns his "miserable sex urges" (Disney 31).[3] The marriage counselor who talks to Thad reassures him, commenting, "I've seen no persuasive evidence that any human being is born condemned by genetic inheritance to lead the life of a sexual deviate" (33). In another article from 1968 in—of all unlikely places—*Seventeen* magazine, the writer warns her readers that "a girl who seeks involvement with another girl usually does so because she is unable to accept her own feminine competence and the challenge of going out with boys" (Wood 284, 322). In a similar article from *Seventeen,* this one from 1969, a psychiatrist informs his readers that "a well-functioning heterosexual certainly ranks higher on the scale of development and mental health than a well-functioning homosexual" (Gould 128). In these early articles, as in others, the writers assumed that homosexuality was a perversion that anyone would want "cured." No hint existed that homosexuality could be a blessing, not a bane. These magazines promulgated the generally held views of 1960s society and facilitated the spread of those ideas.

The connection between the image of lesbianism in women's magazines and in society as a whole became more evident in the 1970s. In 1973 homosexuality was declared not to be a mental illness by the American Psychiatric Association, and in response women's magazines began to veer away from the language of perversion that characterized the 1960s. There was still a great deal of attention given to the "natural" inferiority of lesbianism, and writers frequently assumed that psychological turmoil was responsible for lesbianism. For instance, in Anne Roiphe's 1977 *Vogue* article "Who's Afraid of Lesbian Sex?" the author suggests that "the lack of good mothering, the lack of good fathering in a landscape of female second-class citizenship may drive more women to the Lesbian choice than would be the case in a more equal, liberated society" (198). Clearly, Roiphe presents lesbian relationships as inferior to heterosexual ones. She also condemns lesbians who adopt masculine signifiers, stating, "In the extreme, this identification with the opposite sex has a pathological look that frightens the rest of womankind" (198). Although Roiphe's article is generally positive and she defends the right of lesbians to equal treatment, her homophobia and fear of lesbianism as a "pathology," particularly in some "extreme" cases, are evident.

Another 1970s article that perceives homosexuality as a disease, "When Women Love Other Women: A Frank Discussion of Female Homosexuality" (1971), musters the opinions of experts—two psychiatrists, two psychologists, and a sociologist—to answer questions about homosexuality, assuming that such professionals are necessary to understand the complex nuances of such a pathology. Although this article does a good job of representing a variety of opinions about lesbianism, it still presents an argument that is targeted at voyeuristic heterosexuals. But one can praise this article, and similar ones, for at least presenting a great deal of information about lesbianism and attempting to provide what the magazine identifies as the most "full and factual . . . treatment of lesbianism . . . it could" (84), even including the observations of lesbian activist Barbara Gittings.

Women's magazines in the 1970s varied in how accepting they were of lesbianism, but sometimes they ran articles that appeared surprisingly tolerant. *Mademoiselle,* in particular, published a number of articles that discussed lesbianism positively, including Karen Durbin's 1976 article where she comments that homosexuality "is an ordinary, integral part of the human experience and should be regarded as such" (46). Similarly, Amy Gross's article "If Lesbians Make You Nervous . . ." (1978) calls on heterosexual women to recognize that their fear of lesbians is ludicrous. These different reactions to lesbianism in articles from the 1970s are representative of a society struggling between an older concept of homosexuality as a sickness and a newer concept, made more public by gay rights activists, of homosexuality as a sexual orientation that signifies little or nothing about a person's mental state. The magazines were and continue to be involved in the project of changing society's views about the medical etiology of homosexuality.

In the 1980s, lesbianism became an even more popular topic for women's magazines, and it cropped up in a vast variety of contexts. The *Ladies' Home Journal* even ran an article entitled "Why Is Grandma Different?" in 1985 about Sarah Hatfield's lesbian mother. If Grandma could come out as a lesbian and not be threatened with trips to prison or to the psychologist, *Ladies' Home Journal* and other women's magazines were presenting a very different image of homosexuality than that put forth in 1965 when the *Ladies' Home Journal* could label homosexuality a "perversion." In the 1980s, lesbianism became chic, at least in the pages of some magazines, and racy or mildly scandalous stories about it appeared frequently. *Cosmopolitan,* in particular, could not seem to discuss lesbianism enough, and articles on the subject kept appearing, such as Marsha Kimmelman's "I Had a Lesbian Lover" (1981); Candace Lyle's "Lesbian Life Style" (1982); Linda Harrington's "What a Woman Taught Me about Love" (1983); Kiki Olson's "Women Who Have Lesbian Affairs" (1986); and Valerie Louis's "What It's Like to Be a Gay Woman Now" (1989).[4] Although other magazines did not match *Cosmopolitan's* rate of production when it came to articles about lesbianism in the 1980s, they still discussed the issue. *Essence* published Alan Ebert's "Lea Hopkins: Just Different" (1980). *Glamour* published Jane Adams's "When Your Friend Tells You She's Gay" (1982) and Martha Barrett's "Double Lives: What It's Like to Be a Lesbian Today" (1989). *Mademoiselle* published Pam Black's "When a Friend Tells You She's Gay" (1983). All of these magazines published as many, if not more, articles about male homosexuality, as well as numerous nonfeature articles about lesbian or gay issues. I do not wish to suggest that lesbianism or male homosexuality in any way became as prevalent as such women's magazine staples as thin thighs in thirty days, the grapefruit (or orange or papaya or banana or cranberry or watermelon . . .) diet, or ninety-nine ways to flatter your man. Such subjects overwhelmed—and continue to overwhelm—the limited amount of attention these magazines give to lesbianism. Still, even the relatively few articles that do appear can have a large impact because of society's deep ambivalence about lesbianism and the hidden nature of lesbianism in United States culture.

The content of the articles that appeared in the late 1980s shows some improvement over earlier years. Martha Barrett's "Double Lives: What It's Like to Be Lesbian Today" presents a fairly straightforward, factual account of lesbianism, although readers might notice that the disclaimer is included, "Names in personal stories have been changed" (316). Even the pictures in Barrett's essay are more realistic than ear lier pictures of lesbians with roses in their hands, wandering around in silk teddies, which were apt to appear in *Cosmopolitan* in the early 1980s. On the negative side, Barrett's heavy use of the first-person accounts of various lesbians works to distance her from the subject and her subjects; this perspective perpetuates voyeurism and encourages the reader to think of lesbians as Other.

In the 1990s, articles about lesbians and gay men continue to proliferate in women's magazines, with *Mademoiselle* publishing Elise Harris's "Women in Love" (1993), *Redbook* publishing Stephanie Salter's "My Two Moms" (1992), *Essence* publishing Linda Villarosa's "Coming Out" (1991) and Nadine Smith's "Homophobia: Will It Divide Us?" (1994), *Cosmopolitan* publishing S. Catherine Eaton's "A Matter of Pride: Being a Gay Woman in the Nineties" (1993), and *Glamour* publishing Amy Cunningham's "Not Just Another Prom Night" (1992) as well as Louise Sloan's "Do Ask, Do Tell: Lesbians Come Out at Work" (1994). Even the fairly conservative *Woman's Day* jumped into the fray with the article, "'Mom, I'm Gay': Coping with the News No Parent Wants to Hear" (Bartocci, 1992). These articles, at least on the surface, are becoming increasingly liberal and progressive. For example, Louise Sloan's "Do Ask, Do Tell" presents a clear, well-supported analysis of the different approaches lesbians adopt to being out at the workplace. The article even has two different sections about ways to work on coming-out issues, one labeled "if you're straight" and the other "if you're lesbian." Sloan also identifies herself as a lesbian at the beginning of the essay and describes homosexuality as being little dissimilar from heterosexuality, quite a different approach from the more sensation-filled approaches to lesbianism of the late 1970s and early 1980s.

In the 1990s, women's magazines frequently present lesbianism as trendy, hip, and stylish. In Elise Harris's essay "Women in Love," for instance, the author writes, "young lesbians: they're fresh, they're proud, they're comfortable with their sexuality. [H]aving staked out their own issues, they're now defining a new style" (180). The reference to style is particularly revealing, since style can be a force that confines women, including lesbians. An emphasis on style can encourage an emphasis on surfaces and on buying an endless supply of commodities to keep up the appearance of "style," which thrives on constant consumption. As Stuart Ewen writes about style and its ubiquitous nature in contemporary society, "The ability to stylize anything—toothpaste, clothing, roach spray, dog food, violence, other cultures around the world, ideas, and so on—encourages a comprehension of the world that focuses on its easily manipulated surfaces, while other meanings vanish to all but the critical eye" (262). Ewen's words help to explain the emphasis on lesbian style, fashion, and appearance that is found everywhere in 1990s women's magazines, including the photographs used in the stories. Readers are encouraged to look at the stylish, surface appearance of lesbianism, not to seek beneath the surface for a deeper understanding.

The portrayals of lesbianism from the 1980s and 1990s deserve closer scrutiny. Are they as liberating as they might first appear? Or are there ways in which these "liberating" articles might be functioning to reestablish the status quo? These are two of the questions that the next section seeks to address as it analyzes the significance of the boom years for descriptions of lesbianism in women's magazines.

Fluff and Femininity: Representing Lesbians in the 1980s and 1990s

"The lesbian life—just like *yours!*—is filled with both joy and heartache. Whether sympathetic or not, you'll be fascinated by this peek behind the façade" (Louis 229). This sentence is designed to lure readers into Valerie Louis's article "What It's Like to Be a Gay Woman Now." The words are revealing because they display the heterocentrism that is still such an evident part of women's magazines, despite the occasional appearance of an article about homosexuality. There is the assumption that the reader is looking behind a façade to lesbian life; no assumption exists that the reader might already be on the other side of the façade. And why use the word "façade," which suggests a false front that hides reality? Certainly presenting a false front to the world is generally considered to be negative and "fake." Also, the lesbian is positioned as a passive subject, something to be watched, poked, inspected, just like a laboratory mouse.

Louis's article, as well as other articles in women's magazines from the 1980s and 1990s, is quick to elide the true complexities of lesbianism; for instance, one woman in Louis's essay provides this simplistic story of her first kiss with a woman she has just met at a gay bar: "she walked me to my car and kissed me good night. It was absolute fireworks! I never dreamed anything could feel that good. It was like something out of *Casablanca,* when Humphrey Bogart kisses Ingrid Bergman for the first time. I finally felt I belonged. . . . I didn't feel different anymore" (228).[5] In the logic of women's magazines, it takes only a single kiss to make a lesbian feel entirely at ease with her sexual orientation. The article disregards the frequently complex, time-consuming process of coming out and coming to terms with one's lesbianism.

Louis's article also presents a rather limited portrait of other aspects of lesbian lives, although she does bring up some social issues that affect lesbians. For instance, she discusses being in the closet at work. However, she describes only women who are closeted; there is no similar discussion of women who are open about their sexual orientation at work. This omission creates an impression that all lesbians are fearful for job security and can never be open about their sexual orientation. Louis positively describes other aspects of lesbian life. She presents lesbians as normal women: "You work, shop, go to the health club, and sit in church right beside [lesbians]—because most lesbians look and act pretty much like other women in many ways—and you probably don't even know it" (229). Louis also gives her approval to lesbians acting as parents. In addition, she points out the negative stereotypes that heterosexual society holds about lesbians, concluding her article, "The only thing that appears to stand between [lesbians] and more completely satisfying lives is the falling away of stereotypes about what living the lesbian life is all about" (231). The impact of Louis's last words, however, is lessened when one notes that the creators of this article found it necessary to include the following warning with the photograph that accompanied the essay: "The models in the photo are not associated with the content of this article" (228). This disclaimer undermines the whole article's supposedly prolesbian stance. Readers are reminded of the glaring fact that many heterosexual women still worry about being mistaken for lesbians, so much so that a disclaimer is necessary. This article also mentions that "strong societal pressures" against lesbianism made it necessary for nearly all the lesbians with whom Louis talked to insist on anonymity "out of fear of losing jobs or the respect of family and friends who know nothing of their sexual preference" (229). This article sends ambivalent messages about the position of lesbians in United States society. The pressure of the real temporarily threatens to overthrow the fiction of the narrative, revealing the true social problems facing lesbians.

Louis's article, like many others, emphasizes the physical attractiveness of lesbians: "Ann . . . has a mane of dark, wavy hair and a winning manner. Yvette . . . has the exotic good looks of her Indian heritage" (229). "Many gay men behave, dress, and speak in certain styles that make them conspicuous. But most lesbians, precisely because they are attractive and traditionally feminine, pass in straight society, leaving many people to assume that only the few obviously butch-looking women are gay" (231). Louis's essay is far from alone in its emphasis on physical attractiveness. For example, Candace Lyle's "Lesbian Life Style" repeatedly emphasizes the beauty of the lesbians with whom the author speaks, describing one woman as "beautiful" and a second as a "tall, slim, auburn-haired stunner" (234). Yet another woman is described in the following fashion: "Her high-cheekboned face and lean, athletic body give her what she calls an androgynous appearance. This look is considered attractive today—think of lovely Patrice Donnelly in *Personal Best*" (235). In this fictional world, dowdy lesbians are in the minority. The reader is reassured that "Lesbians who outfit themselves to turn men *off*—or who dress *like* men—are in the minority" (234). Lest Louis's and Lyle's words fail to convince their readers, photographs of supposed lesbians are included. The models used in the photographs would not be out of place in a Frederick's of Hollywood catalogue; the women are beautiful and feminine, wear silken lingerie, and fail to look like any lesbians I have ever encountered, although I recognize that some exist.[6] Viewers are given a fantasy image of lesbians, which is as unrealistic as the image that all lesbians are ugly. Also, using models who look stereotypically heterosexual pretending to be lesbians provides titillation without threat as there is an implicit understanding that these are not "real" lesbians.

In yet another article, Linda Harrington's "What a Woman Taught Me about Love," the narrator emphasizes that the main lesbian character, Caroline, is stereotypically pretty: "She was a beautiful woman, my age, thirty, with strawberry blond hair she wore shoulder length, a marvelously smooth, lightly tanned complexion, and a figure I envied. I'd noticed men trying to attract her attention, but she never seemed to be aware of them" (104). In the land of *Cosmo,* it is important that the lesbian be highly attractive and appealing to men. What this emphasis on beauty does is leave in place stereotypical notions about what is attractive in women. By no means does *Cosmo,* or any other mass-market women's magazine, ever suggest that husky, tattoo-sporting, swaggering, leather-jacketed butch dykes are attractive; they simply are not considered. For *Cosmo* and other women's magazines, such nonfeminine images must be deleted or hidden, because what the magazines do not wish to convey is that other standards of beauty exist, particularly when a great deal of the magazines' advertising revenue comes from manufacturers of cosmetics, perfumes, and women's clothing, not businesses in a rush for women to adopt lesbian butch styles, which can be constructed with relatively few commodities (i.e., short hair, jeans and a white t-shirt, maybe a leather jacket) in contrast to more traditionally feminine styles.

Creating a stereotype of lesbian attractiveness conveys a false impression not only to heterosexual women but also to homosexual ones, who are led to believe that they, just like their heterosexual sisters, should strive to achieve the images that the magazines tout. In other words, lesbians potentially can become entrapped in what Naomi Wolf identifies as the endless fruitless search for the Professional Beauty Qualification, her term for the idea that every woman can and must strive to achieve the flawless beauty of a professional model. Women's magazines are one of the sites that Wolf points out as a breeding ground for belief in the PBQ, and this belief applies as much to the images of lesbians in these magazines as it does to the images of heterosexual women. The repeated descriptions and pictures of extremely attractive women create a standard that the majority of lesbians, just like the majority of heterosexual women, can never achieve. Thus lesbian readers, like heterosexual ones, are pulled into the consumer ethos that forms the heart of the magazines.

But why are women's magazines so intent on portraying the lesbian as a shop-till-you-drop type of gal? One of the reasons for this appropriation is that the magazines are specifically designed to sell items to women, targeting them as consumers of soap, shampoo, body lotion, foundation cream, mink coats, Cartier watches, and countless other products. Because the magazines depend heavily on advertising for their revenues, their designers need to think of some way to contain the lesbian, who is commonly depicted as a woman who burned her Neiman Marcus credit card and who frequents thrift stores to maintain her wardrobe of pre-grunge flannel shirts, torn jeans, and Birkenstocks, which she has owned for fifteen years. Discussing such an antishopper in women's magazines, which offer a paean to our commodity-choked culture, requires careful maneuvering. One effective way to present lesbians is to re-create them, whether they are willing or not, as happy, all-American girls who want to shop every bit as much as their heterosexual sisters.

By emphasizing that lesbians are beautiful, well dressed, and born to shop, Louis, Lyle, Harrington, and other writers build up an image of lesbians as being "just like us"—or, in other words, "homosexual = heterosexual"—a strategy with possible dangers for lesbians and lesbian culture. Discussing lesbian images that appear in mainstream texts, Danae Clark mentions some of the potential dangers to lesbians from such images in her well-known essay "Commodity Lesbianism" (1991): "Mainstream media texts employ representational strategies that generally refer to gays and lesbians in *anti-essentialist* terms. That is, homosexuals are not depicted as inherently different from heterosexuals; neither does there exist a unified or authentic 'gay sensibility'" (192). She continues: "when a sense of lesbian or gay identity is lost, the straight world finds it easier to ignore social and political issues that directly affect gays and lesbians as a group" (193). Clark's words aptly describe the operations of women's magazines in the 1980s and 1990s. The magazines defuse the potential threat posed by lesbianism to heterosexual hegemony by suggesting that lesbians in the past have been sadly misrepresented; actually, the magazines reassure readers, lesbians have exactly the same concerns as heterosexual women. Nowhere is this strategy more blatant than in Amy Cunningham's "Not Just Another Prom Night" (1992), a lengthy essay that discusses how Heidi and Missy, two lesbians attending a high school senior prom, are very much like any other young women worrying about the prom. They fuss about what to wear, take a limousine to the prom, have photographs taken, and buy each other lavender rose boutonnieres. Anything distinctive about lesbians must be smoothed over, ignored, "normalized," making heterosexual and homosexual women appear little different and defusing the threat of lesbian organization and unity. A group of man-hating lesbians dressing as men might be a potential threat to heterosexual harmony, but an isolated few lesbians, attractive and well dressed, seem to pose little danger and do not remind readers of the many other real lesbians who might not be so polite and decorous.

If articles from the last two decades were not busy insisting on the physical beauty of lesbians or making them into "normal" girls, more interested in proms than politics, they were frequently intent on depicting them as primarily sexual creatures, who, it was implied, lacked the moral standards of heterosexuals. An example of this appears in the article "What a Woman Taught Me about Love," which recounts the story of Linda Harrington, who lives with an abusive husband, Howard.[7] She leaves him, and—surprise, surprise—meets a lesbian, Caroline, who introduces her to the pleasures of lesbian lovemaking. What follows is a lesbian affair with a woman who seems too self-sacrificing to be true. Caroline even tells Linda that her two children "need a father. . . . You're doing a magnificent job with them now, but they need a man's influence" (108). Caroline is obviously not a great threat to the patriarchal status quo. Sexually, however, Caroline does seem to have an edge, which Linda describes: "I had never experienced with Howard or any other man the strange thrills she could arouse. . . . I never knew love-making could have such variety, such passion and warmth" (108). Caroline's prowess seems unnerving to heterosexuals, until readers are informed that she "couldn't remain happy with one person for very long" (108). The narrative perpetuates the cultural stereotype that lesbian relationships are fleeting, and it comes as no surprise to readers when Linda and Caroline go their separate ways. At this point, in true storybook fashion, Bruce appears, and Linda is swept off her feet and into his bed in short order: "I'd never believed love-making could be so exquisite, so warm and friendly and passionate at the same time" (112). Linda's description of Bruce's lovemaking, which sounds remarkably similar to her description of Caroline's, shows readers that men have nothing to fear from the sexual prowess of lesbians; a woman just has to be careful to get the "right" man, not a dud like Howard. Conveniently, the two women remain friends, and Caroline even offers to baby-sit so that Bruce and Linda will have more time together, but the reader is left with a clear understanding about where the lasting relationships are. Linda concludes, "I'm thirty-three, Bruce is thirty-five, and we figure we have a pretty good chance of celebrating our fiftieth wedding anniversary together" (112). Compared to Caroline's flightiness, Linda's husband is all stability. The message is plain: Lesbian desire, no matter how sensual or passionate, is doomed to be temporary; one should not assume that homosexuals can have the durable, lasting relationships that heterosexuals can.

The representation of lesbian relationships as brief sexual flings, which fail to have the lasting quality of heterosexual relationships, is emphasized repeatedly in women's magazines. One of my favorite examples is Kiki Olson's "Women Who Have Lesbian Affairs" (1986), an article that begins: "You and a pretty girlfriend are gabbing, laughing . . . then somebody is *kissing* somebody. Not possible, you say? Listen to these stories from women who stumbled innocently into surprisingly *delicious* same-sex liaisons!" (192). This description makes lesbianism sound like an accident, as well as a primarily sexual relationship. Olson's article goes out of its way to reassure its presumed heterosexual readers: "psychologists hold that one—or even several— gay affairs don't establish a homosexual identity. . . . Often, women involved in a lesbian relationship see it as a 'rest stop' between heterosexual entanglements. For them, the relationship is less sexually com-

pelling than it is warmly reassuring" (192). Again, Olson emphasizes
that lesbianism is only a brief break between the more "compelling"
relationships women have with men.

Another article that emphasizes the primarily sexual nature of
lesbian affairs is Marsha Kimmelman's "I Had a Lesbian Lover" (1981),
which tells the story of a heterosexual woman who has a lesbian
relationship. Happily (?), the woman recognizes that she prefers sex
with men, and she can dismiss her relationship with another woman
as merely a sexual adventure: "I'm glad I let myself experiment with a
sexual variation I know must seem shocking to some" (86). Her
lesbian affair only leaves her "more confident and giving with men"
(86). This article is remarkably similar to "What a Woman Taught Me
about Love." Heterosexual woman meets lesbian, has lesbian affair,
but goes back to men, better able to interact with them. This philosophy is familiar: Lesbianism is just a phase that will ultimately vanish; lesbianism is also primarily a sexual relationship that, ironically
enough, will better prepare a woman for her future relationships with
men.

What readers discover repeatedly in *Cosmopolitan, Essence,
Glamour, Mademoiselle, Vogue,* and other women's magazines is a fantasy about lesbian and heterosexual women's lives. Inevitably, these
fantasies assure the implied readers (heterosexual women) that lesbianism might offer fleeting sexual satisfaction but no long-term commitment and that heterosexual relationships are still superior to homosexual ones. This strategy of seeming to critique heterosexual
relationships but, ultimately, working to shore them up is one that
many popular women's texts follow, as feminist critic Tania Modleski
notes in her book *Loving with a Vengeance: Mass-Produced Fantasies for
Women* (1982): "while popular feminine texts provide outlets for
women's dissatisfaction with male-female relationships, they never
question the primacy of these relationships. Nor do they overtly
question the myth of male superiority or the institutions of marriage
and the family. Indeed, patriarchal myths and institutions are, on the
manifest level, wholeheartedly embraced, although the anxieties and
tensions they give rise to may be said to provoke the need for the texts
in the first place" (113). *Cosmopolitan* and other similar magazines

might explore lesbianism, but in no way do these magazines suggest that the patriarchal, heterosexual order should be abandoned. Lesbianism is inevitably swallowed up by the overwhelming heterosexuality of the magazines, which is all-pervasive; as Erica Rand notes, the threat posed by lesbians in *Cosmopolitan* is made to seem less significant because of "the obviously heterosexual context in which each lesbian article occurs, amid advice columns, ads, and articles that presume or articulate a quest for heterosexual bliss" ("Lesbian" 125). In such an environment, lesbianism will inevitably seem a weak option in comparison to the dominance of heterosexuality. Homosexuality and heterosexuality will never appear to be equal choices because lesbianism remains ghettoized in the magazine's universe in the form of a single article, which can easily be swept away by the glut of advertisements, articles, and photographs directed at a heterosexual audience.

Since women's magazines adopt a predominantly heterosexual subject position when discussing lesbianism, it is difficult for the reader to avoid being seduced by the idea that heterosexuality is the norm and lesbianism is always the Other. *Cosmopolitan,* like other women's magazines, possesses "the ability to make heterosexuality look like the natural and most significant referent toward which even homoerotic depictions point" (Rand, "Lesbian" 135). This strategy appears in Jane Adams's article "When Your Friend Tells You She's Gay." The very title presupposes that the reader is heterosexual and her friend is a lesbian, not vice versa; the article is not entitled "When Your Friend Tells You She's Straight." The entire article is directed at counseling a heterosexual woman about how she should react to a friend who suddenly announces her lesbianism. Heterosexuality is presented as the very explicit norm for behavior. In a similar fashion, the implied reader of Renita Weems's "Just Friends" or Pam Black's "When a Friend Tells You She's Gay" is heterosexual. Like the other two articles, Black's is filled with information about what the presumably fearful heterosexual woman should do when a friend admits to being a lesbian. Black repeatedly uses advice from experts, such as psychologists and psychotherapists, to assure the heterosexual woman that her fears are perfectly acceptable. Through this emphasis on the

reader's presumed heterosexuality, the magazines implicitly undermine some of their more positive statements about lesbianism. Also,
lesbian readers are pushed into the margins; their reading experience
is simply not considered, which reveals the superficiality of the magazines' attention to lesbianism.

A central paradox with which women's magazines wrestle is that
they wish to maintain the centrality and dominance of heterosexuality,
but they also want to defuse the potential threat of lesbianism by
making it seem as "normal" (i.e., heterosexual) as possible. Even the
most recent articles about lesbianism function to "normalize" the
lesbian, a strategy that might make heterosexual readers more comfortable but that elides some of the significant differences between
lesbians and heterosexual women. For instance, S. Catherine Eaton's
essay "A Matter of Pride: Being a Gay Woman in the Nineties" (1993)
is an improvement over other articles, perhaps because a lesbian wrote
it, but it still presents a skewed vision of lesbian life. Notably, the two
women featured in the article's sole photograph both have long hair
and appear suitably attractive and feminine, typical of the emphasis on
femininity in the magazines' portrayal of lesbians. Femininity is again
emphasized at the beginning of the article: "My long hair and dresses
don't fit the image most people have of lesbians" (226). Eaton's article
also tends to make lesbianism look like a decision that is largely
concerned with whether a woman will ever go to parties again: "Even
at the start, being gay wasn't the social disaster I feared. Nobody I cared
about treated me differently, and I got more invitations than ever to
college parties from those who found it trendy to have a homosexual
or two in attendance. And when my straight friends began getting
married, they all asked me to bring my girlfriend to their weddings"
(227). Although Eaton's words sound as though lesbianism is primarily an issue of whether a woman is going to be popular on the party
circuit, this essay also includes sections on parents' reactions to their
children being gay and about antilesbian violence; these sections are
mixed in with comments about the lesbianism of such stars as k. d.
lang, Sandra Bernhard, and Martina Navratilova. To borrow Alisa
Solomon's words, Eaton's article "takes the tone of a *National Geographic* special" ("*Cosmo*" 24), providing a broad overview of the

"natural" habitat of the lesbian. The lesbian appears very much like a cheetah, rhinoceros, elephant, ocelot, or any other rare species that is being scrutinized by the writer. This *National Geographic* style, which seems to be endemic in women's magazines, does have drawbacks. Although Eaton is able to bring up some important social issues regarding lesbianism, lumping these issues in with a survey of lesbian "stars" and a review of the author's party invitations both before and after coming out trivializes the importance of such issues as anti-lesbian violence.

Eaton's article, like many others from the 1980s and 1990s, focuses on lesbians as chic and fashionable. This perspective on lesbian life would not have been possible without some dramatic changes in the lesbian community itself. In the 1970s many lesbians strove to appear as unfashionable as possible in a protest against society's beauty dictates, but this image changed in the 1980s when what have been called "the fashion wars" erupted.[8] During this period, many lesbians, particularly young, urban ones, reevaluated their attitudes toward fashion and style. Many lesbians recognized that being lesbian did not necessarily entail shopping at Goodwill or wearing their brothers' hand-me-downs. In the 1980s, lesbian fashion changed dramatically, as lesbians from coast to coast played with combining sequins and combat boots or a tuxedo and a feather boa. Play was in. Fashion became a way for lesbians to re-create, redesign, reimagine, reexplore their lesbian identities, and perhaps to discover new ones.

Nowhere was the heightened lesbian interest in fashion more apparent than in the group of women known as "lipstick lesbians" for their combination of stereotypically feminine styles with lesbianism. Danae Clark describes the radical potential of these lesbians and their rethinking of their relationship to fashion: "there is more to 'lipstick lesbians' or 'style nomads' than a freewheeling attitude toward their status as consumers or a boredom with the relatively static nature of the 'natural look.' . . . Fashion-conscious dykes are rebelling against the idea that there is a clear one-to-one correspondence between fashion and identity" (185). Veronica Groocock writes positively about the prevalence of lipstick lesbians in the media: "It would be all too easy to dismiss the 1990s vogue for 'designer dykes' or 'lipstick lesbians' as a

myth or ploy concocted by a male-dominated media to sell newspapers. There may indeed be some element of escapism in this particular image, a reaction against the 'right-on' earnestness of lesbian feminism, a way of putting back the 'sex' into sexual politics. However, I
believe that in the process it has helped remove any remaining stigma
attached to lesbianism, making society less inclined to regard dykes as
victims or objects of ridicule" (118). Although I agree with Clark and
Groocock that lipstick lesbians are too complicated to be viewed as
merely a sign of lesbian cooption, I am far more ambivalent about how
representations of lipstick lesbians or "designer dykes" are manipulated in the mainstream press, such as women's magazines. Do wom-
en's magazines recognize that lipstick lesbians are rebellious, or do
such media forms simply try to incorporate lipstick lesbians into
dominant forms of acceptable femininity? As I have argued, descriptions or pictures of lesbians in the popular media can work to assure
heterosexual women that lesbians are just like heterosexuals, an assumption that might offer lesbians more status in the dominant society but that can also negate the differences that make up their
cultural identity.

Beyond *Cosmo*

"The *Cosmo* dyke cannot roam free in the *Cosmo* world, and the vision
that appears total is only partial" (Rand, "Lesbian" 128). Erica Rand's
statement describes the boundaries that limit the *Cosmo* dyke, the
Essence dyke, the *Glamour* dyke, the *Vogue* dyke, or the dyke that
appears in any other popular women's magazine. Lesbians are carefully contained in these magazines. Although the magazines give lip
service to lesbianism as an acceptable choice for a woman's sexual
orientation, the notion that heterosexuality is the desired norm goes
unchallenged and is supported by the overall heterosexual focus of the
magazines. The magazines' attention to lesbianism, which might seem
progressive, actually functions to delineate lesbians as deserving *some*
human rights but in no way having the unquestioned centrality or
importance of heterosexuals.

Also, the magazines, particularly in the 1980s and 1990s, enforce the idea of the "correct" lesbian being a consumer and a style maven, who is as obsessed with the PBQ as a heterosexual woman. This is a disturbing image, one that negates or denies the identity and political commitment of countless lesbians. As I have suggested, what is even more disturbing is that readers can assume that this mythical vision of lesbianism is a mimetic reflection of reality, particularly because women's magazines through their use of realism and personal narratives encourage readers to think of their articles as realistic portraits of life, rather than as texts that mythologize lesbian lives. These strangely distorted representations of lesbians have the potential power to create an image of lesbianism that has little or no basis in reality.

But it is unreasonable to interpret the lesbian representations in women's magazines as possessing only the power to coopt. The magazines can be read in many different ways. As popular culture theorist John Fiske, writing about the varied readings of popular texts, argues, "A reading, like a text, cannot of itself be essentially resistant or conformist: it is its use by a socially situated reader that determines its politics" (44–45). Readers, whether lesbian or not, bring different backgrounds and beliefs to their reading of *Cosmopolitan, Essence, Redbook, Glamour,* or other magazines; thus the reading experiences are bound to be unique. My friends and I, when we read *Cosmopolitan* together in college, were certainly not the readers that the magazine had in mind. Other readers will read these magazines, or other popular texts, in a subversive fashion. Whether applied to women's magazines or Nancy Drew books, such reading strategies, however, do not negate the fact that these popular images of lesbians are being read "straight" by countless readers and are, whether we like it or not, influencing lesbian identities or the perceptions of lesbian identities.

Nor are women's magazines alone as a source that shapes lesbians' lives today. The media, whether popular magazines, television, or movies, are increasingly filled with images of lesbians. Whether in magazines such as *Cosmopolitan* and *Essence,* television shows such as "Oprah" and "Roseanne," or other media formats, depictions of lesbianism are becoming increasingly prevalent and are far from ideologically neutral. Instead, such representations are shaping, both positively and negatively, lesbian identities in the United States today. As this chapter has demonstrated, such representations can work to contain the threat of lesbianism even when they might appear liberal and tolerant. Such popular images, I believe, will become an even more important battle site for changing portrayals of lesbianism, as queer activism and agitation for civil rights for lesbians and gay men make lesbians even more visible in United States society, resulting in the popular media redoubling their efforts to contain the threat to the dominant order posed by homosexuality.

2

Forms of Resistance

4

Is Nancy Drew Queer?
Popular Reading Strategies for
the Lesbian Reader

"She is as immaculate and self-possessed as a Miss America on tour. She is as cool as Mata Hari and as sweet as Betty Crocker," writes Bobbie Ann Mason about a supersleuth with whom we are all familiar: Nancy Drew (50). No one can question her prominence as a cultural icon. Along with the 80 million-plus Nancy Drew books (in seventeen different languages) that have been sold (Watson 60), Nancy also has had, at various times, her own television series ("The Nancy Drew/ Hardy Boys Mystery Hour"),[1] lunch box, cookbook, two coloring books, datebook, diary, and a "Nancy Drew Mystery Game" that Parker Brothers sold from 1957 to 1959 (Chapman 31). If this is not enough Drew miscellanea to pique your interest, you might wish to hunt down the three Nancy Drew movies that Warner Brothers produced between 1938 and 1939, join the official Nancy Drew fan club, or look up the *Playboy* story on Pamela Sue Martin that promises "TV's Nancy Drew undraped" (Caprio 181). Nancy's fame is such that the first academic conference on Nancy Drew in 1993 was featured on the front page of the *New York Times*.

Lesbians have read the Drew books, imagining that they, too, could be like Nancy or be part of her world. As evidence of lesbian fascination with the girl detective, she has been the subject of a number of lesbian novels and short stories. For example, Mabel Maney wrote the novel *The Case of the Not-So-Nice Nurse* (1993), a lesbian spoof on the Nancy Drew and Cherry Ames stories. In this book, "Nancy Clue" is a superhuman character who manages to tie up three villains with only one short piece of rope, thanks to her Girl Scout training. At one point in her adventures, Nancy Clue reminisces about being trapped in a tunnel for three days, commenting, "Luckily I had a loaf of bread, chocolate bars, oranges, and some milk in my purse" (142). Maney's work, a parody in which the majority of characters, including Nancy, turn out to be queer, has proven very popular in the lesbian community.[2] This fascination with rewriting the life of a favorite childhood icon demonstrates Nancy's subversive potential.

To understand her subversive possibilities, Nancy can be compared to another omnipresent paragon of popular femininity: Barbie. Nancy Drew and Barbie are names recognized even by those who have never read a Drew book or played with a Barbie doll. Both Nancy Drew and Barbie have been, and continue to be, phenomenally successful. Both Nancy and Barbie in many ways epitomize a vision of socially acceptable and presumably desirable femininity. At first glance, Nancy, with her fashionable wardrobe, football-playing boyfriend, and lawyer daddy, and Barbie, with her long, silken tresses, Malibu beach house, and Ken the wonder boyfriend, might seem to offer little possibility for subversion of the dominant status quo and to display little apparent homosexuality. But is this really true? To borrow Lynda Hart's words from her book, *Fatal Women: Lesbian Sexuality and the Mark of Aggression* (1994), "Homosexuality is . . . most prominently represented when it is virtually under erasure" (66). Sometimes the cultural icon, such as Barbie or Nancy, that *seems* at first glance most representative of mainstream heterosexual values also offers the greatest number of possibilities for alternative homosexual readings. For instance, Erica

Rand writes that Barbie "has some features particularly conducive to lesbian reappropriation: the nifty Barbie-of-the-eighties slogan 'We girls can do anything' . . . and a series of wardrobe-crafted identities to pull out of her closet" ("We Girls" 190). Barbie has been dressed in drag, redrawn as "AIDS" Barbie, and had her computer chip replaced with one from a GI Joe so that she snarls, "Vengeance is mine!"[3] All of these actions by various groups—such as one that calls itself the Barbie Liberation Organization—endlessly re-create and provide new readings of Barbie and the complex symbology that surrounds her. In a similar fashion, this chapter will focus on a related destabilizing strategy: analyzing the Nancy Drew books as speaking not only to mainstream heterosexual society but also to lesbian society. By examining the homoerotic counterplot of these books and discussing the reactions of lesbian readers to these works, this essay will help to explain how lesbians read texts targeted to a largely heterosexual society.

I must include a caveat at this point. I am not suggesting that lesbians *always* read differently than heterosexual women. This is not true. Despite different sexual orientations, readers might receive the very same message when reading a book from the Nancy Drew series, but this is not always the case. Often lesbians do read differently than heterosexual women. In this chapter, I shall discuss messages that both heterosexual and homosexual women receive from the Nancy Drew books, as well as focusing on some messages that heterosexual readers most likely will not discover in the Drew novels. Such an approach, I believe, will show how lesbian readings may overlap, but are not identical to, heterosexual readings. Examining these lesbian subtexts is important because their outsider status allows lesbians to critique heterosexual norms and to question the myth of heterosexual hegemony.

This essay is far from the first to adopt a feminist approach to Nancy Drew. Nancy has attracted approval as well as criticism from feminists.[4] Eileen Goudge Zuckerman claims that the girl detective was her "first feminist role model" (74), and Joanne Furtak argues that Nancy was "a feminist's dream before the dream became fashionable" (90). Others are more doubtful about Nancy's feminist potential, including Ellen Brown, who discusses what she perceives to be Nancy's wasted life: "doomed forever to be eighteen, sexually frozen, unmothered and unmothering, married to the masculine world of order and reason, with avocation but no vocation, dependent on the Great White Father for economic security and permission, driving around in daddy's car" (10). Although she calls Nancy the "most independent of girl sleuths" (49), Bobbie Ann Mason also questions Nancy's appeal for feminists: "She always has it both ways—protected and free. She is an eternal girl, a stage which is a false ideal for women in our time" (75). These critics are correct in pointing out Nancy's ambiguous character, yet it is this very ambiguity that makes the Nancy Drew books such a fruitful site for contesting cultural norms and gender values, as I shall show throughout this chapter. The apparent "normality" of the stories calls for reading strategies that emphasize alternative approaches and perspectives in order to destabilize the work's surface meaning.

I should also point out that not all lesbian readers have unambivalent responses to the Drew books. Some of the women whom I interviewed clearly feel alienated because, for them, Nancy represents mainstream heterosexual values. Elaine, for instance, comments, "I read many of the Nancy Drew books, but I preferred the Hardy Boys and the Alfred Hitchcock Adventurer series as Nancy kept getting silly over boys." Many lesbians prefer the Hardy Boys, Frank and Joe, and their wilder adventures to Nancy's milder exploits. Another woman, Jill, writes, "My sister (who is straight) read the Nancy Drew series while I read the Hardy Boys series; we traded books but we each thought our series was better." Other lesbians rejected Nancy for other reasons; Laura, for example, explains: "I only read about three or four Nancy Drew books. The books I read were from the 'newer edition' where Nancy always has to have help—usually from a male counterpart. I didn't like that and so went off in search of books where the leading character was more independent—like *Harriet the Spy*." The Nancy Drew books, like so many forms of popular media, are always going to be shifting, ambiguous texts; they will never have a fixed meaning for an entire group of readers, including lesbians. But we should explore how some lesbian readers turn the Drew books into a subversive reading experience, reading against the grain of the implied text.

How Lesbians Read

Before turning to the novels themselves, it is necessary to discuss how lesbians read texts that are targeted chiefly at a heterosexual market. A number of influential essays have been published on this subject.[5] One of the most astute is Danae Clark's discussion of how gays and lesbians read gayness into an advertisement that might seem to have no overt homosexual content: "gays and lesbians can read into an ad certain subtextual elements that correspond to experiences with or representations of gay/lesbian culture" (183). This subtextual reading strategy works when lesbians read fiction, too. They look for meanings that lurk behind the text's apparently heterosexual surface, knowing that lesbian experiences, whether in fiction or reality, are rarely overt. When lesbians read, they actively disassemble the dominant heterosexual plot, demonstrating that heterosexuality does not hold its culturally prescribed central role for all readers. Clark goes on to discuss how lesbians view advertisements: "because lesbians (as members of a heterosexist culture) have been taught to read the heterosexual possibilities of representations, the 'straight' reading is never entirely erased or replaced" (187). She cautions, "The straight readings, however, do not simply exist alongside alternative readings, nor do they necessarily diminish the pleasure found in the alternative readings" (188). Although Clark is discussing advertising, her words are equally applicable to novels, including the Nancy Drew books. Lesbians are always aware that the dominant heterosexual narrative of most fiction is a myth that fails to reveal the content of lesbian lives. Thus lesbian readers search for the lesbian subtext that speaks to them and their experiences. Lesbians read and interpret aspects of a text that heterosexual readers might not notice in the same way (such as George's evident butchness). Lesbian readers do more, as Jean E. Kennard points out, than merely "substituting 'woman' wherever the word 'man' appears" (651); they are constantly involved in altering the entire text. As Gabriele Griffin suggests in her book *Heavenly Love? Lesbian Images in Twentieth-Century Women's Writing* (1993), "The lesbian reader has two positions open to her in her engagement with a text: identification and dissociation. Through her reading she can impose on the text a lesbian identity simply by asserting it. Similarly, she can declare a text *'not that.'* However she argues her position, it will not inevitably be shared by others" (7). This suggests not that lesbian readers ignore entirely the "straight" reading but that they are reading multiple levels simultaneously.

Reading the Nancy Drew books from a lesbian perspective entails being a resistant reader who refuses to accept the books' apparent messages about society, cultural values, and gender. What exactly do I mean by a "lesbian perspective"? Julia Penelope provides an excellent explanation of this term: "[T]he 'Lesbian Perspective' is a 'turn of mind,' a stance in the world, that asks unpopular questions, that can be comfortable only when it confronts the sources of its discomfort, a frame of mind that refuses to accept what most people believe to be 'true.' . . . The Lesbian Perspective makes it possible to challenge the accuracy of male consensus reality, and to create a reality that is Lesbian-defined and Lesbian sustaining. Once we learn to perceive the world from our own perspective, outside the edges of the pale male map, we'll find it not only recognizable, but familiar" ("The Lesbian" 90, 107). By asking "unpopular questions" about a text, lesbian readers decenter the assumed "normalcy" of heterosexuality. In this way lesbians create realities that might be far more intriguing. Such an alternative reading strategy produces a text that might be unrecognizable to Carolyn Keene's implied readers (prepubescent, heterosexual girls) but one that is easily recognizable to countless lesbians. (Mabel Maney made this way of reading overt and public in her novel and its two sequels—she brought the lesbian subtext to the foreground.)

But why bother with untangling the lesbian plot or plots in a seemingly "straight" text? What does this process actually achieve? Marilyn Farwell provides the most accurate explanation of the value of this approach in her essay "Heterosexual Plots and Lesbian Subtexts: Toward a Theory of Lesbian Narrative Space." According to Farwell, "many feminist theorists, whatever their theoretical allegiances, have explored the importance of women's bonding, often termed lesbian whatever the sexuality of the women, as a powerful tool for breaking narrative codes. . . . in opening a new narrative space the reader can forge a subtext that explores female desire while the main text does not. The subtext gives us the possibility for a transgressive narrative that can be more fully realized in other narratives or that can be part of our readings of other texts that seem to reinforce the bonding between heterosexuality and the narrative" (93, 102). Such a subversive reading approach to Nancy Drew opens up new avenues for women by showing that heterosexuality, even when it seems most stable, can be undermined. Lesbianism cannot easily be separated from the text, despite the book's apparent allegiance to heterosexual values. In a society that privileges the heterosexual narrative, such a reading strategy, although applied in this chapter primarily to Carolyn Keene's fiction, is a method of interpretation that has relevance far beyond this particular series.

A Few Words about Nancy's Roots

Before turning to the series and its lesbian readers, we must first know a little about Nancy's origin. From where did this titian-haired (sometimes it is golden-haired) WASP detective spring? Many unwittingly assume that "Carolyn Keene"—the name that appears on all the books' covers—created Nancy Drew, but Keene is only a pseudonym used by a large number of writers responsible for creating the series. Actually, Nancy was originally the creation of Edward Stratemeyer, who has been called the "Henry Ford" of the serial book business, cranking out thousands of juvenile books in an assembly-line process (Nye 78).[6] The Stratemeyer syndicate was phenomenally successful; over 200 million copies of Stratemeyer's serial novels have been sold (Johnson ix). The Nancy Drew series was far from the only product of the huge Stratemeyer syndicate, which at one point produced over 700 book titles (Soderbergh 865). Among all the characters in these volumes, however, Nancy is the star, outshining a number of other girl detectives, such as Ruth Fielding, Betty Gordon, and Nan Sherwood, who were already in the Stratemeyer lineup when Nancy appeared on the scene. The Nancy Drew series started in 1930 with the publication of *The Secret of the Old Clock,* which was an immediate hit, as were all the other books in the series. Not even the Depression dampened their success, and the books have continued to sell throughout the years, developing an almost cultlike following. Of the Stratemeyer books, the Nancy Drew and Hardy Boys mysteries account for over half the estimated sales, with the Nancy Drew books outselling by millions even the popular Hardy Boys (Johnson 142).[7]

When Edward Stratemeyer died, his daughters took over the syndicate. One daughter in particular, Harriet S. Adams, provided the impetus for the Nancy Drew series throughout much of the twentieth century and ran the syndicate until her death. Along with her partner Andrew Svenson and assorted ghost writers, including Walter Karing and Mildred Wirt Benson, whom most consider the true "mother" of Nancy, Harriet Adams wrote the Nancy Drew books until her death in 1982, when Nancy Axelrad took over. Although there is an ongoing battle about exactly what writer wrote which Drew novel, everyone acknowledges that Adams had a crucial role.[8] Early on, she was responsible for introducing Bess Marvin, George Fayne—Nancy's primary companions, who replaced Nancy's first pal Helen Corning—and Ned Nickerson, Nancy's boyfriend (Felder 31). Adams, during her fifty years of involvement with the Drew series, deeply influenced the development and characterization of Nancy according to her own standards, even referring to Nancy as her "daughter" (Caprio 157).

Adams also played a crucial role in implementing the extensive revisions of the Drew series in 1959 (mostly eliminating racial stereotypes and updating references to technology) to keep it current (Johnson 145). Some of these alterations were no doubt an improvement, like doing away with the crude ethnic stereotypes of the earlier volumes and making Hannah Gruen almost a substitute mother for Nancy rather than merely a servant. Other alterations were less beneficial. Adams thought Nancy was "too bold and bossy" and sought to tone down her character (qtd. in Caprio 22). Reflecting the cultural changes of the 1950s, Nancy lost some of the vigor that had been associated with her in the past, which is one of the reasons some women readers search out the older versions.

Since Adams's death, the Drew books have continued to do well for their new publisher, Simon and Schuster, with close to a million copies a year sold throughout the 1980s (Johnson 147). The Drew books even led to a spinoff series in 1986 for teenage readers, the

Nancy Drew Files, whose volumes have more in common with Gothic romances than with the early Drew books (Johnson 153). Another series, the Nancy Drew/Hardy Boys Super Mysteries, started in 1988, features stories that star both Nancy Drew and the Hardy Boys, an easy way to get more boy-girl interaction into the novels and, presumably, to attract a greater number of readers. The latter books will not be the focus of this chapter for a variety of reasons. First, they have not been around long enough to analyze their impact on lesbian readers. Second, the books have actually become less interesting: Recent writers have stressed girl-boy relationships ad nauseam, devoting much less space to how Nancy relates to other women, such as her crime-fighting friends Bess and George. These changes, moreover, have come at the expense of the novels' plots, which appear far less developed than in earlier books. Third, for the sake of this essay, I am primarily interested in how past lesbian readers have experienced and interpreted the older Drew stories, as well as the queer subtext that can be uncovered in these books.

Nancy Drew and Company

Nancy leads a life that any lesbian would envy.[9] The eighteen-year-old daughter (she was originally sixteen, but her age was changed so she could drive in every state) of a famous criminal lawyer, she has a remarkable amount of freedom, despite her youth. Conveniently, her mother died when Nancy was three, leaving her with a father who is "the most elusive parent anybody ever owned" (Keene, *Nancy's Mysterious Letter* 178), freeing his daughter to sleuth to her heart's content. Not even Nancy's schooling holds her back; readers never actually see her in attendance at high school, although we are informed in later books that she did go to high school and did attend art school briefly. This apparent lack of education does not seem to interfere with Nancy's intellectual accomplishments, as she speaks German, French, and Spanish and has reasoning skills that would be a match for Sherlock Holmes.

Nancy's intelligence is fortunate, because her skills are certainly put to the test in her hometown of River Heights, which must be the most crime-ridden suburban town in all the Midwest. In book after book, she encounters villains lurking in her garden, burglarizing her house, slipping away with her possessions, and hiding behind every shrub and tree. Any normal girl would know that it was time to find a new home, but Nancy is no normal girl: She glories in her crime-ridden surroundings, welcoming each new exploit. The formulaic plot of each book revolves around her being introduced to a new central mystery, which turns out to be interconnected with two or three other mysterious affairs. Trying to solve the mystery, she searches for clues, questions a variety of suspects, and travels widely. While in pursuit of her goal, she is constantly menaced by evil characters. Typically, near the book's conclusion, she is locked in some confined area, which is always dark, dreary, dank, dangerous, and so excessively dirty that it is obvious her dry-cleaning bills must be astronomical. Just when things look bleakest for Nancy, her father (or Ned or Bess and George or the police) appears and rescues her. The book concludes with a summary about what has happened to the central characters; the good have been rewarded, typically with wealth, while the bad have been revealed as impostors and imprisoned. The last few pages provide a glowing review of all of Nancy's skills. She is thanked by all those who have been aided. Not atypical is a business owner in *The Clue of the Velvet Mask* (1953) who, when his mystery is solved, says "I owe everything to Nancy" (176). Despite such praise, the girl detective is always suitably modest and only reluctantly consents to accept a little trinket (an antique clock, an aquamarine ring, a diamond pin, and other assorted booty) from her admirers.

One reason for the appeal of the Drew books to lesbian readers is that the books' formulaic plots suggest a possible path through a lesbian's life. The young lesbian who has yet to discover her sexual identification has a secret in her life (her lesbianism) that she must search to discover, although she will be hindered at every step of the way by individuals who would prefer that she did not solve this mystery. At one point, the lesbian, although she most likely does not find herself trapped in a dark basement, does find herself trapped by society's conventions. Only when she discovers the secret of her lesbianism is the lesbian finally rewarded. On a mythical level, the books reassure lesbian readers that there is a path to lesbianism that can be negotiated, no matter how dangerous it might appear at first.

Also reassuring to lesbian readers is Nancy's amazing ability to excel at anything she attempts, showing that a girl does not need to pursue only traditional feminine activities. Nancy is an excellent swimmer, diver, and skin diver, an admirable equestrienne, a talented ballet dancer and actress, a champion golfer and ice skater, a terrific tennis player, *and* a good mechanic. Nancy seems to have little regard for activities deemed appropriate for men and women; she simply does well at everything, making her a particularly appealing figure to young lesbians who do not wish to be bound by gender conventions. Nancy also has a photographic memory and quickly becomes an expert or near expert in the many diverse fields she is called to master in the course of her sleuthing. For instance, in *The Clue of the Leaning Chimney*, Nancy learns all about rare Chinese porcelain. In *The Hidden Window Mystery*, she finds out how to make stained-glass windows. On top of all these skills, Nancy is also described as "courageous and resourceful" with "an amazing ability to fight her own battles in the world" (*The Mystery of the Ivory Charm* 13).

In addition to all these traits, she is always impeccably turned out for crime fighting: "Titian-haired Nancy was a trim figure in her olive-green knit with matching shoes. Beige accessories and knitting bag completed her costume" (*The Secret of Shadow Ranch* 2). Never, never does Nancy run outside in her nightgown to chase a criminal, even though it might be three in the morning. On all occasions— including breakfast—she is perfectly groomed, her costume carefully chosen and color-coordinated. Her brains and beauty make her the match of any man, which is appealing to lesbian readers in particular because she presents an image of female empowerment. Even her careful attention to her clothing fails to conceal that she is remarkably sharp and capable.

All these abilities, and more, Nancy uses to fight the criminals who seem not only irresistibly drawn to her but also delight in threatening the girl sleuth. A typical description of Nancy's encounter with a villain occurs in *The Secret in the Old Attic* when Nancy is captured: "Nancy fought to escape from the man, but his clutch was like an iron vise. He whipped out a handkerchief and stuffed it into Nancy's mouth. . . . When [Trott] had her completely at his mercy, he stood looking down at her, grinning evilly" (197). Anyone other than Nancy might be in a sticky situation, but she escapes, as she does time after time. It is all in a day's work for her to handle situations like those that confront her in *The Spider Sapphire Mystery:* She is trapped in her car, is knocked down, has her purse stolen, is held at gunpoint, has her suitcase and clothing destroyed, burns her hands with acid, and is locked in a dungeon. Although she is constantly being threatened or attacked, such as having her living quarters destroyed by a time bomb (*The Mystery at Lilac Inn*) or being temporarily blinded by acid (*The Ringmaster's Secret*), Nancy is not unnerved by her experiences. Even after being kidnapped and dumped into an airplane, Nancy, with hands and ankles bound, can whip a lipstick out of her pocket and scrawl a large "SOS" on a window (*The Mystery of the Fire Dragon*). For her, it is just a typical afternoon's work to break up a house burglary ring, crack a counterfeit ring, or restore an Indian ruler to his throne. All of these exploits establish Nancy as a nontraditional heroine, who appeals to nontraditional readers. Her life is a fantasy where, despite all perils, she always emerges unscathed, which is one of the reasons why many lesbians might be attracted to the Drew novels. Lesbian readers are able to enter a society in which a woman manages to remain unhurt, even though the world around her is filled with people who wish to do her harm. For lesbians, who frequently face persecution, this fantasy is alluring.

Nancy is also a nontraditional woman in other ways that could appeal to lesbian readers. Even her eating patterns are not typically "ladylike." Between adventures, she always makes it home for a snack, lunch, or dinner produced by Hannah, her father's trusty housekeeper. Nancy thinks nothing of consuming a meal consisting of cream of mushroom soup, tomato salad, lamb chops, French fries, peas, and chocolate pie. Chasing crooks must burn a lot of calories, because she maintains her svelte figure even when partaking of Hannah's daily gustatory excesses. Whether Nancy eats peas or pineapple might seem of little import, until one recognizes that the consumption of food in

the Keene books is further developing a largely all-women community, since Nancy is most frequently found to be eating with George
and Bess or Hannah. Besides building a sense of female community,
Nancy's elaborate meals show lesbian and nonlesbian readers alike
that consuming food is a pleasure they should relish, rather than
considering a healthy appetite inappropriate for "ladies."

No discussion of Nancy Drew would be complete without consideration of her car, a vehicle that offers the promise of endless
mobility to the lesbian reader. What starts out as a battered maroon
roadster in the earliest volumes evolves into a long series of shiny
brand-new cars for Nancy, culminating in the famous blue convertible.
She receives more new cars than a Chrysler showroom. In *The Haunted
Showboat,* she is presented with a new yellow convertible. In *The
Password to Larkspur Lane,* her father gives her a "powerful black and
green roadster" (122). But Nancy's cars have short life spans. They are
frequently stolen (*The Witch Tree Symbol, The Haunted Showboat, The
Moonstone Castle Mystery*) or smashed up (*The Clue of the Dancing
Puppet* and *The Clue of the Whistling Bagpipes*). Every crook in town
seems to desire nothing more than to destroy Nancy's latest prize, but
she is never left without a car for long because the car represents
freedom and autonomy; with it, she is able to travel anywhere.[10] As
Carol Billman points out in *The Secret of the Stratemeyer Syndicate:
Nancy Drew, the Hardy Boys, and the Million Dollar Fiction Factory*
(1986), "The lasting effect of Nancy Drew's all-encompassing independence is that she can be supremely active and mobile, free-wheeling in
a word. Always on the go, she merely stops in at home to refuel and
collect late-breaking news about her cases from Carson Drew. Then
she is off again in her car, or her motor-boat, or her plane" (113).
Nancy creates a fantasy of endless mobility for any reader, particularly
young readers who might not yet have access to a vehicle. Readers also
learn, however, that driving a car is not supposed to make a woman
less feminine; Nancy always maintains her feminine appearance. Even
after a high-speed car chase in *The Sign of the Twisted Candles,* she has
not a hair "out of place or a pleat wrinkled." Clearly, these novels send
ambivalent messages to their readers about desirable gender behavior,

which is one of the reasons why the lesbian reader does not just read the text but redesigns it, paying little attention to messages that she might consider irrelevant to her own experiences.

Nancy's attention to presenting a feminine appearance, however, should not lull one into assuming that she is more interested in her image than in crime solving. Crime always comes first for the ace detective, and she is endlessly on the lookout for codes and clues. She cannot even walk to the corner store without finding one or more clues on the way. In her world, everything is a clue that must be uncovered, sometimes with the aid of her magnifying glass, which she uses obsessively, often finding clues that others have missed. She glories in clues, telling one woman who complains that she would have no patience for Nancy's work, "That's the fun of being a detective. You look and keep on looking. And suddenly, when you least expect it, you find a clue" (*The Clue of the Black Keys* 137). It is a rare house that doesn't have a secret passage, room, or compartment for Nancy to discover. Codes, too, pose little difficulty for her; she breaks them with ease in *The Secret of Red Gate Farm, The Clue of the Velvet Mask*, and other volumes. Nancy even manages to create her own clues, such as in *The Clue of the Tapping Heels* (1939), in which the young detective learns how to tap dance in Morse code in order to send secret messages. Her obsession with codes and clues shows readers that the world is an understandable, logical place, but only for those who look closely. Girls are also shown that they, just like Nancy, can figure out puzzles that leave grown-ups baffled. Additionally, we can look at the search for clues as being metaphorically the search for homosexuality that any lesbian must conduct when reading the Nancy Drew novels or other literature. Lesbianism is a "clue," a "secret," a "mystery" that must be detangled from the surface narrative. This is the quest that any lesbian reader must pursue, because mainstream fiction is typically inimical to lesbian representation.

Lesbians also read the Drew books for the release they provide from the conventions of the real world. Clearly, the novels fail to provide a mimetic replication of reality. Instead, these books create a fantasy world in which society's conventions about correct behavior for young women never seem to hinder Nancy in the least. The serial stories provide a sense of order in an apparently random world, as Lee Zacharias writes: "The Nancy stories tell us life is a mystery which can be solved. Each volume contains several mysteries which eventually come together in one solution; this common solution reassures the reader that there is order in chaos, that the seemingly random events of her life and the confusion she perceives in the world do have a pattern" (1027). This fantasy world, which is so much more orderly than the real world, is alluring to any reader, heterosexual or homosexual. Lesbian readers, in particular, might find an escape into the ordered world of Nancy Drew appealing, because their own world is often chaotic and frightening. One lesbian recalls: "The books must have definitely been an escape/fantasy for me because I grew up in a very sheltered and overprotective environment. I loved Nancy's self-confidence, persistence, independence, and leadership. She was everything I wasn't and did everything I couldn't. She had her own car, had her own business, and engaged in all sorts of interesting, challenging, and scary activities." Another lesbian, Sarah, thinks back to reading the books: "I was simply delighted to read about another girl, I think. I would stop in the middle of a sentence and literally hug the book. I think I was proud to be a girl, like her. I always envied the fellas in books who got to go fishing and camping and got to play detective and have clubhouses. So I guess Nancy Drew and friends gave me a character with whom to identify." A third lesbian, Kate, remarks: "I loved Nancy Drew! I enjoyed the action and the fact that she had to think so much. My mom said that I read every Nancy Drew book the library had. When I was sick, she would offer to go out and get me books. She said I would list off all the ones not to get." Another woman, Sue, remembers as a young girl pretending to be like Nancy and her friends and "sleuthing around, finding mysteries to solve." These readers used Nancy's experiences to explain their own lives and perhaps to serve as a model for their own behavior. Nancy showed that women do not have to follow society's dictates about desirable behavior. Readers could see in the Drew books that male companionship is sometimes far less absorbing than the friendship and company of other women. Certainly, at least until the most recent books, Nancy appeared far more interested in George and Bess than in Ned. Ned has a difficult time even wheedling a date out of her, whereas George and Bess seem to spend most of their waking hours with Nancy.

Other reasons exist for Nancy's appeal to lesbians. She shows herself to be remarkably free from the dictates of men and is able to twist any man around her little finger. Only Nancy would have the nerve to ask her father if he would fly to London with her "right away" (*The Ringmaster's Secret* 164). Without blinking an eye, Carson Drew agrees to leave that very day. (Why couldn't my father take a lesson from Nancy's dad?) Nor does he ever complain when his daughter sends him the bill for her extensive wardrobe and her trips to such exotic locales as Belgium, Greece, France, Turkey, Hong Kong, Mexico City, Peru, Scotland, Venice, and Africa. It takes Nancy to make grown men gush, "Miss Drew, you're the most ingenious girl I've ever met" (*The Bungalow Mystery* 140) or "you certainly have the best ordered mind and the keenest ability to put two and two together of any person I ever met" (*The Sign of the Twisted Candles* 160). Instead of men controlling Nancy, she controls them, and they are eager to do her bidding. She is a model of feminine strength that would appeal to many lesbians (as well as nonlesbians).

The most tractable man of all is Ned Nickerson, star football player of Emerson College, who is Nancy's "special friend" through many volumes. Ned isn't even rewarded with a kiss until some of the later books, and he must always recognize that sleuthing is far more important to Nancy than a date with him. In one book, he even begs, "Nancy, how about taking your mind off mysteries for a while and thinking of me instead" (*The Quest of the Missing Map* 178). Nancy only laughs, paying little heed to his words. Although his physical strength sometimes helps Nancy to escape from a difficult situation, she does not always need Ned as backup; when he pleads to be taken along one time, she leaves him behind, remarking blithely that, if Ned is not around, she will "depend on George and her judo to take care of troublemakers" (*The Clue in the Crossword Cipher* 16–17). Poor Ned.

Like Nancy, lesbian readers tend to minimize Ned's role. One lesbian, Marilyn, remembers "Nancy's strength and self-sufficiency" and recalls little about the assistance provided by the boys in her life. Megan, another lesbian who read the Nancy Drew books in the late

1960s, explains: "I loved the books because Nancy was smart and she was doing something, not just watching boys doing something. She was the protagonist, George and Bess secondary characters, and Ned merely tertiary or less. Ned seemed an okay guy, but who needed him? It did get irritating that he had to rescue Nancy so often." Yet another lesbian, Winifred, wrote about the Keene novels, "I have a vague recollection of some boyfriends, but I never paid much attention to them. I actively disliked Nancy's boyfriend. I remember that pretty clearly." Other lesbian readers reported similar feelings about Ned and Burt Eddleton and Dave Evans, George's and Bess's respective boyfriends.[11] For these readers, the book's apparent plot is malleable. Individuals can perceive Ned as either crucial or completely dispensable to the narrative. In this way, lesbians refashion a text that is superficially heterosexual into a homosexual work. Ned is perceived as being merely camouflage for Nancy; she seems heterosexual by having him around, despite her far greater interest in bonds with other women. Thus, just as Danae Clark argues, lesbians create a vision of the world that is more in line with their own experiences. They call into question the assumed import of the heterosexual romance by showing that it is an insignificant part of the text, at least for them. Such a perspective recrafts canonical and noncanonical texts, revealing the lesbian subtexts.

George and Bess: Butch and Femme?

Looking beyond the heterosexual-oriented surface plot, the lesbian reader finds extensive support for seeing the Nancy Drew books as having a lesbian subtext. Particularly revealing is the relationship between Nancy and George and Bess. The three young women form a cohesive community that not even Ned can disrupt. In fact, the Keene novels revolve around women's community. One has only to think of the women who help Nancy—like Hannah Gruen, Helen Corning, and Nancy's Aunt Eloise—or the women whom Nancy helps—like Nancy and Allison Hoover in *The Secret of the Old Clock*, Manda Kreutz in *The Witch Tree Symbol*, or Millie Burd in *The Secret of Red Gate Farm*—to recognize that men play a minor role in these novels. Nancy's father is frequently away on business trips, and the only male characters are typically crooks or relatively superfluous figures like the police or Ned.

Bess and George, who are easy to slight in favor of the more glamorous Nancy, must be studied in order to understand the Nancy Drew books' strong lesbian subtext. George Fayne and Bess Marvin, who are cousins, are introduced in the fifth volume of the series, replacing Nancy's original crime-solving friend, Helen Corning (who always seemed a trifle lackluster). The two cousins are opposites: George enthusiastically supports Nancy and her pursuit of mysteries, while Bess quails at the thought of adventure.

> Bess and George were cousins, but there any likeness ended. Bess, blond and pretty, had a penchant for second desserts and frilly dresses. She shared Nancy's adventures out of deep loyalty to her but was constantly fearful of the dangers involved.
>
> George was as boyish as her name. Her hair was dark, her face handsomely pert. George wore simple clothes and craved adventure. (*The Secret of the Wooden Lady* 20)

Beth is all that is feminine, and George is all that is masculine. Curiously enough, the writers of the early Nancy Drew novels frequently tried to build up George's masculinity rather than downplay it. The books commonly mention George's short haircut: In 1932, "George had cropped her straight dark hair as short as the style would permit, and combed and brushed it as infrequently as possible" (*The Clue in the Diary* 2). In *The Secret in the Old Attic* (1944), Nancy tells George, "If you have much more hair cut off, people will think you're a boy" (10). George's masculine name is stressed: In 1932, she was described as "proud of her masculine name, and dressed the part. Woe to the person who called her Georgette or even Georgie, let alone Georgiana or any other feminization of her real name!" (*Nancy's Mysterious Letter* 95). George is also proud of her athletic form, boasting in 1932 to Bess, "Look at my brawn! I assure you I haven't wasted all the time I spent in the gym" (*The Clue in the Diary* 174).

George is truly butch. Even today, when I read the older Nancy Drew books, I find myself surprised at George's masculinity. It is difficult to *avoid* seeing her as a butch lesbian. She fits neatly into the category of the mannish lesbian described by late-nineteenth-century sexologists, such as Krafft-Ebing, who discussed in the 1880s what he named the "female urning" who ignored "girlish occupations," neglected her toilet, and affected "rough boyish manners" (418), or Ellis, who wrote that "the commonest characteristic of the sexually inverted woman is a certain degree of masculinity or boyishness" (244). Freud, too, emphasized the masculinity of the "true" lesbian. Since the supposed linkage between lesbianism and masculinity was already apparent to a general audience by the 1920s and has been assumed to be true throughout this century, it is surprising from our historical perspective that George was depicted as so butch.

Some critics have sought to downplay George's (and Bess's) apparent lesbianism. In 1964 Arthur Daigon claimed that George "introduces a suggestion of sexual ambivalence" (668). He does not elaborate on his ideas. A few years later, Russel Nye wrote that George is "a masculine girl who cuts her hair short and wears mannish clothes (facts which are absolutely not to be misconstrued in this context)" (86–87). In 1976 Lee Zacharias was more outspoken: "The extremes of possibility for female characters push Bess and George into stereotyped sex roles. To conclude that the girls are lesbians, however, is a camp but erroneous interpretation" (1032). I would have to concur with Nye and Zacharias that the writers of the Nancy Drew series probably did not intend to portray George and Bess as the stereotypical butch and femme couple; Nye and Zacharias overlook, however, that the text created by homosexual readers is as "real" as the text heterosexual readers construct.

Lesbian readers quickly spot Bess and George as lesbians, understanding these unusually close cousins as a butch and femme couple, a duo that has existed in the lesbian community since at least the 1920s.[12] Few lesbian readers could avoid thinking about George as butch, which tells us why she is frequently their favorite character in these books. One lesbian, Megan, writes, "I preferred George to Bess because George was the tomboy like me." Another woman comments, "I always thought that George and Bess were a couple." Sarah, who read the Drew books in the late 1970s, writes, "George was my favorite character, probably just due to her male name and her short haircut.

God, was I a tomboy. Anyhow, I hated Bess. All I can remember about her was her boyfriend." Other lesbians comment favorably on George's name and her general appeal as a character. In order to increase their reading pleasure, these readers are consciously manipulating the text's codes. By reading the narrative as lesbian, the readers also question the idea that the dominant heterosexual text is "naturally" right.

George, unfortunately, was too openly lesbian to last. In the later books from the 1950s until the present, she has undergone some disconcerting changes. In *The Legend of Miner's Creek* (1992), she is described as "tall and athletic. Her short, curly, dark-brown hair was full of bounce and seemed to reflect her energetic personality" (2). Although modern-day George has developed a talent for judo that makes her a match for any villain, she has simultaneously become less apparently masculine. No longer does she have a boy's haircut. No longer does she wear the most masculine clothing possible. Despite her judo skills, she has lost some of her appeal and certainly some of her butchness. In 1932, George had been "too blunt and boyish to captivate the young men" (*The Clue in the Diary* 118). When *The Haunted Showboat* was written in 1957, George was already being described as an "attractive brunette" (1) with a boyfriend. The most recent Nancy Drew novels seem intent on demonstrating George's heterosexuality. There is an evident uneasiness that George could be interpreted as anything other than an all-American girl. The books' writers seem to struggle with the anxiety-provoking fact that creating women characters who appear adventuresome, outgoing, and courageous imbues them with some of the traits that also supposedly identify lesbians in our culture.

Bess and George are an obvious lesbian sign, but there are many other ways in which these books are queer. As I have mentioned, Nancy's independence, her allegiance to Bess and George, and the emphasis on the women's community throughout the novels point to a lesbian-centered universe. Nancy, her aunt, Bess, and George might not be lesbians if one narrowly defines lesbians as women who have sex with other women, but they certainly are if one uses a broader definition, such as Adrienne Rich's philosophy of a lesbian continuum in which many women can be identified as lesbian, even women who never have sex with other women. According to Rich, "we can see ourselves as moving in and out of this continuum, whether we identify ourselves as lesbian or not" (219). Although I feel it is important to recognize the unique problems faced by lesbians who self-identify as lesbian and, thus, face the dominant society's wrath, I believe Rich's continuum can help us to understand the lesbian subtexts that exist in the Drew novels. Nancy, Bess, and George in their women's community are part of the lesbian continuum.

Nancy Today

In their attempts to make the modern Nancy Drew books appear nonthreatening to heterosexual girls, the current-day publisher and writers have deemphasized the all-female community and included new boys wherever possible.[13] The girls' boyfriends gain new prominence, and Bess always seems to be ogling a new male rock star or movie star. Nancy is far more concerned about Ned (and the other men she dates) than she ever was in earlier volumes. Critic Jackie Vivelo remarks that the new Nancy is evolving into a "Barbie doll detective" (76), and it does appear that Nancy is more one-dimensional these days, more interested in rock and roll and boys than in learning yet another foreign language or translating Middle English (which she actually does in an earlier volume). Yet are Nancy's changes truly that drastic? In popular culture, everything changes—even Nancy. In former years, Nancy quoted Shakespeare and learned foreign languages; now she studies karate and frequents shopping malls. In past years, she relied on her trusty magnifying glass; now she has the help of computers, fax machines, video cameras, and cellular telephones. Nancy is still primarily absorbed with crime solving, but usually on a larger scale, such as tracking down the culprits in a million-dollar jewel heist (*The Case of the Disappearing Diamonds,* 1987), ferreting out who is stealing top-secret government information (*The Ghost of Craven Cove,* 1989), or capturing the kidnappers who demand a million dollars for the return of a missing girl (*The Mystery of the Missing Millionairess,* 1991). No matter what activities engage Nancy's time, there is always room for subversion of the dominant story lines.

Readers will still receive messages radically different from those that the publisher intended. Examining the Nancy Drew novels has shown that popular texts, even though aimed at a heterosexual audience, can be interpreted in a queer fashion, a reading that is no less significant because it probably is *not* what the writers intended.

Such an approach to popular reading and popular culture studies in general is tremendously empowering to lesbian readers. So many texts that seem closed off to lesbians or at least distanced from their experiences open up and become more relevant when the lesbian subtext(s) lurking beneath many dominantly heterosexual texts is recognized. Watching the 1960s television show "Bewitched," viewing the film *Thelma and Louise,* reading Nancy Drew books or Harlequin romances, one finds a textual universe filled with lesbian interpretations and lesbian meanings. Studying this universe starts a person along the long and laborious path of decentering heterosexuality as the "norm." In addition, such lesbian-centered interpretations of popular culture—whether the subject is a Barbie doll or a Nancy Drew mystery—allow critics to better understand the multiplicity and complexity of popular culture. Popular culture has as much to say about nondominant groups and forms of cultural resistance as it has to say about the white, heterosexual, middle-class public.[14]

5

"Candy-coated cyanide"

Children's Books and
Lesbian Images

They have been flung into bonfires, stolen from libraries across the country, and censored, at least in recent years, more frequently than any other form of literature. When even the slightest hint of homosexuality appears in a children's or young adult book, controversy inevitably erupts. Conservatives go to absurd lengths to ensure that books about homosexuality are removed from libraries, while liberals are just as ardent about keeping such books on the shelves. Why are these books at the center of such a maelstrom? What images of homosexuality do they present that are objectionable? How subversive are most of these books? To try to answer these questions and others, I visited my local gay and lesbian bookstore.

On seeing how many books with gay and lesbian themes are available for children and teenagers, I was at first impressed. A greater number of gay and lesbian books for young readers are being published by the large mainstream publishing houses as well as by traditional bastions of lesbian/gay publishing, such as Alyson Publishers in Boston. The situation certainly had changed since I was young and had to be content with checking out from the library *The Well of Loneliness* (1928) or *Patience and Sarah* (1969), both novels about lesbianism that appeared to have little to do with my own experiences in the seventies. I also read avidly *Harriet the Spy* (1964) and *The Long Secret* (1965), but I did not know then that the books' author, Louise Fitzhugh, was a lesbian, and the implicit references to homosexuality that her works contained went right over my head.[1] While I was growing up, books focusing on lesbianism that were aimed explicitly at a young audience were almost nonexistent. During this period, homosexuality was considered an abnormality, not something that should be discussed in polite society and definitely not a topic fit for young people. Now, perusing the store's bookshelves, I was amazed at the far larger selection of titles. At first glance, it seemed as if everyone and her mother were writing children's books with lesbian and gay themes. Writers such as Francesca Lia Block, Forman Brown, Aidan Chambers, Stacey Donovan, B. A. Ecker, Paula Fox, Jane Futcher, Nancy Garden, Bette Greene, M. E. Kerr, Norma Klein, Hilary Mullins, Lesléa Newman, Christina Salat, Sandra Scoppettone, Johnny Valentine, Elaine Wickens, Michael Willhoite, and Jacqueline Woodson all had books on the shelves that discussed lesbianism.[2] It was only later when I visited a nonspecialized bookstore that I realized gay and lesbian youth continue to have a difficult time gaining access to reading materials that relate to their own lives. This bookstore, which is probably far more representative of bookstores across the United States, had on its shelves only copies of those old standbys *The Well of Loneliness* and *Patience and Sarah*, although the sales clerk informed me that the store could special order any of the other books that I wanted. It seemed that children's and young adult books containing lesbian and gay themes were still rare finds in a mainstream bookstore. Since the availability had changed less than I would have assumed, I wondered whether the image of lesbian and gay characters or the depiction of homosexual issues had also changed little. To try to answer this question, I decided to read many of the dozens of books addressing lesbian issues that were written in the 1980s and 1990s,

seeking to discover in what ways the depiction of lesbianism in children's books had changed, if at all.

This chapter focuses on representations of lesbians rather than
on depictions of both gay men and lesbians because of the relative
invisibility of lesbians in children's fiction. As late as 1988, Christine
Jenkins could write: "One of the most obvious trends in the young
adult portrayal of gay people is the predominance of males. Despite
increased visibility of lesbians within the gay movement, the large
number of female authors of these books, and the perceived majority
of female teenage readers, there are few books with lesbian themes"
(82). Even in the mid 1990s, children's books, particularly young
adult novels, about gay men largely outnumber the ones about lesbians.[3] Similarly, scholarship on gay and lesbian images in juvenile
fiction, which is in its infancy, consists primarily of studies that focus
on gay men and boys.[4] The emphasis on males in both fiction and
critical studies made me wonder what messages about lesbianism were
being given to young women and how those messages have changed.

When I examined texts aimed specifically at young women, I
discovered that lesbians are some of the most underrepresented and
misrepresented characters in children's literature.[5] Although there
have been significant improvements in the last fifteen years and lesbians are being portrayed more frequently than ever, they still appear
in only a minority of books and their depiction is apt to be stereotypical. Compared to the ever-increasing richness of contemporary children's literature when it comes to the representation of other minority
groups, such as African Americans, Native Americans, Asian Americans, or Hispanics, the omission of lesbians is even more noticeable.[6]

This essay examines books for both young children and teenagers, although the two are often considered to be two distinct genres.
I chose to adopt such an approach because I am primarily interested in
how lesbianism is represented in books for *all* young readers, whether
aged five or fifteen. I recognize, of course, that picture books need to
be judged by different criteria than young adult novels. The books
targeted at older readers have a more sophisticated analysis of homosexuality and often discuss sexuality in far more open terms than
books directed at younger readers. Although they have significant

stylistic differences, picture books and young adult novels can be studied together to gain a more complete view of the broad variety of ways that lesbians are represented to young people today.

Censorship and the Need for Lesbian Juvenile Literature

Another reason gay and lesbian children's literature deserves critical attention is the great frequency with which it is censored by different individuals: "Those who are threatened—and who fear [a] work's persuasive power—may try to limit the work's accessibility to young minds; and thus we have ideological rejection of manuscripts by publishers, the writing of negative book reviews to discourage sales, official silence (nonmention) on the part of librarians and teachers, and moves to censorship and banning" (Sutherland 151).[7] Children's literature has become a battleground,[8] and the battle often grows bitter: "Keep this candy-coated cyanide out of the reach of my children," demanded one parent in a debate to keep Michael Willhoite's picture book *Daddy's Roommate* (1990) out of schools (qtd. in Sadowski 11). Willhoite's book has the dubious distinction of being the most challenged library book of 1993 (Sadowski 11) and 1994 ("*Daddy's*" 368). It has even been challenged at a college library (Minot State University in Minot, North Dakota) and has been relentlessly attacked by groups across the United States. The book, which one parent described as "a predatory attempt to seduce the minds and bodies of . . . children" (qtd. in Sadowski 12), is, from most perspectives, fairly mild. It tells the story of a boy who visits his divorced father and his father's "roommate," Frank. Daddy and Frank read the newspaper, clean the house, cook dinner, and shave together. There is one picture of them in bed, but it is devoid of any sexual implications. The most open display of physical love is a friendly hug between the two. I could criticize this book for its greeting-card perception of gay men, but I find nothing especially risqué about it. However, because homosexuality is still the ultimate taboo, something that most parents do not even want their children to be aware of, *Daddy's Roommate* caused an uproar that continues today. Nor is this a debate only about reading materials. It is also about how the family should or should not be constituted, and this is an issue with far-ranging implications for young gays and lesbians. The relationship between homosexual parents and children is still hotly debated in courthouses across the United States, and the courts often look with disfavor on gays and lesbians who want to keep their biological children or adopt.[9]

The censorship of Daddy's Roommate is far from an isolated case. The American Library Association has recorded "224 challenges to lesbian and gay material in children's books since it started keeping track in September 1990" (Ford 25);[10] there were 40 such challenges in 1991, 64 in 1992, and 111 in 1993 (Cart 127). In 1994, the numbers diminished, but only slightly, to 91 challenges ("Daddy's" 368). These figures, of course, include only official challenges, not the countless times that libraries simply decide not to stock such books or schools do not include books with lesbian and gay themes in their curriculum. Censors pounce on a book with a homosexual theme; it makes little difference whether the characters are female or male. Even critically acclaimed books, such as Nancy Garden's Annie on My Mind (1982), are not free from censorship. Her novel was burned on Kansas City school district grounds in 1993 (Cart 127) and was the subject of a lawsuit instigated by a group of parents and children (Garden, "Banned" 11). The harsh treatment of Daddy's Roommate, Annie on My Mind, and other gay and lesbian children's books reveals an ideological battle that has far more serious ramifications than just whether a particular book will appear on library shelves. The war being waged is over the much larger issue of whether homosexuality should be considered "normal," which would suggest there is no innate difference between homosexuality and heterosexuality, a thought that many members of society find abhorrent.

Gay and lesbian children's literature also deserves critical scrutiny because it has the potential to influence how young gays and lesbians understand homosexuality. The role of fiction is particularly important because lesbian and gay youth live in a typically hostile environment, one in which they are very much outcasts. "Gay and lesbian youth are engulfed in a culture in which antihomosexual attitudes proliferate" (Savin-Williams 182). In many ways, the status of gay and lesbian youth has changed shockingly little in the last quarter of a century. A few large cities, such as New York, Los Angeles, Chicago, and San Francisco, have developed special outreach programs for young gays and lesbians, and many gay and lesbian community centers in urban areas have discussion groups particularly designed for youth, but these changes cannot conceal the fact that our schools are still virulently homophobic and that being gay or lesbian is a sure way to be a social outcast:

> It would be hard to imagine a group more deprived of significant, independent "political bases" than homosexual youth (particularly those who are also poor, female, or people of color). They share with all children the basic restrictions imposed upon political, economic, and social expression. And though they exist within the additional constraints imposed upon any minority, gay and lesbian youth do not share in the array of key social allegiances, specific educational resources, and cultural support routinely established for other youth subcultures. (Kielwasser and Wolf 355)

Because young gays and lesbians are considered by many to be a marginal and despised group, fiction has the potential to serve a doubly important role for them, affirming the positive aspects of homosexuality and reassuring them that their sexual orientation is shared by many and is perfectly "normal." Teenager Virginia Dunn, the heroine of Stacey Donovan's novel *Dive* (1994), aptly describes the role of books in her life and their role for other young gays: "Books have saved my life, or stopped me from thinking I'm purely crazy anyway" (46). At least in regard in their sexual orientation, lesbian and gay youths have an intense need to affirm themselves through literature—to prove that they are not "purely crazy"—since the entire culture functions to assure them that they are not normal.

Homosexual youths also need fiction and nonfiction accounts about what it means to grow up gay or lesbian because the mainstream media typically ignore this issue: "A lesbian teenager is no more likely to have her identity validated on a situation comedy than in her high school history book or a copy of *Seventeen* magazine" (Kielwasser and Wolf 363).[11] This can have a devastating effect. "[T]he symbolic annihilation of gay and lesbian youth exhibited by television in the extreme, and by most mass media in general, can contribute to a dysfunctional isolation that is supported by the mutually reinforcing invisibility of homosexual adolescents on the television screen and in the real world" (Kielwasser and Wolf 352). Watching television or reading mainstream magazines and books, young gays and lesbians might all too easily conclude that they are alone in society. This feeling of alienation and isolation is not apt to be greatly lessened by reading discussions about homosexuality even in gay-targeted magazines and newspapers, since they often focus on adults. Youth are thus pushed to the very margins of the gay/lesbian community. These doubly marginalized young people need gay and lesbian literature because it has the power to affirm their lives and to address issues of particular concern to them. Also, since talking about homosexuality is still taboo, particularly for adolescents and children, there are few places where homosexuality can be discussed openly, whether between young people or between children and adults. Fiction is one of the few sources that discusses homosexuality openly and offers young people affirmation of their sexual orientation.

Ideology and the Politics of Assent

Since literature is a primary source for gay and lesbian youth looking for representations of their experiences, critics should study with great care what messages are being conveyed by these texts. As children's literature critic Peter Hollindale succinctly remarks, "[I]deology is an inevitable, untamable and largely uncontrollable factor in the transaction between books and children" (10). Because our society regards children's literature as an important tool for socializing young people and teaching them cultural mores, children's books often suggest more about the values and concerns of adults than they do about those of children, as Peter Hunt affirms in his book *An Introduction to Children's Literature* (1994): "what a culture thinks of as childhood is reflected very closely in the books produced for its citizens. Despite the fact that what adults intend is not directly related to what children perceive, children's books very often contain what adults think children can understand, and what they should be allowed to understand; and this applies to 'literariness' as well as to vocabulary or content" (5). In other words, since they are written, designed, sold, read, and taught by adults, children's books present an adultocentric view of the world, which gains legitimacy simply by being presented as "natural" or "real." When adult writers of children's books depict only heterosexual characters and disregard lesbians entirely, they are creating a world view that they wish a child or young adult to adopt. In a similar fashion, when authors of children's books fail to depict lesbians or gay men because they assume that children should remain uninformed about homosexuality, the writers are censoring homosexuality and suggesting that homosexual relationships are less worthy than heterosexual ones, which fill the pages even of picture books for the youngest of children.

Robert Sutherland's discussion of what he calls "the politics of assent" can help to explain how ideology functions in children's literature. He writes: " 'assent' is an author's passive, unquestioning acceptance and internalization of an established ideology, which is then transmitted in the author's writing in an unconscious manner. The ideology subscribed to is a set of values and beliefs widely held in the society at large which reflects the society's assumptions about what the world *is*. When this received ideology informs and shapes a literary work, that work becomes a vehicle expressing it" (151). Sutherland describes one of the reasons why lesbians and gays in children's literature are so hotly contested. It is always profoundly destabilizing and uncomfortable to abandon a foundational belief about how the world *is*. People try to avoid this at all costs, as they generally do not wish their children to grow up with concepts different from their own. With fiction, the politics of assent functions for readers as well as for writers. Whether children or adults, readers accept with few questions the ideology of a particular children's book because the text appears to state what is "natural." Children's books are particularly susceptible to the politics of assent because a large segment of society prefers to believe that children's books are naive, simple, and nonideological, which they are not. In juvenile literature, the politics of assent operates in numerous ways, such as reinforcing parental beliefs about acceptable topics for young readers.

The politics of assent is insidious, since its effects are concealed, as Sutherland points out: "The politics of assent not only affirms the status quo but continually reinforces it. Since its underlying ideology is rendered invisible to authors and readers alike . . . , its influence is especially potent, for its persuasive force is hidden" (155). The hidden politics of assent is at work in the universe of children's books when all the characters a reader encounters are heterosexual, reaffirming the idea that heterosexuality is the one "normal" sexual orientation. A juvenile book may not make specific derogatory comments about homosexuality, but when it fails to include any gay or lesbian characters, it suggests that homosexuals do not exist. The invisibility of gays and lesbians in children's books has created a fertile environment for a small group of authors to attempt to be more inclusive in portraying gay or lesbian characters—an attempt, as we shall discover, that has met with limited success.

I have mentioned that before the 1960s young readers could find at the library *The Well of Loneliness,* if it escaped the censor, but books specifically aimed at children and young adults that featured gay or lesbian characters did not appear until the 1969 publication of John Donovan's novel *I'll Get There: It Better Be Worth the Trip,* which is considered to be the first young adult novel to discuss gay themes, the second being Isabelle Holland's *The Man without a Face* (1972). Other early books include Lynn Hall's *Sticks and Stones* (1972), Sandra Scoppettone's *Trying Hard to Hear You* (1974), Mary W. Sullivan's *What's This about Pete?* (1976), and M. E. Kerr's *I'll Love You When You're More like Me* (1977). These early young adult novels share one feature: They all focus on gay men, not lesbians. This textual absence, as I have already pointed out, continues today, because lesbians have always been "invisible" in comparison to gay men. Western society has long regarded male experience as generic, meaning that it was assumed to express the experiences of *all* humans; women's voices were considered nonessential. Lesbian stories have often been pushed into the margins or never even heard.

A few writers in the last twenty years have tried to address this absence by writing juvenile books that concentrate on lesbian characters and battling what Michael Thomas Ford calls the "paralysis that grips the children's publishing community when it comes to gay topics" (24). This paralysis is gradually diminishing, and even some of the big publishing houses are now willing to address homosexuality in children's and young adult books. For instance, HarperCollins has recently published *Am I Blue? Coming Out from the Silence* (1994), edited by Marion Bauer, a collection of short stories about gay and lesbian issues aimed at a young adult audience. Despite these small gains, getting a juvenile book about a lesbian character published is still difficult, and once published, the book is apt to be stigmatized as being by a "lesbian author," resulting in potentially lower book sales and the loss of future publishers for such writers as Stacey Donovan, Nancy Garden, M. E. Kerr, Norma Klein, Lesléa Newman, J. P. Reading, Sandra Scoppettone, and Jacqueline Woodson.

"I had to be queer": The Evolution of Lesbian Depictions in Children's Literature

But what portrait of lesbianism have these writers and others created in the last two decades? How have these writers challenged lesbian stereotypes? In what ways have those stereotypes gone unchallenged? How has the depiction of lesbianism in children's books changed since the 1970s, and is this change positive? These are a few of the questions that I wish to answer by examining two dozen children's and young adult novels from the last two decades. I have chosen to discuss a greater number of young adult novels than books for younger readers because this is an accurate reflection of the marketplace where young adult books about homosexuality far outnumber such books for children. I have also decided to examine these books chronologically because I am interested in the evolution of lesbian depictions in the texts that I study. By no means is this survey definitive, but I do believe that the chosen books display the variety that is available and show the evolution of the lesbian juvenile novel up to the present. As we shall find, in children's books published in the last five years, lesbians are portrayed in a more complex and thoughtful fashion than ever before, but lesbian stereotypes are hard to eradicate, even in the most recent books. Lesbian children's books from the 1990s also suffer from other

problems. For instance, their characters, with a few notable exceptions, are largely white and middle-class, a problem that also plagues
images of gay men in children's books. Even more so than depictions
of heterosexuals in picture books, picture book descriptions of lesbians are apt to be wooden and one-dimensional. Too many recent
children's books still become didactic and dull when they attempt to
explain lesbianism.

Despite their flaws, 1990s children's books with lesbian characters are a significant improvement over many earlier works. Except for
Patience and Sarah, children's and young adult books about lesbianism
were nonexistent in the twentieth century through the 1960s, and
even *Patience and Sarah* was not targeted directly at young readers.
The situation did not improve greatly in the 1970s, although a few
books began to appear. These novels, however, were apt to depict
lesbianism as "just a phase," rather than as an enduring aspect of a
young woman's life. For instance, at the end of Rosa Guy's novel *Ruby*
(1976), which describes the developing relationship between Harlem
teenagers Ruby and Daphne, Daphne goes straight and Ruby presumably does, too. Although Guy's novel is notable as one of the very few
that describes lesbian life as experienced by nonwhites, ultimately the
book falls into stereotypical conventions about the nature of lesbian
relationships as temporary and as something that the "normal" girl
outgrows. Like Guy's, Deborah Hautzig's novel *Hey, Dollface* (1978)
depicts lesbianism as only a phase. The novel records the erotic
tension that a high school girl feels when she is with her best friend,
but the book makes it clear that their passion is fleeting. Although
these two novels are tolerant of lesbianism, both imply that lesbianism
is not very serious and is childish compared to the male-female relationships of mature adulthood. Guy's and Hautzig's novels reveal how
even books that adopt a seemingly supportive attitude toward lesbianism can function to assert that heterosexuality is better than homosexuality. As I have already mentioned, contemporary women's magazines
operate in a similar fashion by adopting a position toward lesbianism
that seems, at least on the surface, to be supportive, yet still functions
to affirm the superior status of heterosexuality.

Unlike Guy and Hautzig, Sandra Scoppettone does not insist on ending the relationship between her heroines in *Happy Endings Are All Alike* (1978). But this book is entrapped by the conventions of the romance and unable to present a realistic portrait of lesbian lives. This young adult novel recounts the story of Jaret Tyler and Peggy Danziger, teenage lesbians who live in a small New York town, Gardener's Point. The narrative focuses on Jaret and Peggy's developing romance and their experiences during the summer before they go away to college. Unfortunately, the young women are portrayed as such perfect characters that one loses interest in them rapidly. They both are described as extremely attractive. They share the same favorite poet: Edna St. Vincent Millay. And they are both about to attend one of the Seven Sisters colleges. Although some readers might be able to identify with these paragons, many readers will not. In *Happy Endings Are All Alike,* as well as many other lesbian novels aimed at a youthful audience, a common flaw creeps in. In fighting against the more common social stereotypes of lesbians as twisted, ugly women, children's novelists often make their lesbians too good and too glamorous to be true.

Scoppettone's novel, however, deserves recognition for its vivid description of what happens when Mid Summers, a young man obsessed with girls and sex, rapes and beats up Jaret. He had seen the girls making love in the woods and decided to "get Jaret Tyler" (85). The aftermath of the crime is horrific. Mid's defense is that Jaret's lesbianism drove him to rape her. A bigoted police chief believes that Jaret should not pursue the prosecution. Most harmful, Peggy wants Jaret to drop the charges so that Peggy will not have to reveal her lesbianism. When Jaret insists on a trial, Peggy vows never to see her again.

Even though Scoppettone's description of the legal system is accurate and only too plausible, she cannot prevent this novel from being little more than a potboiler, which suffers from an abundance of purple prose that could have come right out of a Harlequin romance: "[Peggy and Jaret] returned to looking into each other's eyes. . . . [A] different kind of tension began and finally ended as they naturally, sweetly kissed for the first time" (35). When Peggy comes back to Jaret just before she leaves for college and confesses that she still loves Jaret, the book ends, with the girls in each other's arms: "Looking into each other's eyes, a moment passed and then they glided easily into one another's arms, holding, loving" (201). These incidents and others turn the novel into a traditional romance, a book that simply sticks two girls, instead of a girl and a boy, into a formulaic plot.

Lesbian juvenile novels remained trapped within genre constraints in 1980 and 1981, when a number of banal books that focused on crushes or schooling were published. J. P. Reading's *Bouquets for Brimbal* (1980) is one of the novels that focused on crushes, a subject that threatens to overwhelm lesbian literature for girls.[12] Oddly enough, crush stories, rather than decentralizing heterosexuality, often affirm its centrality, since the lesbian crushes are commonly revealed to be brief episodes in a girl's life. *Bouquets for Brimbal* tells the story of Annie and Macy, who are best friends until Annie gets a crush on Lola Marion. Macy's jealousy and alienation grow as she recognizes that Annie and Lola are lovers. The book's attitude toward lesbianism is accepting, but sometimes the novel can read as if it were a treatise by Miss Manners on how a well-brought-up young lady ought to behave toward a lesbian, a common flaw of lesbian juvenile books, which are sometimes targeted at an implied reader who is heterosexual.

Two other 1980s books that focused on crushes, Elizabeth Levy's *Come Out Smiling* (1981) and Jane Futcher's *Crush* (1981), were no improvement over Reading's novel. *Come Out Smiling* details the experiences of Jennifer Mandel at her summer camp. A central issue in the book is Jenny's experience when she discovers that two of her camp counselors, Peggy and Ann, are lovers. Jenny wonders about her own sexual orientation when she develops a crush: "Did this whole thing mean I was a lesbian? If I were not a lesbian, maybe I would never have had a crush on Peggy in the first place. It might be normal to have crushes, but it was definitely not normal to have a crush on a lesbian. I had to be queer" (126). Futcher's novel is a boarding school story about Jinx Tuckwell, who attends the prestigious Huntington Hill and who develops a crush on manipulative, self-centered Lexie Yves. (Where do writers find these names?) This is yet another book (along with Judith St. George's juvenile novel *Call Me Margo* [1981]) to add to the scores of novels that talk about women's colleges and high schools as hotbeds of lesbianism. The book is ambivalent toward lesbianism. It is never clear whether Jinx is a lesbian, and Lexie certainly is not. Lesbianism is presented only as a pathological illness and is not dealt with in much depth. Despite the visibility of lesbianism in these crush novels, the books function to show lesbianism as a fleeting part of a girl's maturation, not as a permanent part of her adult life. We then have to wonder how progressive these novels really were when they were first published. Yes, they depict lesbianism, but they represent it in such a fashion that it appears less appealing than heterosexuality. Like the college novels discussed in chapter 2, these juvenile books depicting lesbianism also serve to reaffirm the centrality of heterosexuality.

Another way that lesbianism was contained in juvenile books of the early 1980s was by downplaying the sexuality of lesbian relationships. This approach is apparent in Norma Klein's novel *Breaking Up* (1980), which addresses lesbianism only superficially. *Breaking Up* focuses on fifteen-year-old Ali Rose, who travels to California to spend a summer with her father after moving to New York City with her divorced mother. The main plot concerns Ali's developing relationship with a boy, but a fair amount of the book focuses on the conflict between Ali and her father when he discovers his ex-wife is a lesbian and tries to persuade Ali to stay with him. Although she chooses to stay with her mother and decides that lesbianism might not be as negative as it is commonly portrayed, lesbianism is handled in a cursory fashion and made to appear less threatening by portraying no physical contact between Ali's mother and her girlfriend; "they just joke around and act like good friends. They still don't call each other 'darling' or kiss a lot" (193). In this fashion, the threat of the women's sexuality is negated. The lack of lesbian sexuality is even more evident because the sexuality between Ali and her boyfriend is repeatedly emphasized. Thus, lesbianism is reduced to being merely a form of close friendship.

What can only be described as the dreary state of lesbian literature for juvenile readers in the early 1980s changed abruptly in 1982 with the publication of Nancy Garden's *Annie on My Mind*, a book that ushered in a number of other lesbian juvenile novels in the 1980s and 1990s. Garden's novel begins as Eliza ("Liza") Winthrop recalls meet-

ing Annie Kenyon when they were both high school students and
reflects on the gradual growth of their romantic relationship. A book
that begins like just another run-of-the-mill romance develops into far
more. *Annie on My Mind* is remarkably convincing, depicting a world
that appears very much like the world many teenage lesbians face
every day. Annie, for instance, lives in a rough neighborhood and
attends a dilapidated and dangerous urban school that looks like "a
military bunker" (71). The novel deserves praise for the attention that
Garden gives to the many details that make up the relationship between Annie and Liza, like the time Annie bursts into tears because
she cannot afford to give Eliza a present or when Eliza looks up
"homosexuality" in the encyclopedia and is chagrined that the article
fails to mention love. The novel makes no attempt to whitewash the
uneasy feelings the two girls have about the physical aspect of their
new relationship. The book also does a fine job describing the all-
consuming nature of falling in love: "We saw each other every afternoon that we could, and on weekends, and called each other just
about every night, and even that didn't seem enough" (107). With the
publication of *Annie on My Mind,* young readers finally had a book that
addressed their concerns in a plausible fashion. Eliza and Annie are
two ordinary teenagers living ordinary lives.

Toward the end of the novel, Eliza and Annie are cat-sitting for
two teachers from Annie's school, Ms. Stevenson and Ms. Widmer.
When Eliza and Annie are caught in a compromising position, we
learn that Ms. Stevenson and Ms. Widmer are lesbians. Although the
girls escape punishment, the teachers both lose their jobs, an indication of the rampant homophobia in our society. Eliza then leaves to
attend MIT and Annie goes off to Berkeley, but Eliza does not write
Annie. Only after reflecting on all of her experiences and recognizing
the strength of her love for Annie does Eliza finally call. The novel
concludes with the two young women making plans to meet for
Christmas vacation and clearly determined not to allow society to
sunder their relationship. In many ways, *Annie on My Mind* is an
affirming account of lesbian lives and lesbian love. Neither Annie nor
Eliza dies, and the relationship continues to develop rather than being
terminated as often happened in earlier young adult novels with

lesbian characters. Garden's book also has realistic characters and situations and does not attempt to avoid the problems that confront lesbians in contemporary society. Due to Garden's skillful writing, her depiction of intelligent and likable teenage lesbians, and her creation of plausible scenarios, *Annie on My Mind* is one of the best juvenile books addressing lesbianism that has been written in the last fifteen years.

After this groundbreaking novel's publication, the following years produced a mixed bag of lesbian juvenile literature. *Annie* has led to a broader acceptance of lesbianism in children's literature, but this acceptance is limited. Even after the publication of *Annie on My Mind*, lesbian juvenile novels, not surprisingly, still suffered from stereotypical representations of lesbianism, frequently showing lesbians as masculine man haters. Typical of this style is Norma Klein's novel *My Life as a Body* (1987), in which the heroine, Augie, has a best friend, Claudia, who is an out lesbian. The novel deserves praise because Claudia's lesbianism and Augie's musings about her sexual orientation are presented as perfectly normal, even though the girls have different sexual orientations. Claudia, however, is stereotyped: She has a low opinion of men and has numerous hopeless crushes on heterosexual women. She is also stocky and athletic. In many ways, she conforms to heterosexual assumptions about how lesbians look and behave. Stereotypes such as these have proven to be remarkably durable in the world of juvenile literature.

A few juvenile writers in the mid and late 1980s tried to move beyond the stereotypes of lesbians as masculine man haters. One such writer was Madeleine L'Engle, who wrote *A House like a Lotus* (1984), a book for teenage readers that focuses on the experiences of Polly O'Keefe, a seventeen-year-old visiting Greece, and reflects on her relationship with Maximiliana Horne, a lesbian artist. On the positive side, Max is older and far from stereotypical. Her love, Dr. Ursula Heschel, is also older. On the negative side, Max and Ursula are too good to be true: a brilliant, wealthy artist living with a world-renowned brain surgeon on an estate that would make Donald Trump envious. Perhaps I do not socialize with the right women, but I rarely encounter such couples. Because Max and Ursula are such extremes, a common problem with depictions of lesbians in fiction for children and young adults, they are not as convincing as they could be. Also, since the book is narrated from Polly's first-person perspective and she states that she is not a lesbian, it is difficult to feel that Max and Ursula are not something of an oddity. This feeling is only reinforced when the reader learns that Max had a wretched childhood that included a domineering, demanding father; although not explicitly stated, it is hard to avoid the assumption that these childhood experiences influenced Max's sexual orientation.

Like L'Engel's novel, Lesléa Newman's picture book *Heather Has Two Mommies* (1989) depicts lesbians in a positive fashion, perhaps too positively. *Heather Has Two Mommies* describes a white upper-middle-class family, whose members live in "the little house with the big apple tree in the front yard and the tall grass in the back yard and they [are] all very happy" (5). No money problems plague this family, probably because Mama Kate is a physician (Mama Jane is a carpenter). Newman is determined to make her family appear as "normal" as possible, which results in it becoming as colorless as possible. Perhaps in an attempt to make the book appear nonthreatening to heterosexual readers, signs of lesbianism are at a minimum. The mothers hug when they discover they are going to have a baby, but they seem more like good friends than lovers.

Halfway through the book, I found myself wondering whether it was ever going to deal with homophobia and the real-life difficulties that most lesbians confront. I wished that just once Mama Kate and Mama Jane would squabble over who was to do the dishes or that they would send little Heather to her room without any supper because she had not picked up her toys. Such hopes were bound to be dashed. Instead, the family members "do lots of fun things. On sunny days they go to the park. On rainy days they stay inside and bake cookies. Heather likes to eat gingersnaps and drink a big glass of milk" (14).[13]

The one moment of tension in the whole story occurs when Heather goes to a play group, where she realizes that, unlike many of the other children, she does not have a daddy. My hopes for some attention to more serious issues faded, however, as the members of the politically correct classroom discuss their diverse family structures, including one boy who announces he has two daddies. After the children draw pictures of their different families, they all seem reconciled to difference. The teacher reassures them, "It doesn't matter how many mommies or how many daddies your family has. . . . It doesn't matter if your family has sisters or brothers or cousins or grandmothers or grandfathers or uncles or aunts. Each family is special. The most important thing about a family is that all the people in it love each other" (30). The only problem with this glib statement is that it *does* matter how many mommies or daddies a child might have, at least to the general heterosexual society. After her play group ends, Heather walks home with her two mommies and everything is fine. Or is it?

Newman's slightly later picture book *Gloria Goes to Gay Pride* (1991) has a few of the same weaknesses as *Heather Has Two Mommies*, including being so saccharine that it makes my teeth ache. The story's plot is simple. A young girl, Gloria, goes to a gay pride march and along the way encounters what appears to be her whole neighborhood, including her mail carrier, music teacher, and a man who works with one of her two mothers. Even the local store owners come out to cheer on the parade as it passes. In this happy, happy world, the one intrusion occurs when Gloria notices three people who "aren't singing or clapping" and who carry signs that read "Gays go away" (24). She is quickly reassured by her mothers, however, who tell her that love is the "most important thing of all" (26). Nothing destroys the serenity of the rest of the day. This unrealistic account of a gay pride march implies that any child could have a similar experience, when in actuality a gay pride march where a child might run into numerous lesbian and gay adults from her life is apt to be confined to a few large cities (San Francisco, Los Angeles, and New York) and a handful of small towns (e.g., Northampton, Massachusetts).

Newman's picture books suffer from a form of revisioning that plagues gay and lesbian children's books, particularly those for the youngest readers. Intent on challenging the negative depictions of lesbians and gay men that have dominated in this century, writers go to the opposite extreme and portray a lesbian or gay family that appears perfect and is little affected by the rampant homophobia of our society. A third example of this approach is seen in Elaine

Wickens's picture book *Anna Day and the O-ring* (1994), in which the two lesbian mothers and their child are portrayed in a loving relationship that is untouched by social problems; even when the two mothers take a walk while holding hands on a city street, they are not harassed. Another book that creates an unrealistically positive view of what it means to be a lesbian is Rosamund Elwin and Michele Paulse's picture book *Asha's Mums* (1990), in which a small girl, Asha, has two mothers. The book describes what happens when Asha's teacher doubts that Asha has two mothers. Although the book portrays lesbianism positively and depicts women of color (Asha's two mums), it also depicts homosexuality as something that is relatively easy to address. Asha's fellow students are first shown as being intolerant of her two mothers, but they change quickly when they actually meet Asha's mothers. Despite their positive depiction of lesbians and gays, books such as these simplify lesbian lives in a way that can be potentially destructive. In a fashion similar to 1950s television shows, such as "Leave It to Beaver" and "Father Knows Best," the books present a distorted image of family relations that might make some young boys or girls feel that their families are inadequate because they fail to achieve the perfection of such fictional ones.

An improvement on the picture book scene was the publication of Johnny Valentine's *The Daddy Machine* in 1992. This children's book tells the amusing story of two girls who have two moms but no dads. They invent a daddy machine and soon are inundated with daddies of all sorts. The girls quickly realize that they are actually content with their two mothers and manage to make all the daddies vanish with the help of the machine. The shortcoming of this book is that lesbianism is an incidental issue and there is little discussion of any specifically lesbian concerns.

Despite the shortcomings of the picture books by Newman, Wickens, Elwin and Paulse, and Valentine, I wish to emphasize that none of these books should be perceived as entirely without merit. These picture books and others do serve an important ideological purpose. They inform children that it is acceptable to have different forms of families, a message from which all children can benefit and that might help them grow up to be more tolerant individuals. Thus it is far better that these books exist than that they not exist at all. However, I am also interested in how the politics of assent functions in these picture books. By repeatedly emphasizing happy, happy families, these books send a message to readers that all families must be as unproblematic lest they be labeled as deviant. Though these books do affirm the importance of diverse families, they also, paradoxically, negate the possibility that families are not always lighthearted and free from strife.

Like recent picture books, contemporary young adult novels struggle with how to reenvision lesbianism, how to challenge and change the century-old notion of lesbians as sexual deviants. In the process, some writers have become firmly stuck in conventional genres, mainly the romance, which has resulted in some less than successful books. Typical is Hilary Mullins's novel *The Cat Came Back* (1993), a Naiad Press potboiler. The book is the journal of seventeen-year-old Stevie Roughgarden, who records her experiences coming out as well as her growing attraction to Andrea Snyder, one of her ice hockey teammates. This book is overblown, overwrought, and over-done, and there is nothing in Stevie and Andrea's romance that has not been told many times before.

M. E. Kerr's novel *Deliver Us from Evie* (1994) runs into similar problems. The novel describes what happens to a rural farming family in Missouri when it is revealed that their teenage daughter, Evie, is a lesbian. Evie's life gets even more complicated when she falls in love with Patsy Duff, a girl from a wealthy family. Evie and Patsy are a stereotypical butch-femme couple. The book repeatedly emphasizes what Evie's brother calls her "deep-down" difference (66), and Evie's mother worries that her daughter all too neatly fits the classic butch lesbian stereotype. In this fashion, the book reaffirms the notion that one is born a lesbian, an unproven idea that oversimplifies the com-plexity of lesbian lives. The story becomes increasingly improbable as readers discover that Patsy drives a black-cherry Porsche and has her own trust fund, which enables her to fly herself and Evie to France and to move to New York City, far away, we presume, from the bigots of their hometown. At the book's conclusion, it has lost any impact that it could have had because it is so entirely unrealistic. How many young lesbians with trust funds and brand-new $70,000 German sports cars does the typical teenage lesbian living in the rural South meet in the course of a lifetime? Although I recognize that fantasy is important for any young reader, including a lesbian, I believe that lesbian readers also need plausible fiction after which they can model their own lives. Because there are only a handful of real lesbian role models in our society, lesbian readers are likely to turn to fiction to gain an understanding of how to behave in the world. As a young teenager, I can remember reading *The Well of Loneliness* not only as fiction but also as an accurate account of how lesbians actually lived, since I myself had met no "real" lesbians of which I knew.

Despite the lack of realism displayed by many contemporary juvenile books that address lesbianism, all hope is not lost. A few juvenile writers are trying to depict lesbianism in far more complex ways than could be imagined in the 1970s and 1980s. Authors are exploring the intersections between lesbianism and such issues as race, ethnicity, and social class, developing a richer and more nuanced portrait of lesbian lives. One of these writers is Jacqueline Woodson, who discusses such controversial subjects as teenage pregnancy, biracial couples, and lesbian parents in her books. In her first juvenile novel, *The Dear One* (1991), Marion and Bernadette are a lesbian couple who have been together for eight years, and their relationship is a significant one. Lesbian issues, such as the gay and lesbian teachers' group that Bernadette attends, are openly mentioned and, even more notable, Marion is the daughter of a white mother and a black father. Woodson's next book, *From the Notebooks of Melanin Sun* (1995), is also concerned with race and biracial relationships. Melanin Sun is an African American teenager growing up in Brooklyn who discovers that his mother is a lesbian and that her lover, Kristen, is white. He reacts with violence and anger, refusing to speak to his mother and punching holes in the walls of their apartment. He gets into a fight when a friend calls his mother a "dyke." Ultimately, however, after Melanin meets and talks to Kristen, he recognizes that she might not be as objectionable as he had assumed. Unfortunately, this conclusion is too pat. After going to the beach with Kristen for only one day, already Melanin is reconciled to her presence in his mother's life.

Other 1990s writers address different controversial issues. In her novel *Lark in the Morning* (1991), Nancy Garden discusses homelessness, runaway children, and child abuse as she explores a teenage lesbian's relationship with two young runaways. Christina Salat also handles problems with family dynamics in her novel *Living in Secret* (1993), which portrays a lesbian mother as perfectly acceptable. This novel focuses on the experiences of eleven-year-old Amelia Monet. When her parents divorced, her father was given custody of Amelia because of his former wife's "deviant" lifestyle, and at the novel's beginning, Amelia is "kidnapped" by her mother and her mother's girlfriend, Janey. Although she lives a new life in San Francisco, Amelia knows that her father is searching for her. He finds her, forcing her to return to live with him. A court battle over her custody, however, seems to be in the future at the book's conclusion. Lesbianism is discussed openly, and the relationship of Amelia's mother and Janey is portrayed far more positively than the heterosexual relationships depicted in the novel. In each of these novels, the writers focus on family dynamics to reaffirm that not all heterosexual families are good and not all homosexual families are bad.

Like Woodson, Garden, and Salat, Stacey Donovan complicates the depiction of lesbianism. Donovan's novel *Dive* (1994), which is one of the best—perhaps the best—young adult novel discussing lesbianism that I have read, addresses a wide range of subjects. *Dive* is narrated by Virginia Dunn, also known as "V," a teenager whose life is falling apart. Her dog is seriously hurt by a hit-and-run driver. Her best friend starts avoiding her. And, worst of all, her father is in the hospital with a mysterious disease.

V comes alive as a character. Her reflections on what it means to be a young woman growing up in the suburbs are acute and sometimes painful:

> No, life doesn't make sense.
> But I am alive anyway. I live in the suburbs, land of car rides to the Dairy Barn. Around here, nobody ever walks. (112)

> The sky slants. Before dusk, it hurts my eyes. Soon it will be completely dark. I'm walking home. Nothing exists except my breath. (44)

Virginia lives in a world that often seems more like a dream than reality: "Sometimes the night never ends; it just breaks into light and we pretend. I am alive, though I tend to forget that when I am pretending" (97). She experiences the loneliness, alienation, and isolation that fill everyone's life to a certain extent. Lesbianism is one facet of her character, but there are many others that are also significant.

Dive juxtaposes the agonizingly slow decline of Virginia's father to her developing relationship with Jane, a new student at Virginia's school. These two experiences are woven together with great skill, with neither one being more important than the other. In this fashion, Donovan reveals the ways in which lesbianism is woven into the larger tapestry of a woman's life. At the same time, Donovan does not shortchange lesbianism and its significance to Virginia. She spends a great deal of time reflecting on her feelings about lesbianism and what her relationship with Jane means: "Even I think there's something wrong with it, and I don't know how that happened. Or I think I thought I did. But I don't. . . . I wonder how I arrived at the idea that it's wrong without even thinking about it. I guess that's where the danger is. In the things that aren't mentioned" (225). Like Garden's Annie and Eliza, Virginia is very much a thoughtful heroine, one who reflects on how society constructs lesbianism and refuses to accept what others tell her about lesbianism being "wrong." Virginia is a lesbian heroine for the 1990s, but I could not help but wish she had been around in the 1970s when I had to content myself with Stephen Gordon.

Nor does Donovan merely end this book with the happily-ever-after conclusion that so many recent lesbian juvenile books share. The finish leaves Jane and Virginia's relationship up in the air. It is an affair in its early stages. But Virginia's father has died. Life and death are intertwined in this book, reflecting the cyclic nature of our brief days on this planet.

Despite its thoughtful consideration of Virginia's developing relationship with Jane, Donovan's novel has failings. For instance, Jane and Virginia are incredibly good-looking, recalling the scores of other beauties that choke the pages of lesbian novels for young adults. Virginia's first impressions of Jane are described vividly: "[L]ike some Mediterranean model with a deep olive complexion that glowed,

[Jane] sauntered up the aisle, sauntered in her silent black boots and skintight faded jeans with her motorcycle jacket draped off one shoulder" (129). This sounds as if Donovan has been reading too many issues of *Vogue*. As I argued in chapter 3, images of glamorous pseudo-lesbians in women's magazines create an image of lesbianism that is inaccessible to the majority of women. In a similar fashion, the stunning lesbians that fill juvenile books show a standard of beauty that only a few can attain.

Not only Donovan herself but also her publishing company seem to be suffering from a *Vogue* overdose, which is made more evident when one looks at the book's cover art of two long-haired, high-cheekboned beauties, looking as if they would be at home in the pages of *Glamour*. In addition, the two women are never pictured kissing or even hugging. Instead, one woman gazes at the other, who stares into space. As is common in novels with a gay or lesbian focus, the cover art operates to take the edge off the controversial subject matter. *Dive's* cover is so nondescript that the only way to discover the book's lesbian content is by browsing through it. The description on the dust jacket is just as coy; it fails to mention lesbianism at all except in the most oblique fashion: "[F]ollowing the captivating Jane are other questions that both arouse and disturb. The wrenching answers to these seem to break every rule, and beyond that, all limitations." The often non-revealing cover art and dust jacket copy of lesbian books for children reveal a publishing industry that continues to be edgy about homosexuality, particularly when it comes to the marketing of children's and young adult fiction. Lesbianism is making more frequent appearances, but it is still a topic that is carefully regulated by major publishers seeking large audiences.

Into the Future

As this chapter has pointed out, even today lesbianism is by no means accepted as standard fare in children's literature. Children's and young adult books about lesbians, for the most part, exist in a ghetto, where they are produced by lesbian and gay publishers for lesbian and gay bookstores and lesbian and gay readers. Although these books are sometimes found in bookstores or libraries, they are not mainstreamed nearly as much as are children's books about other minority groups. It is sobering to recognize how frequently juvenile books about lesbianism are censored even in recent years. As late as 1994, *Annie on My Mind* was removed from the shelves of Olathe South High School in Kansas because four members of the school board objected to its content, even though no complaints had been filed ("Board" C-4). In addition, lesbian characters have made few inroads into the huge realm of popular fiction for children and young adults, where countless thousands of books still feature the stereotypical boy-meets-girl romance. Lesbian children's books have a tenuous foothold, one that could vanish abruptly. This must not be allowed to happen because all young readers, particularly lesbians, need books that portray lesbianism, since it is commonly elided from other media forms targeted at juveniles.

The tremendous need for lesbian and gay images in juvenile books, as well as in other media forms directed at young people, was made more apparent to me after I took a walk through the campus of a local high school, which, just like the high school that I attended over ten years ago, appeared overwhelmingly heterosexual. Boy-and-girl couples, hand in hand, strolled across the yard. Plastered across every available bulletin board, neon pink signs, showing a picture of a girl and boy dancing, advertised the weekend's upcoming event. Carfuls of boys drove slowly across the campus, ogling the girls. A group of giggling, permed girls sporting identical long, lacquered, Chinese-red nails, wandered across the campus, stopping to exchange flirtatious comments with the boys in the cars. Such an environment, which is typical of the majority of schools across the United States, makes heterosexuality appear not as one choice but as the *only* choice. Given the dominance of heterosexuality and its often unquestioned status, fiction has the potential to make readers aware that heterosexuality is not the only sexual orientation.

Not only is it important to ensure that gay and lesbian juvenile books continue to be published, despite the conservative pressure to abolish or censor such work, but it is equally important to analyze the ideological messages of such texts. As I have demonstrated, even the books that seem most positive can function to create and perpetuate lesbian stereotypes, such as the stereotype that all lesbians are masculine. Books, too, can perpetuate reverse stereotypes, such as the idea that all lesbians are gorgeous. Lesbian depictions in juvenile books are especially vital to critique because such representations might be the first image of lesbianism that young people encounter and thus may have a lasting influence on how they perceive lesbianism.

At the same time that we recognize the importance of the ideology displayed in children's literature, we must also recognize the limitations of such books. Their influence is limited because it is part of a far larger ideological realm. A vast range of societal influences shape children's perceptions of homosexuality. Children do not read in a vacuum. "Ideology is not something which is transferred to children as if they were empty receptacles," Hollindale writes. "It is something which they already possess, having drawn it from a mass of experiences far more powerful than literature" (17). Literature is important and can influence how people perceive homosexuality; it is not, however, such an overpowering force that it will induce young boys and girls to become homosexuals, an argument that is made by some conservatives.

Along with the previous four chapters, this one has shown that representation *does* matter. Representations of lesbians not only have depicted lesbian experiences but have also helped to constitute them. Lesbianism and its place in society can only be understood by recognizing how representations have functioned to maintain the status of the lesbian as a hated and feared outsider. Representations, however, have also been used to alter that cultural stereotype and to create new, empowering ways to depict lesbian lives. The last chapters have explored how lesbians have been marginalized by mainstream culture and how this position in the margins has encouraged lesbians to find new approaches to creating a culture of their own, whether through an alternative reading approach to mainstream books or by writing children's books of their own.

Part III examines how lesbian and gay communities create internal margins of their own. By analyzing geography, passing, and butch identities, I shall show ways that lesbians become marginal members of their own communities. These three chapters will reveal some of the ways that lesbians are marginalized not only by heterosexual society but also by lesbian and gay society itself.

3
Writing in the Margins

6

Lost in Space

Queer Geography and the
Politics of Location

Imagine that a mischievous fairy disrupted our space–time continuum and threw us all into an alternate reality in which Cincinnati,
instead of San Francisco, were the queer capital of the United States.
How would queer culture, queer studies, and queer theory in that new
universe compare to how we know them in this familiar one? Would
they be identical, similar, or radically divergent? Perhaps the differences would be minor. If Cincinnati were the queer mecca instead of
San Francisco, there might be an explosion of gay and lesbian chefs
coast to coast concocting Cincinnati's renowned "Cincinnati chili,"
which seems to be sold on every block, rather than cooking the Pacific
Rim dishes so trendy in the city of our world. Possibly Cincinnati's
Northside neighborhood would have the fame that the Castro has
achieved. But perhaps the differences would be far more dramatic. The
Cincinnati of our universe is a very conservative city. What impact
would that fact have on gay and lesbian cultural evolution? How far-

reaching would be the effects? Would Stonewall still have occurred in New York City? Would ACT UP ever have come into being?

These musings are designed in part to highlight the preeminence of San Francisco in the queer cultural imagination. Cincinnati will not soon eclipse San Francisco as the most prominent city in the United States' queer geography, nor will any other city. It seems a trifle sacrilegious—like the idea of painting a moustache on the Mona Lisa— even to suggest that another city or town could replace the fabled City by the Bay. San Francisco, after all, does have a large, flourishing gay culture and a long history of providing refuge to lesbians and gay men, particularly after the end of World War II when the city's gay and lesbian community expanded rapidly as veterans of the armed forces moved to the city rather than move back to the more conservative cities and towns where they grew up. This sense of uneasiness about displacing San Francisco as the "queer capital" points out how taken for granted queer geography has become in the United States. It is this fixity that this chapter seeks to destabilize. I wish to reinspect queer geography to study the margins that queer studies—an area that is very much in the margins already—is creating within itself, whether intentionally or unintentionally.

I am turning my attention not only to San Francisco, although that city does play a significant role in my argument, but to the entire "queer geography" of the United States to make four points: (1) The geography of the United States, particularly what I identify as its "queer" geography, shapes queer studies in ways that might be harmful as well as beneficial. (2) The dominance of gay and lesbian culture in San Francisco, Los Angeles, New York and a few other enclaves (Northampton, Provincetown, Fire Island, Key West) overshadows the true multiplicity of lesbian/gay culture in the United States today. (3) Geography helps to constitute the queer subject in such a way that the queer subject par excellence becomes a lesbian or gay man from a major urban city on one of the coasts, particularly someone from New York City or San Francisco. (4) Geography shapes, in part, a person's understanding of his or her homosexuality.

Although this chapter draws much from recent work in postmodern and feminist geography, it should not be categorized solely

as a geographical analysis.[1] Geographers traditionally have been the
scholars most concerned with space, but there is growing interest
among other social and cultural theorists in the study of space, spatial
relationships, and the processes of space. This chapter has been influenced not only by researchers interested primarily in geography, such
as Alison Blunt, J. Nicholas Entrikin, Gillian Rose, and Edward H.
Soja, but also by scholars, such as Gloria Anzaldúa and María Lugones, who are interested in how minority communities construct
their identities in relationship to the mainstream, as well as by theorists, such as Mark Blasius, Judith Butler, and Michel Foucault, whose
main focus of research lies elsewhere. This interdisciplinary approach
is necessary to bridge the gap between geography and queer studies
and to demonstrate the importance of place for gay and lesbian theory.

Since a person's locatedness in space inevitably influences his/
her perceptions of the world, there are limitations to my approach in
this chapter. I am white, middle-class, highly educated, and female;
thus my view of the United States' queer geography will be colored
accordingly. In addition, my subject position as a lesbian who has
experienced life in a variety of locations in the United States, including San Francisco, Boston, Cincinnati, San Diego, and Northampton,
creates an unavoidable bias to this chapter, a geographical bias that no
person can escape. A working-class African American man living in
the South or an upper-class Asian American woman working in the
Northwest might have completely different stories to tell about how
they perceive the queer geography of the United States. I hope, however, that this chapter will be a starting point for a larger discussion of
the way queer geography is constituted both by individual lesbians
and gay men and by much larger cultural forces.[2]

Standard geographical descriptions of the United States typically
fail to allow a space for the lives and experiences of gays and lesbians.
As a result, we have to create our own worlds and words to describe
our spaces; only in this way can we maintain existence where existence is denied. As lesbian philosopher Joyce Trebilcot writes, "Dykes
especially cannot be expected to live in worlds made by others. A
commitment to being a dyke is partly a commitment to invention—a
commitment to making up one's own world, or parts of it, anyway"

(138). Lesbians and gays need not only to create a new, inclusive
geography but also to analyze the dominant, exclusive geography
around them. This is a difficult task. Since people tend to normalize
their surroundings, unraveling the network of relationships that constitute a place can be an arduous task. We are used to seeing space as
no more than a void to be filled. Yet geography is socially constructed,
though it takes on the appearance of naturalness and the authority of
reality, just as do constructs of gender, sexuality, race, and ethnicity.

Scholars and theorists need to recognize and acknowledge the
biases implicit or explicit in queer cultures and queer scholarship
today and guard against the creation of a queer version of what Donna
Haraway calls the "master subject," which she defines as "an autonomous subject who observes social conflicts from a privileged and
unconflicted place" and whose claim to pure objectivity "can be con-
verted from fantasy into reality only by denying the relational character of subjectivity and by relegating other viewpoints—different subjectivities—to invisible, subordinate, or competing positions" (qtd. in
Blunt and Rose 5). Variations on the "master subject" already exist in
the gay and lesbian world; although "[c]ontemporary lesbian and gay
male cultures evidence a heightened sensitivity to issues of difference
and the social formation of desire, sexuality, and identity" (Seidman
105), this sensitivity, as Steven Seidman points out, has its limitations,
and lesbian and gay research still tends to privilege Anglo-American
accounts. The elision of differing subjectivities that constitute gayness
is based not only on factors such as race, ethnicity, age, gender, and
class but also on geographic region. A regional bias exists in contemporary research on gays and lesbians, with a large amount of work
concentrating on a relative paucity of locations. The opening of new,
prestigious lesbian/gay research centers in Los Angeles and New York,
the creation of the Harvey Milk Institute in San Francisco, or the
production of books such as George Chauncey's *Gay New York: Gender, Urban Culture, and the Making of the Gay Male World, 1890–1940*
(1994), Martin Duberman's *Stonewall* (1993), Esther Newton's *Cherry
Grove, Fire Island: Sixty Years in America's First Gay and Lesbian Town*
(1993), and Kath Weston's *Families We Choose: Lesbians, Gays, Kinship*
(1991) all demonstrate a tendency toward privileging specific geo-

graphical locations, notably on the East or West Coast, particularly San Francisco, New York, and, to a lesser extent, Key West, Provincetown, or Fire Island.[3]

To avoid simply giving status or attention to the cities and towns with the highest concentration of gays and lesbians, scholars need to construct a new queer geography. This is not to suggest that there is no value in studying preeminently gay areas. To the contrary, much valuable information can be gained about how gay people formulate identity and create institutions in areas where they are numerous, visible, and relatively powerful. As Weston points out in *Families We Choose,* which is based on fieldwork conducted in the San Francisco bay area, "With its unique history and reputation as a gay city, San Francisco hardly presents a 'typical' lesbian and gay population for study. Yet the Bay Area proved to be a valuable field site because it brought together gay men and lesbians from very different colors and classes, identities and backgrounds" (8). Further, large cities are a "hotbed" of diversity and "fringe" activity—this is the case for everyone, not just gays. This element of diversity means that newer movements, such as queer politics, are more likely to emerge in locations like San Francisco, Los Angeles, or New York before moving inland to the more conservative areas of the country where they might eventually be assimilated even into the mainstream. As Denyse Lockard writes, "the East and West Coasts are at the forefront of cultural innovation" (88) for many lesbians.

But, as exciting and important as studying new behaviors and trends is, scholars should not lose sight of the fact that the majority of lesbians and gay men in the United States are not in the vanguard of the movement and do not live in the cradles of gay civilization. Many gays and lesbians live in areas with small gay communities or no discernible gay presence; they are trying to survive in what are often inhospitable, conservative environments. In some ways their situation is akin to that of gays and lesbians before Stonewall, but it is not identical. The antagonism they face is similar, but the gay culture has changed. Gays and lesbians today are much more visible and vocal in demanding rights and recognition than ever before and have managed to change a number of institutionalized homophobias, including the

classification of homosexuality as a psychiatric disorder. Gays and
lesbians are also creating a national culture by disseminating a multi-
tude of cultural artifacts, including travel books, magazines, comics,
clothing, postcards, and a host of other commodities that are accessible to nearly every gay person in the United States (sometimes travel
to a gay cultural center is required, sometimes items must be borrowed
from well-traveled friends). Though these cultural artifacts and signs
travel across spatial geographies and engender a sense of cohesive gay
culture, they never entirely negate the differences that are produced by
living in places that have disparate perceptions about what it means to
be queer. Overall, the United States remains hostile to gays and lesbians—the *Bowers* v. *Hardwick* Supreme Court case and the debate
over whether homosexuals should be allowed to serve in the military
are perfect examples of America's unwillingness to accept homosexuality—though some areas are more welcoming than others. In effect,
most gays are living in a curious mixture of pre- and post-Stonewall
gay/lesbian culture. So while some of the writings that center on
gay/lesbian cultural centers are outstanding and deserve high praise,
this intense concentration on only a few sites of gay/lesbian culture
provides a distorted glass through which to view the gay/lesbian
"hinterlands."

This is not to suggest, of course, that *no* work has been done on
smaller gay and lesbian communities across the United States. A great
deal of such work has been accomplished, and this scholarship continues to grow, as do calls for recognition of the diversity of gay
cultures.[4] Elizabeth Kennedy and Madeline Davis, Susan Krieger,
James T. Sears, Edmund White, and numerous other writers have
looked at lesbian and gay experience in a variety of different regions.
This chapter is concerned, however, with the damaging effects of
universalizing certain types of gay experiences while relegating others
to a marginalized position. Studies of gay men and lesbians in San
Francisco and New York are often universalized, whereas the work of
those concentrating on other locations is particularized. Simply because the experiences of gay men and women in certain areas, such as
San Francisco and New York, are so visible, it is all too easy for writers,
both academic and nonacademic, to assume that the experiences of

such gays reflect the experiences of other gays in the rest of the United States. Lesbian/gay studies should be wary of creating universal theories from looking at only a small number of locations. Shane Phelan's words about how grand theories operate are useful here: "Grand theories work by subsuming all struggles under a single rubric, delaying or denying the importance of other categories" ("(Be)coming" 784). It is important to avoid creating grand theories about lesbian/gay studies that do not account for regional differences in gay/lesbian identity and culture. Gays and lesbians may acknowledge that obvious superficial differences exist among communities in various regions, but there is an expectation of a universal "gayness" that denies the profound differences between gay cultures in different regions. I shall explore some of these differences, particularly for lesbians, in the following section.

Queer Culture Shock

In the South industrialization and the end of segregation reoriented all values. In the West the frontier spirit, no matter how faint, can still be sensed. In the East, wave after wave of social change has made everything seem transient.

Only in the Midwest has so little changed over such a long period. Only here can people sneer at the antics of less stable populations. (White 192)

I first became interested in queer geography when I moved with my girlfriend from California to Hamilton, Ohio, a small working-class city located about twenty miles north of Cincinnati. As transplants from San Francisco and Northampton, Massachusetts (dubbed "Lesbianville, USA" by the *National Enquirer*), who had lived in Boston and San Diego, we were disconcerted by what constituted gay/lesbian culture and community in the Cincinnati area. The semiotics of lesbian identity in Cincinnati was unfamiliar; the social institutions were different; the backgrounds and values of most lesbians we met were unlike our own; the diversity of cultural institutions was minuscule compared to what had been available in our previous home regions. Our profound sense of dislocation was more than geographic; we suffered a dislocation of identity as well. What did it mean for us to identify as lesbian when what constituted "lesbian," as reflected in the culture and community, had apparently shifted under our feet? This rupture in our sense of lesbian selves made it clear that our subjectivities as lesbians were constructed in relation to a specific culture in a particular place.[5]

The recognition that place affects one's sense of identity is not new, yet what became clear to us was how place operated specifically on our lesbian identities, creating a universalizing perception of lesbian identity and lifestyle based on where we had learned what it meant to be homosexual. This experience echoes the work of Mark Blasius, who argues that "coming out is a lifelong process of *becoming* lesbian or gay" (654–55), which involves the feedback of one's community. A number of other theorists, including Judith Butler in *Gender Trouble: Feminism and the Subversion of Identity* (1990) and Cindy Patton in her essay "Tremble, Hetero Swine!" (1993), concur with Blasius: Gay identity is not constituted in a singular moment of "coming out"; rather, it is a lifelong process that is influenced by one's community. Butler, for instance, writes about gender identities: "gender intersects with racial, class, ethnic, sexual, and regional modalities of discursively constituted identities. As a result, it becomes impossible to separate 'gender' from the political and cultural intersections in which it is invariably produced and maintained" (3). According to her, numerous factors shape a lesbian's gender display, including the region of the nation where she lives, and if one accepts that gay identity is similarly constructed, then it follows that *where* one comes out has a profound effect on how one perceives one's gay identity. Michele, a thirty-four-year-old computer systems analyst, who spent ten formative years in San Francisco, comments:

> In San Francisco, part of my sense of dyke identity lay in being on the fringe. I relied on markers such as a leather jacket and extensive tattoos to anchor my sense of self as different from the mainstream, and I moved within a community of others who utilized similar symbols. But in Ohio, in an area where I saw few lesbians, and even fewer who looked like me, I experienced a disruption in my sense of identity. Surrounded by conservative

heterosexuals, with little "lesbian feedback," I found that the
meaning of the concept "being a lesbian" as I had conceived it in
San Francisco was growing increasingly fuzzy.

When a person leaves a familiar community and enters another that
has unfamiliar norms and values, the resulting sense of internal dis-
ruption is commonly known as culture shock. Gays and lesbians
experience a culture shock related specifically to their experience of
gay community and identity. As Blasius notes, "one enters into a
specific discourse and practice about what it means to be lesbian or
gay that the existence of community has made possible and through
which one voluntarily forms oneself as an ethical subject *in relation to
the values of that community*" (657; emphasis added). Because gay
communities are influenced by the character of the larger region in
which they are found, there can be enormous variance in norms and
values among gay communities, despite a relatively high cultural
congruence at a more superficial level. Members of one gay or lesbian
community might be surprised at the values of another: The rainbow
flag could be the same as the one at home, but other differences might
surface that surprise and confound the unwary.[6]

An excellent example of the subtleties of difference among places
is the reaction to the film *Go Fish*. This full-length feature film is the
first one about lesbian life that I had viewed that reflected my own
experiences in the gay community. All of my friends whose gay communities of origin were big coastal cities like San Francisco, New York,
or Boston loved the film for similar reasons. Yet reactions from lesbians
in other parts of the country were not always as favorable. One woman,
Susan, who recently moved to Austin, Texas, from San Francisco,
reported her experience at a party where Austin lesbians were discussing the film. None of the Austin lesbians liked the film, not because
they thought it was poorly made or too arty but rather because they
could not "relate" to the characters and their lifestyles. As one woman
put it, she could not understand why the characters were living "as if
they were poor or something," a reference to the communal households portrayed in the film. Some lesbians found the depiction of
communal living to be an authentic and endearing representation of

lesbian life, while others could not recognize themselves in that picture. Nor was this response unique to Austin—another San Francisco transplant, in North Carolina, reported the same reaction to the movie there. Although it is obvious that not all lesbians live or have lived in communal households, what was surprising to me was that some lesbians could not even *conceive* of the possibility of living in such a household: Communal households are not a part of their experience or of their conception of lesbian community. This may be because they live in areas where the American Dream of owning one's own home is still realizable by the average working person, including most lesbians. Cities like Austin and many midwestern cities, including Cincinnati, are also influenced by the strong religious and "family values" attitudes of the surrounding area, which insist upon households based on couple relationships. The economic and cultural values of Texas, in this case, had a strong influence on how lesbians constructed their identities, an influence that, in the case of *Go Fish,* took precedence over a common bond of lesbianism.

Hence, "being a lesbian" in suburban Cincinnati means something different from "being a lesbian" in San Francisco. Judith Butler tells an anecdote about being a lesbian in her essay "Imitation and Gender Insubordination": "When I spoke at the conference on homosexuality in 1989, I found myself telling my friends beforehand that I was off to Yale to be a lesbian, which of course didn't mean that I wasn't one before, but that somehow then, as I spoke in that context, I was one in some more thorough and totalizing way, at least for the time being. . . . To say that I 'play' at being [a lesbian] is not to say that I am not one 'really'; rather, how and where I play at being one is the way in which that 'being' gets established, instituted, circulated, and confirmed" (18). Here, Butler's ideas echo those of Blasius, acknowledging the crucial role of the arena in which gay identity is enacted. One can interpret Butler's words as describing the difference between simply living as a lesbian in a more or less nonreflective manner and *being* a lesbian as that distinction was highlighted by her recognition that being a lesbian publicly, for an audience, connoted something different from the being of daily life. Blasius and Butler agree that audience matters in the formation and enactment of gay identity: The actor is shaped in part by the audience for which she is performing. I apply this idea to geography, using it to explain why my experience of myself as a lesbian in San Francisco was different from my experience in Cincinnati.

In moving from queer-saturated areas to the Cincinnati suburbs, my girlfriend and I felt the shock of moving from a very public community to a very private one. Having coastal-big-city aesthetics, we had both come to expect certain signifiers and a certain level of visibility from other members of the gay community. One such signifier is what I call "the look"—eye contact between lesbians on the street that extends just a few seconds longer than between casual passers-by.[7] It's a look that is meant to say "I see you," a secret sign in a society where overt recognition of lesbianism is not done. "The look" was a common feature of life in urban areas, but where I live in the suburbs it does not exist. To the trained observer, my girlfriend and I are obviously lesbian, yet we have passed other lesbian couples in the local mall who give no indication of any kind of having seen us.

Another important identifier of lesbians is clothing style. In Cincinnati, we found a city where the dress codes that identified lesbians were notably toned down from what we were used to in San Francisco and Northampton, areas where lesbians enjoy a public community and culture. That element of public-versus-private culture makes it easy to focus on the "gay cities" when writing about gay cultural expressions such as fashion. For instance, Inge Blackman and Kathryn Perry write: "Today's lesbian 'self' is a thoroughly urban creature who interprets fashion as something to be worn and discarded. Nothing is sacred for very long. Constantly changing, she dabbles in fashion, constructing one self after another, expressing her desires in a continual process of experimentation" (77). Blackman and Perry are concentrating on English lesbian culture, but their words are equally applicable in the United States where many lesbians assume that the "real" lesbian is the urban one, particularly the woman who lives in Los Angeles, San Francisco, New York, or, to a lesser extent, Chicago, Boston, or Seattle. Northampton and Provincetown are special cases because, despite their small size, they have large proportions of lesbians and gays. Another description of lesbian fashion appears in

Lisa Duggan's essay "The Anguished Cry of an 80s Fem: 'I Want to Be a
Drag Queen,'" which focuses chiefly on San Francisco, New York, and
Cherry Grove. She remarks: "Dykes in their 20s in the major urban
centers are looking less like nuns and more like motorcycle club
members and their molls" (63). Duggan's words might describe lesbian fashion in San Francisco but have little to do with Cincinnati,
where the fashions are apt to be far more conservative. This example
shows the tendency of writers to focus on what is happening to
lesbians in San Francisco or New York, while intentionally or unintentionally overlooking other areas.[8] The emphasis on lesbian fashions in
these cities tends to promote the idea that *all* lesbians have the same
lifestyle as a few East or West Coast urban-chic dykes.

But you cannot always identify a lesbian by her style. I sometimes wish that lesbians had some universal, cross-cultural signal of
identity, because not only are the lesbian codes and fashions in this
part of Ohio different from those in San Francisco, but so are codes for
heterosexual women. I frequently mistake straight women for lesbians
because they use many of the signifiers I associate with lesbians, including short hair, no makeup, and comfortable, androgynous clothing. This constant misinterpretation of my environment has, at times,
led to serious feelings of disorientation and a sense of "not belonging."
I am missing what John Jackson identifies as a sense of place, which he
associates with "a lively awareness of the familiar environment, a ritual
repetition, a sense of fellowship based on shared experience" (159). I
am missing that sense of place, and I find myself longing for the
familiar forms of lesbian culture with which I was "raised." I long for
"home."

Slowly, my girlfriend and I are learning how to "read" midwestern lesbian culture, and we are finding that it is profoundly
influenced by the social geography in which it is located, as is the
lesbian culture of any other region. The Cincinnati area differs in some
fundamental aspects from San Francisco and Northampton. Cincinnati is a conservative city in the part of the country known as the Bible
Belt. A strong fundamentalist Christian presence exists here, with the
attendant homophobia. Cincinnati voters overwhelmingly passed Issue 3, which struck gays, lesbians, and bisexuals from the city's human

rights amendment. Do not forget the attempt to close down the Robert Mapplethorpe exhibit here in 1992; that fiasco is a quintessential example of Cincinnati's obsession with what it calls "decency." This conservative backdrop inevitably affects the form gay and lesbian culture takes.

Where I live, just north of Cincinnati, I can go for weeks without meeting with another obvious lesbian.[9] Contrast this with a recent trip my girlfriend made back to Northampton, where she counted twenty lesbians during a half-hour walk along Main Street. The Cincinnati area is not a very hospitable environment for gays and lesbians, yet, in my research on the area before moving there, I was told more than once that there was a large and thriving lesbian community. There is, but it does not look like what I, having had my gay identity shaped in "queer hotbeds," think a lesbian community should look like. Cincinnati proper, as a fairly large city, does have a more visible gay presence than the outlying suburbs, including a gay ghetto located in an area called Northside. Many lesbians and gay men own property there, and rainbow flags are not an uncommon sight. The women's bookstore, considered by many to be the center of lesbian activity, is in that neighborhood, along with a new lesbian-owned cafe and a new lesbian bar. But there is simply no comparison between Northside and San Francisco's gay ghetto, the Castro. That lesbians and gay men are not as visible here as in San Francisco or Northampton makes sense in an area like Cincinnati (and much of the rest of the United States). Lesbianism is less of a public identity here; the trendy urban dyke styles of San Francisco or Los Angeles are seldom visible. Lesbians are far more likely to wear clothing that allows them to blend in with heterosexual society. While this serves as a protection against potential threats, it has the side effect of making it difficult for lesbians to identify each other, weakening or inhibiting the sense of public community that is such a marked feature of the Castro.

Perhaps I can best describe my current experiences by referring to Gloria Anzaldúa's discussion of what she calls "*mestiza* consciousness." In her influential book *Borderlands/La Frontera: The New Mestiza* (1987), she writes: "Living on borders and in margins, keeping intact one's shifting and multiple identity and integrity, is like trying to swim in a new element, an 'alien' element" (preface). She describes borderlands as being "physically present wherever two or more cultures edge each other, where people of different races occupy the same territory, where under, lower, middle and upper classes touch" (preface). Although Anzaldúa is writing about her experiences living on the Texas/Mexico border, her words are equally germane to our experiences in Ohio where we straddle the border between homosexual and heterosexual communities. A form of *mestiza* consciousness arises for lesbians and gays in the Midwest. They need to circulate in a variety of different cultures, always negotiating their way between cultural systems that share little in common and may even be diametrically opposed.[10] They must learn how to negotiate in those different cultures to survive—their "straight" jobs are frequently necessary for their economic well-being. But living in different cultures can carry a price—a heavy one. Sometimes I feel as if my lesbianism were being diminished—becoming almost ghostlike—because there are so few times when it is acceptable to show it.

Place helps constitute my lesbianism far more than I realized before moving to Cincinnati. Place is always shaping people, just as people are always shaping it. This is why queer theorists need to gain a better understanding of how place functions, particularly for queers, and how queer geography influences our interactions in queer communities across the United States.

Lost in Space

> The space in which we live, which draws us out of ourselves, in which the erosion of our lives, our time and our history occurs, the space that claws and knaws [sic] at us, is . . . , in itself, a heterogeneous space. In other words, we do not live in a kind of void, inside of which we could place individuals and things. We do not live inside a void that could be colored with different shades of light, we live inside a set of relations that delineates sites which are irreducible to one another and absolutely not superimposable on one another. (Foucault, "Other Spaces" 23)

Geography is, in the most basic sense, the study of space. The above quotation from Foucault presents an evocative description of what it feels like to live in space, the human condition none of us can escape. Space, as he points out, is more than measured volumes of air molecules that we displace by our presence. It is also constituted by the relationships between the things "inside" of it—including relationships between people. Hence, it makes sense to say that queer people inhabit and create a different kind of space than do heterosexuals, and the terrain of queer space needs to be explored and mapped to understand more fully its multivalent nature. But queer space is equally defined by its relationship to power and its relationship to the heterosexual spaces into which it is woven, and for that reason queer studies cannot afford to overlook the impact of geography on its turf.

I am using the term "queer geography" to refer to the particular geography that is uniquely significant to the lesbian/gay community. For instance, in thinking about queer geography, it is evident that San Francisco would be equivalent to the capital of the United States. Similarly, Provincetown and Northampton would be far more important than their small sizes would seem to suggest. Obviously, queer geography creates a map that shares similarities with the "real" United States but also varies widely in places. To better conceptualize queer geography, consider one of those maps of the United States that graphic artists create using the world view of a particular city or town. For instance, a New York inhabitant views New York as taking up much of the map, with the entire Midwest taking up very little room. For a lesbian, San Francisco and Northampton might have room on a queer map that is far disproportionate to their actual size. When looking at the United States from a lesbian or gay perspective, what emerges is a map that bears little resemblance to the more traditional map found hanging in a geography classroom.

Though the term "queer geography" initially elicits images of physical space, geophysical terrain, and mapping strategies, geography as a discipline and space as its subject encompass more than our eighth-grade geography teachers let on. Space, in its most rudimentary and recognizable form, is conceived of as a static, concrete backdrop to human endeavors as humanity marches forward through time; it is the arena in which people play out their social lives. Such a view emphasizes the ways that space can be measured and described and assumes that these accounts of space serve as mimetic representations achieved through objective observation.

Yet, increasingly, theorists have been disputing this perception of space, arguing that space is actually dynamic and "constituted through struggles over power/knowledge" (Blunt and Rose 5). Maps are a good example of these differing perceptions of geography. Under the first view, a map is a truthful representation of the space it describes. From this perspective, the "queer" map of the United States I described earlier would be considered a parodic distortion of reality. But under the second view, mapping is inherently political, creating "a spatial image that directly addresses the politics of representation as they are bound into the politics of location" (Blunt and Rose 8). For example, many of the popular maps of the world that were manufactured in the United States or Europe have been shown to be politically influenced: Europe and North America appear larger than they actually are in relation to other countries and continents and tend to be centrally located in the map's image.

Space is more than terrain; space is socially produced as "a set of relations between individuals and groups" (Soja 120), and social life is both the producer and the product of spatiality (Soja 129). Every space becomes imbued with political meaning: The bathroom, the closet, the cemetery, the body, all are sites that are simultaneously constituted within a sociopolitical schema and shape it as well. For example, in *Gender Trouble,* Butler describes the impact of social constructions on the female body (a physical space) as being "constituted through discursively constrained performative acts that produce the body through and with the categories of sex" (viii). She goes on to note that acts of parody and gender rebellion highlight the constructedness of hegemonic categories of sex; she postulates that such acts are effective strategies for destabilizing the established order. Her argument demonstrates that not only does space influence the social world but the social world in turn affects space.

Because space is imbued with many meanings, its study is crucial in order to understand the workings of the world and the operations of power. As Foucault wrote, "A whole history remains to be written of *spaces*—which would at the same time be the history of *powers* (both of these terms in the plural)—from the great strategies of geopolitics to the little tactics of the habitat" (qtd. in Soja 21). Feminists and feminist geographers, in their critiques of masculine-dominated geographies, have already begun this project, focusing on the diversity of experience and what Adrienne Rich termed "the politics of location." Much of this scholarship has consisted of breaking down earlier essentializing and universalizing feminisms, which tended to homogenize the female experience without regard for the variations in women's lives due to the effects of racism, classism, colonialism, and religion on their lives, and of bringing multicultural voices into feminism. I am pursuing one small fragment of such a project as I explore the significance of geographical location in the United States for queers.

If space consists of both concrete spatialities *and* networks of relationships, queer geography can be seen to be constituted, in part, by the relations between queers and nonqueers within different spatial regions. By this argument, areas that tend toward liberal politics, for example, will shape the gay communities that exist within them differently than will more conservative parts of the country. Queer geography can then be used to discuss how gay identity is influenced by traditional geographical divisions of the United States. The Bureau of the Census recognizes four regions and nine divisions of the United States—the West (Pacific and Mountain), the Midwest (West North Central and East North Central), the Northeast (Middle Atlantic and New England), and the South (West South Central, East South Central, and South Atlantic)[11]—each of which is commonly considered to have a unique "character," manifested in the personalities of its inhabitants. For instance, a popular stereotype of southern people portrays them as friendly and welcoming on the surface but likely to stab a person in the back. They are also depicted as suffering still over their defeat in the Civil War. New Englanders, on the other hand, are spoken of as initially cold and difficult to get to know but also as intensely loyal to trusted friends. These stereotypes about regions and their inhabitants have an overwhelming influence. "We recognize upon reflection that such place references are often based on stereotypes and misconceptions," J. Nicholas Entrikin writes, "but they are nonetheless a real and an important part of everyday discourse" (12).

Among geographers, the word "place" is often used to describe these spatial "personalities." Gillian Rose discusses how places are unique: "Places differ one from another in that each is a specific set of interrelationships between environmental, economic, social, political and cultural processes" (41). These forces act upon the inhabitants of a given region, and the inhabitants, in turn, act upon each other and the processes around them. Hence, geography is never static; human experience is intimately intertwined with spatial relationships and connections. As Entrikin writes, "Place presents itself to us as a condition of human experience. As agents in the world we are always 'in place,' much as we are always 'in culture.' For this reason our relations to place and culture become elements in the construction of our individual and collective identities" (1). The meaning and enactment of "queer," as a collective identity, are shaped, altered, molded, and created through the interactions of queers with the places that make up the United States and the world.

Because of its overwhelming influence in our lives, space is as vital to our sense of self as is history, although frequently history is understood to be more significant. Foucault discusses the prevalent privileging of time and history over space in "Questions on Geography" (1976): "A critique could be carried out of this devaluation of space that has prevailed for generations. . . . Space was treated as the dead, the fixed, the undialectical, the immobile. Time, on the contrary, was richness, fecundity, life, dialectic. . . . [T]he use of spatial terms seems to have the air of an anti-history. If one started to talk in terms of space that meant one was hostile to time. . . . They didn't understand that to trace the forms of implantation, delimitation and demarcation of objects, the modes of tabulation, the organisation of domains meant the throwing into relief of processes—historical ones, needless to say— of power" (70). Foucault's words help to articulate my project in this chapter. History, of course, is not inconsequential, but I wish to highlight the ways in which the operations and functions of space can grant us a better understanding of historical forces and of how time and space interact in forming queer communities.

Space is too frequently conflated with history by scholars and theorists. It is important to remember that events occur in a temporal-spatial moment, not simply a historical one. Edward H. Soja provides an intelligent summation of historical bias: "An already made geography sets the stage, while the willful making of history dictates the action and defines the story line" (14). If one assumes, as Foucault commented that many people do, that space is the static background against which the "true" story of human affairs, history, plays itself out, then the geographical will seem less important or even unimportant in comparison to the historical. The privilege frequently given to the historical is described by Claudie Lesselier: "The narrative of the past obeys its own codes and is inscribed in the existing structures of narrative and description. In itself it produces meaning, establishes a code and ends, and transforms lived experience by pouring it into molds" (91). These molds eclipse the spatial in favor of the temporal. Lesselier's words reflect the current predilection for the historical over the spatial, but this is changing as more scholars recognize that "spatial relations are . . . no less complex and contradictory than historical processes" (Hebdige, "Subjects" vii). I do not mean that analyzing, studying, and surveying history should be disregarded. In fact, much of my own scholarship is informed by historical understandings. The role of space, however, needs to be scrutinized with greater care; exploring spatial differences can enrich and deepen scholars' understanding of queer studies, showing the ways that space inescapably interacts with history, as Foucault points out.

Foucault considered geography crucial to understanding the present age. He wrote that "The present epoch will perhaps be above all the epoch of space" ("Other Spaces" 22) and that "the anxiety of our era has to do fundamentally with space, no doubt a great deal more than with time" (23). He may have been referring to the phenomenon of the "shrinking world," where transportation and communication technologies are transforming our conceptions of space and distance, causing an increasing homogenization within and between cultures, along with the inevitable reaction of cultural resistance to assimilation. This tension between homogenization and heterogeneity is playing itself out within America in numerous ways. Describing the homogenization of the United States, Michael Bradshaw writes that there "has been a convergence of values, economies and experiences for individuals" (57). He points out that personal mobility is far more feasible today than even thirty years ago, creating something of an internal "melting pot" of American cultures. He also notes that the differences in regional average per capita income have become narrower than at any time throughout this century (57). Though much of the nation's physical terrain remains unique from region to region, the human landscape is becoming more undifferentiated as national chain stores and restaurants proliferate. Anyone who has driven a long distance on the interstate highways will be familiar with the increasing uniformity of the American gastronomic landscape. No matter what medium-sized town you pull into, you have your choice of the same restaurants: Burger King, McDonald's, Wendy's, Taco Bell, Hardee's, and a host of similar restaurants serving similar food for similar prices in similar surroundings. It is possible for a person to travel across the vast expanse of the United States and *never* be exposed to a different culture than that of the fast-food, Wal-Mart world. All across the country, people see the same advertisements, watch the same television shows, eat in the same restaurants, buy the same brands of food, and sleep in the same motels. This confluence of space, this crowding of cultures, is the source of Foucault's anxiety. It is the anxiety of a people losing a sense of unique cultural identity. Identity movements, such as the queer movement, are in part a response to this anxiety, and queer geography becomes a place from which to examine from a new perspective not only queers but the entire field of queer studies as well.

All of this homogenization has helped to create a nation that appears far less diverse than even twenty years ago. These similarities, however, do not fully conceal the countless differences that exist in the United States from region to region, differences that need to be considered when developing the queer studies' agenda. Lesbian/gay cultures, and hence lesbians and gays coming out within them, are tremendously influenced by the external "straight" geography. Further, queer geography contains unique elements that do not occur within straight geography; for instance, queer geography is plagued by gaps and holes in places where gays find life so unbearable that they never come out to themselves at all or, if they do, they flee at the earliest opportunity to more accepting locales.

Queer geography, like traditional geography, is not unitary. Multiple differences, such as race, ethnicity, and socioeconomic background, affect how queer geography is constituted. For instance, a Hispanic lesbian might see Los Angeles as more culturally significant than an Anglo lesbian would, perhaps as even more central to her world view than New York, Provincetown, or San Francisco. The lesbian earning $10,000, and living in the Western Addition, a poor section of San Francisco, is going to have a different experience of gay life in the city than a lesbian making $100,000 and living in a remodeled Victorian in the Castro.

As with all theoretical frameworks, queer geography is made up of a series of concentric rings, emanating from the individual to the general. Geography, as a network of relationships, is in an endless state of flux for the individual. To understand geography and the many ways in which it functions, one must scrutinize it on a macroscopic and microscopic level, recognizing that change can occur on one level and not another. One can live in San Francisco, for instance, and be marked by its metaphors, but moving within the city from the Castro to Hunter's Point, say, will create an entirely new personal environment and a new perception of one's place in the world. The lesbian separatist living on a farm in Oregon is likely to have a different understanding of queer culture than the lesbian ACT UP activist living in New York City.[12] Inexorably, both of these people are shaped to a large extent by their immediate surroundings, a relationship that helps to create an image of what lesbian culture is truly about. However, these two women, one on her farm and another in her Greenwich Village loft, are not only influenced, affected, and altered by their relationships to two distinct places. These women, and all others, are shaped by their relationships to a myriad of places, a process that continues throughout their lives. People never stop being molded by their contacts with different places. Even a temporary geography, such as the Michigan Women's Festival or the "space" of an on-line lesbian/gay e-mail conference, can alter one's experience of queerness.

Queer geography, however, is not created merely through the perceptions of lone individuals. Institutions such as gay/lesbian/heterosexual media, historical accounts, academic discourse, and word-of-mouth dissemination all manufacture and perpetuate geography. One manner in which queer geography is created is what Barbara Ponse terms "gay referencing": "the practice of specifying people, places, and events as gay or straight in conversations among gay people," where "[g]ayness becomes a lens through which the rest of experience is focused. Through reiteration, gay referencing effects a normalization of gayness and simultaneously increases the relevance of gayness as a standard against which experience is measured" (94). In other words, gay referencing, a kind of "gay gaze," actively helps to create gay space. When a place is labeled gay, it becomes part of a common language and enters into the gay discourse. Places that do not receive the label do not become part of the "lens." They are not used in the process of creating a standard against which gay and lesbian experiences are measured. Some places, such as San Francisco, Provincetown, Northampton, and, to a lesser extent, New York and Los Angeles, become imbued with a certain mystique and are elevated in the cultural imagination to queer "utopias" that begin to seem more truly "gay" to queers than the countless other cities, towns, and suburban or rural regions that fill the United States. These areas come to be regarded as the "norm" against which all other places are judged and, often, come up lacking in some respects. San Francisco, in particular, has become identified as the lesbian/gay utopia, a vision that does not always mesh with the reality of living there. Such a view frequently elides the all too real queer bashing and overlooks the city's social problems, such as expensive housing, crime, overcrowding, traffic congestion, poverty, and drugs. In addition, San Francisco is plagued by problems within the lesbian and gay communities, such as divisions between lesbians and gay men with different backgrounds. But the "dream" of San Francisco still fills the imagination of nearly every lesbian or gay man in the United States, as well as much of the world.

San Francisco: The Queer Mecca

The symbolic location of San Francisco in the gay/lesbian community can be better understood if it is compared to the spiritual home of another group: Israel, which many Jews perceive to be their homeland.

In a similar way, lesbians and gay men understand San Francisco to be their homeland, a city that offers the alluring possibility of a better life, whether they currently live in Anchorage, Alaska; Fresno, California; Topeka, Kansas; Tucson, Arizona; or Cincinnati, Ohio. Both Israel and San Francisco are far more than mere geographical locations; they shape the very being of the Jews and gays who live in those locales. Seven days a week, a person can be immersed in a culture that represents his or her singular identity position. Even if a woman chooses to avoid a complete immersion in such a culture, just knowing that culture is there changes the way she views the world. If she lives in a world that is largely inimical to her lived experience, finding a geographical place where she can "be herself" can have a dramatic effect on her being. But there is a negative side to San Francisco and Israel and their unique identities. Whenever an "authentic," "true" culture is postulated, other cultures and regions seem inferior, even "wrong."

Because lesbians and gay men see San Francisco as a semimythical homeland, its position has received little theoretical scrutiny. Why is it such a special place, and how has that shaped the field of queer studies?

San Francisco holds a dual position in my mind: It is the very real city less than thirty miles from where I grew up. This San Francisco has clear geographical areas—the Haight-Ashbury, Chinatown, Fisherman's Wharf, Nob Hill, the Mission District—places I visited with my parents. I saw different areas later in my life as a high school and college student: the Castro, Valencia Street—the gay/lesbian neighborhoods I visited with lesbian friends and lovers. But there is a different San Francisco that has little in common with the actual city that I knew. This version, which is far more idealized than the real city, comes into being only in my mind. It is a city that I imagine as full of gays and lesbians, so full that the heterosexuals do not even appear, at least in my imagination. It is this imaginary city I yearn to move to, conveniently forgetting the real problems of the actual City by the Bay. This dream city is such a potent image in my mind that it thoroughly obscures the actual city, just as the real city is sometimes obscured by dense fog.

Other lesbians share this experience of imagining San Francisco as a semimythical site. For instance, a professor at a small liberal arts college on the East Coast comments, "When I imagine San Francisco, I imagine the light bathing the Victorians, always cast in improbable sun rather than fog. And the Golden Gate stands out sharply (even if it is painted orange rather than the golden yellow of my dreams). As a lesbian, it seems so appropriate to head for a city with a golden gate, a gate that brings up images of Dorothy in *The Wizard of Oz* as well as San Francisco." Another woman, an engineer in New York, writes:

> San Francisco conjures up the same sort of imagery as the first Ann Bannon novel that I read some years before "coming out"—bars full of smoke and women, unfamiliar social codes, and cues and rules to learn—an illicit excitement of being a lesbian in a group of lesbians. I always imagine the streets to be full of gay folks—a perpetual Pride fest with leather and bikes and optional clothing.
>
> I think the most important part of San Francisco for me is the knowledge that it does exist in some form (albeit most likely not as I imagine it to be)—the knowledge that there is some safe place that I could go to if I wanted to. It plays the same sort of role as P-town for me in that it provides an emotional escape hatch just by existing in my imagination. I can tell myself: Well, if things get really bad, I can always move to San Francisco/Provincetown where I can relax, be myself, and truly live.

For many lesbians and gay men, San Francisco is the equivalent of Shangri-la, part of that larger myth of California as paradise, the promised land that has been such a powerful image throughout the twentieth century. Only recently is this image starting to change, as socioeconomic problems turn the California dream into a nightmare. The specter of AIDS has also colored gay and lesbian views of San Francisco, creating a deathly pall that darkens our visions of San Francisco's promise. AIDS has irrevocably changed the queer land-scape in San Francisco; it is a potent force that demonstrates how queer geography, like racial or ethnic geography, is always in the process of alteration as diverse social forces reshape the spaces that make up queer societies. For instance, as more and more gay men die of AIDS, their property in the Castro district goes on the market and can be bought by heterosexuals. Could AIDS force the gay mecca out of San Francisco to another, less stricken, location?

Queer Geography in Queer Studies

Axiom 1: "People are different from each other" (Sedgwick 22). Though generalization is an important, perhaps even necessary, tool of theoretical musings, it always fails to encompass the true diversity of life itself. There is a growing trend, especially in postmodern scholarship, to break down generalities, to attempt to be as specific as possible. As Dick Hebdige writes, "Renouncing generalities means concentrating on the material effects of *specific* organisations of space. . . . It means concentrating on what is at stake in representations of particular places. It means exploring, as openly as possible, the myriad defiles which connect the intermeshing architectures not just of *the* City and the Psyche, but of individual cities, individual psyches" ("Subjects" vii). Queer studies is itself part of a larger movement that challenges globalizing representations, and in this chapter I have sought to challenge queer studies to ferret out its own tendencies toward exclusionary representations, in this case in the spatial arena.

What is evident is that no singular gay/lesbian/queer community exists in the United States, although, in the lesbian community at least, the idea of building a unified community, one that stretches from coast to coast, has a long history. In its most famous appearance, this notion was discussed by Jill Johnston in her book *Lesbian Nation* (1973), which argued that a distinct lesbian community should develop in order to give a home to lesbians across the country. Lesbian Nation depended on women's music, festivals, and literature to build a sense of community among diverse women. But, as Lillian Faderman writes, "Lesbian Nation was doomed finally to failure because of youthful inexperience and inability to compromise unbridled enthusiasms" (*Odd Girls* 220). Efforts to build a single community to represent the needs of lesbians across the United States are always doomed to failure not only because of the class, socioeconomic, racial, ethnic, and age differences that fissure any large group but also because of the differences in community caused by differences in geography. My task in this chapter has been to explain how queer geography affects the lives of all queers in the United States, who cannot help but be influenced by their relationships to places. Only by recognizing that place is as crucial an element in shaping queer identities as is history can lesbians and gay men hope to create a queer studies that more fully understands the various perspectives of the people for whom it claims to speak. Studying space and spatial differences, I hope, will help to ensure that queers, in all their guises, are given equal voices to express their own particular visions about what it means to be queer in the United States.

I would like to add that this inspection of the United States' queer geography has been an intensely personal trip for me, as well as a theoretic one. Debates about the concepts and theories contained in this chapter have followed my girlfriend and me to the dinner table, the bookstore, our local bagel shop, our favorite pizzeria—named "No Anchovies"—where we invariably order the "groovy pizza" (spinach, feta cheese, and garlic). At the same time that we were arguing about how place functions, all of these places were defining us; we continually recognized how caught up in space we were. The personal questions that this chapter has inspired are many. I have debated what queer geography actually means to my friends and me and thought in new ways about how my lesbianism is changed or altered due to place. I have thought about the many ways in which I engage with places on a daily basis and how those encounters shape my identity as a lesbian. I have considered how I "do" lesbianism differently in Cincinnati than in San Francisco and the reasons this is true. I have scrutinized the mestiza consciousness I have developed, circulating as I do between heterosexual and homosexual worlds, and have considered how this form of consciousness, paradoxically, can both imprison and set free. In some ways, writing this chapter has done what all academic work should strive to do: It has destabilized my subject position. It has also called for me to look anew at the way space is constructed for queers. One of my goals in writing this essay will be satisfied if my words have the same destabilizing effect on my readers, who, I hope, will rethink their own relationships to the places that help to constitute them as subjects.

But let us return now, for a moment, to that hypothetical scenario with which I began: Cincinnati as Queen City for the Queers. This picture, however, is not the one with which I wish to close. Instead, I would imagine no city or town as being the "capital" of queer culture, as suggesting by its very location and pride of place that other places lack a queer culture that is equally as significant. Instead, let us imagine a world in which each place, small or large, has a role to play in our creation of queer studies. This idea is crucial in order to understand more fully the multiplicity that makes up queer communities throughout the United States and the rest of the world.

7

To Pass or Not to Pass

Thoughts on Passing and
Lesbian Identities

We all pass. Passing is not the unique experience of a selected few; passing is an experience we all share, in which we are all, willingly or not, complicit. Though we all pass, there are many shades of gray in our passing and many different ways to pass. This chapter will examine some of these shades of gray by exploring how passing functions for lesbians. I shall argue that every lesbian, even the most out, passes whether she wants to or not, and that passing, particularly what I refer to as "partial passing," needs to be acknowledged as an unavoidable part of a lesbian's life. The negative attitude toward passing in lesbian and gay communities must be scrutinized with greater care to determine whether or not such an attitude is truly desirable.

Acknowledging the inevitability of passing is deeply disturbing because passing threatens assumptions about stable identities and raises the fear that we can never know another's "true" self. Further, passing has the potential to lay bare the myth that our culture is built upon: the presumed essential difference between men and women, blacks and whites, or homosexuals and heterosexuals. Passing shows that these binaries are not as "natural" as many might presume and raises the suspicion that many of the boundaries in our lives are no more than artificial constructs and that conceptions of authentic selfhood are suspect as well. Passing threatens to turn society topsy-turvy, which is why it is censured. At the same time, however, passing is also alluring. Despite its potential danger to one's sense of personal, fixed identity and to society's conceptions of stable identities, passing also offers the possibility of freedom from the bonds of identity. Who has not considered at one point or another the possibility of passing for something that one is not? Passing suggests that people can not only reshape their physical appearance but can become entirely new individuals—a tantalizing possibility. I shall examine the dynamics of passing more closely in this chapter, revealing the many ways that passing influences lesbian lives today and arguing that passing needs to be reconceptualized, giving more attention to the various forms in which it is manifested.

This chapter will focus specifically on lesbians who pass as straight, whether for a lifetime or for only a brief period. I shall give limited attention to blacks who pass as whites or lesbians who pass as men, both subjects that have been written about extensively. One of the reasons I wish to discuss passing for lesbians is because *every* lesbian—regardless of whether she deliberately passes or is the most visible lesbian imaginable—is caught up in the dynamics of passing. Since passing is such an essential part of lesbian life, I am adopting what political theorist Shane Phelan calls the philosophy of "getting specific." For her, getting specific means moving away from broad, theoretical judgments and discussing the significance of specific cases. She describes the benefits of such a strategy: "Getting specific . . . is more like storytelling than like analysis though both are required" (*Getting Specific* 32). Getting specific, I believe, will allow space for reflection on passing as it influences my life and the lives of other lesbians.

A Pass or Not a Pass—That Is the Question

The first difficulty one encounters when discussing passing is that it is a word used to define a vast variety of actions in different communities. For instance, passing can refer specifically to a man or woman who passes as a member of the other sex, as critic Anne Herrmann uses the term: "'Passing' relies on cross-dressing—dressing in the clothes of the opposite sex—for the purpose of convincing an 'unknowing audience' that one actually is a member of that sex" ("Passing" 60–61). In her book *Presence and Desire: Essays on Gender, Sexuality, Performance* (1993), theorist Jill Dolan defines passing differently: "Historical necessity has accustomed lesbians to passing, a complex sociological trick that allows a subversive identity to survive, albeit in a compromised, silent state" (139). As Dolan uses the term, "passing" is not limited to women who pass as men. She includes in her definition all the women who have explicitly or implicitly concealed their lesbian identity. A broader definition is found in Pamela L. Caughie's essay "Passing as Pedagogy: Feminism in(to) Cultural Studies" (1994): "Passing takes many forms, from the strategic adoption of a culturally empowered identity to the disempowering mimicry of a threatening difference. But all passing is marked by the double bind that opens a discrepancy between what one professes to be and how one is actually positioned in a society, institution, [or] discourse. . . . The passer must always run the risk of self-betrayal in any particular performance" (78). Alice Parker has a more fluid definition of passing than Herrmann, Dolan, or Caughie: "Passing seems more and more like rereading, reinterpreting the codes, reworking the masks, the disguises. It is a radical refusal of a fixed place" (335).[1] What these four very different definitions reveal is how difficult it is to pin down passing because it adopts many forms and fulfills many functions. None of these definitions is entirely incorrect or correct; rather, they all focus on different facets of passing.

This chapter examines one specific form of passing: when a lesbian passes as heterosexual, whether only briefly or for a more extended period. When this happens, what Marjorie Garber, in her monumental study *Vested Interests: Cross-Dressing & Cultural Anxiety,* calls a "category crisis" occurs. She defines this as "a failure of definitional distinction, a borderline that becomes permeable, that permits of border crossings from one (apparently distinct) category to another: black/white, Jew/Christian, noble/bourgeois, master/servant, master/

slave" (16). The lesbian who passes as heterosexual calls into question the distinction between heterosexual and homosexual. Ultimately, she threatens to overthrow the whole heterosexual order because heterosexuality can only exist in opposition to homosexuality, as Eve Kosofsky Sedgwick argues in *Epistemology of the Closet*. What emerges from such a category crisis is what Garber defines as a third term that is neither male nor female, heterosexual nor homosexual, black nor white. She writes that the third term "questions binary thinking and introduces crisis—a crisis which is symptomatized by *both* the overestimation *and* the underestimation of cross-dressing. But what is crucial here . . . is that the 'third term' is *not a term*. Much less is it a *sex*. . . . The 'third' is a mode of articulation, a way of describing a space of possibility. Three puts in question the idea of one: of identity, self-sufficiency, self-knowledge. . . . The third deconstructs the binary of self and other that was itself a comfortable, because commutable and thus controllable, fiction of complementarity" (11, 12). In other words, the pass threatens to throw into chaos a societal system based on the perceived difference between one's self and others. Because of her existence as a "third term," the lesbian who passes has the potential to wreak havoc. As we saw in chapter 1, Madame d'Aiguines poses a threat precisely because she does not conform to the gender-based binaries that are supposed to confine her.

Passing Grades: Critical Perceptions of Passing

To this day camouflage terrorizes me.

The pattern of skin which makes a being invisible against its habitat.

And—yes—this camouflage exists for its protection. I am not what I seem to be.

I must make myself visible against my habitat. But there exists a certain danger in peeling back. The diamondback without her mottled skin loses a level of defense. (Cliff 19)

Theorists and others commonly react to passing with uneasiness, anger, or even terror. The above quotation from Michelle Cliff's book *The Land of Look Behind* (1985) aptly express the attitude of many about passing. She writes further: "Passing demands a desire to become invisible. A ghost-life. An ignorance of connections" (21). Passing, for Cliff, entails giving up more than one gains. It means sacrificing connections to one's former friends and family members in order to gain new connections, grounded only on the unstable ground of passing, which always threatens to split open under one's feet.

Some feminist philosophers share Cliff's negative conception of passing. In her *Lesbian Choices* (1995), Claudia Card calls passing "highly problematic":

> Hiding can reflect deserved distrust or contempt of others rather than shame regarding what one hides. And yet, letting major wrongful images and judgments of oneself stand uncontested eventually endangers one's sense of self-worth in the way that a continuous pretense of servility does. . . . Passing is analogous to (perhaps an instance of) at least a pretense of servility. Like servility . . . , it impedes one's ability to protest. Lacking evidence of our faith in our own worth, we become superficial or fall prey to self-doubt. Either way, we are demeaned. Complicity in others' passing can likewise threaten our sense of self-worth, as it easily engages us in hypocrisy regarding values applying as much to ourselves as to those we help hide. (198–200)

Card, who views passing as an inevitable evil, focuses on passing that is done with the subject's awareness; she does not mention the times that people pass whether they want to or not, an issue addressed later in this chapter. She also assumes that passing is monolithic and does not dwell on partial or discontinuous passing. Philosopher Julie Inness also criticizes passing, condemning what she calls "its hidden logic of escalating estrangement" and lamenting that "People who pass neither make a complete transition into the world in which they pass nor do they effortlessly step back into the world they left behind" (231). From her perception, the person who passes is alienated from all others, never finding a comfortable home in any of her worlds. These two philosophers express the thoughts of many feminists: Passing is an evil, which ultimately eats away and even destroys one's sense of self.

Twentieth-century fiction also frequently views passing in a negative light. In the dozens of novels that describe a passing experience, most commonly an African American who passes as white, passing is typically depicted as a loss of self and as a failure to acknowledge one's true background. One of the best-known passing novels is Nella Larsen's *Passing* (1929), which tells the story of Clare Kendry, a black woman who passes as white, and her friendship with Irene Redfield, a black woman who does not pass. At first, Clare looks as if she has it all: "Rather than emphasize the pathos of the 'passing' situation, Larsen stresses its attractive veneer. Clare Kendry always looks exquisite, whether wearing a 'superlatively simple cinnamon-brown frock' with a 'little golden bowl of a hat' or a stately black taffeta gown" (Wall 106). Clare's passing carries a price, however. She is married to a racist, so she is forced to guard her secret with great care. Irene wonders whether Clare's life could ever be serene "with the dark secret forever crouching in the background of her consciousness" (201). Ultimately, Clare dies. In this novel and many others, passing leads to disaster.[2]

Critics have had similar negative reactions when considering the relationship between lesbians and passing. Jill Dolan writes that "Passing exacts high costs because it requires the muffling of lesbian identity under layers of culturally constructed gender roles. Yet to survive lesbians often become adept at gender impersonation" (140). Judith F. Fetterley worries about the dangers of passing and about the importance of lesbian visibility: "Straight feminists are always afraid that people will think *they* are lesbians; the more real danger is that people will think we are not. It is far too easy for us to pass as not-dykes because basically nobody but us, and sometimes not even all of us, wants to believe we exist" (21). In the foreword to her essay "Compulsory Heterosexuality and Lesbian Existence" (1980), Adrienne Rich is even more adamant about the dangers of passing: "The retreat into sameness—assimilation for those who can manage it—is the most passive and debilitating of responses to political repression, economic insecurity, and a renewed open season on difference" (204). The problem with Dolan's, Fetterley's, or Rich's statement is that they assume that passing is an either/or state, when, in reality, passing is composed of countless variations, some of which might be more open

to condemnation than others. It is essential to consider the specificity
of passing situations before condemning all forms of passing as necessarily entailing a loss of self. We need to recognize that passing is
something that we must *all* experience in one fashion or another. Even
the most out lesbian cannot ensure that everyone who views her will
necessarily identify her as a lesbian.

Passing brings forth passionate emotions from people of all
backgrounds and classes. Gays and lesbians can react with anger when
someone passes, shunning those who pass or destroying the pass by
revealing a person's hidden sexual orientation. Even if people do not
erupt in rage, they tend to disparage those who pass. African American
Adrian Piper, for instance, tells us that passing is not acceptable in her
family: "Although both of my parents had watched many of their
relatives disappear permanently into the white community, passing for
white was unthinkable within the branches of my father's and mother's
families to which I belonged. That would have been a really, authen-
tically shameful thing to do" (222). One of the reasons passing is so
unthinkable to Piper and many others is that it threatens the very
identity of a minority group. If it were feasible for the majority of
blacks or lesbians and gay men to pass, then, potentially, that group
might vanish, swallowed up by the larger community. This fear is even
more potent in the lesbian community than in the black community
because it is sometimes more feasible for lesbians to pass as heterosexual than for blacks to pass as whites.

Reactions to passing are not always negative, however. We would
probably view with more tolerance the black man who passes as white
because he fears being lynched than the lesbian passing as straight
who remains silent when her acquaintances start making homophobic
comments. What is at stake here? On one hand, sometimes we feel
disdain toward those who pass, even desiring to reveal their hidden
identity; this reaction can be seen in the outings of public figures by
gay and lesbian activist groups. On the other hand, sometimes we are
supportive of those who pass, particularly if lives are in danger. We
seem split down the middle: We understand and sympathize with
passers, yet we wish to distance ourselves from them. They pose a
threat that identities are far less stable than most people would like to

assume. But, at the same time, passers hold out the promise that identities can be malleable, changeable. We fluctuate between the desire for stability and for change, both of which the passer embodies.

I am concerned about the tendency in the lesbian and gay community to marginalize or negate lesbians and gay men who pass, an issue addressed by Lisa M. Walker in her essay "How to Recognize a Lesbian: The Cultural Politics of Looking like What You Are" (1993) on the politics of visibility/invisibility and the limitations of this trope. She argues that marginalized groups, including gays and lesbians, have come to praise the visible signs of difference that set them apart from the mainstream as one strategy of identity politics: "While privileging visibility can be politically and rhetorically effective, it is not without problems. Within the constructs of a given identity that invests certain signifiers with political value, figures that do not present those signifiers are often neglected. Because subjects who can 'pass' exceed the categories of visibility that establish identity, they tend to be regarded as peripheral to the understanding of marginalization" (868). In other words, privileging visibility as the penultimate sign of belonging to an outsider group can have serious drawbacks, because not all members of an outsider group will share the same overt signifiers of their identity. For instance, not all African Americans are black, and not all gay men are flamboyant and feminine. What privileging visibility leads to, Walker argues, is "the displacement from the field of radical subjectivity of those who do not 'look like what they are'—women of color who 'pass' for white and femme lesbians who can pass for straight" (869). She points out that "The paradigm of visibility is totalizing when a signifier of difference becomes synonymous with the identity it signifies. In this situation, members of a given population who do not bear that signifier of difference or who bear visible signs of another identity are rendered invisible and are marginalized within an already marginalized community" (888). I have quoted from Walker's essay at length because it provides an accurate summation of my own thoughts. The lesbian/gay communities have established unofficial hierarchies in which people who might "pass" in one way or another are not considered "real" gays, and thus passing itself is constituted as a strategy that "real" lesbians do not adopt. I wish to look more closely at this dynamic in the following pages, where I argue that "real" lesbians can pass and that all forms of passing do not always entail a loss of self and self-worth.

To Pass or Not to Pass: That Is *Not* the Question

Passing, as I have already mentioned, comes in many forms, one of the most extreme being women who pass as men. Leslie Feinberg's working-class heroine, Jess Goldberg, passes as a man in order to survive economically in Feinberg's autobiographical novel *Stone Butch Blues* (1993). Jess's experience raises the fear that women can usurp men's power and authority, suggesting that these traits are not "naturally" the province of men. The passer is dangerous not only because of her individual passing but because she threatens the entire gender system with her pass. Different forms of passing also seriously endanger the established status quo, threatening to reveal the mythical nature of the claim that men are superior. Other women pass as men for reasons different than Goldberg's. For instance, world traveler Sarah Hobson camouflaged herself as a boy in order to travel with greater freedom as she explored Iran, an experience she recounts in her travel narrative *Through Persia in Disguise* (1973). Another version of a girl who passes as a boy is found in L. Frank Baum's novel *The Marvelous Land of Oz* (1904) in which the hero, a boy named Tip, is revealed actually to be Princess Ozma, who has been transformed into a boy by the magic powers of the witch Mombi. Tip's words when he discovers he is in reality a she are revealing: "I want to stay a boy, and travel with the Scarecrow and the Tin Woodman, and the Woggle-Bug, and Jack. . . . I don't want to be a girl!" Being "a girl" is regarded as a poor second to being a boy because of the greater physical freedom offered to males. Jess, Sarah, and Tip all find physical autonomy by passing as men.

Women passed as men far earlier in history than the twentieth-century adventures of Jess, Sarah, and Tip.[3] As early as the 1570s a female transvestite movement raised fears that women dressed in men's clothing and styles were becoming too prevalent, and the tradition of women passing as men, no doubt, goes back much earlier

(Herrmann, "Travesty" 296). As scholar Julie Wheelwright points out in *Amazons and Military Maids* (1989), numerous women passed as men in the 1700s, too, including Hannah Snell, Mary Anne Talbott, and Deborah Sampson. These women and others, such as Cora Anderson, Charlotte Charke, Mary Fields, Mary Hamilton, Harry Gorman, Lucy Ann Lobdell, and Charles Warner, passed as men for a variety of reasons. Lillian Faderman emphasizes the "desire for adventure" that could be fulfilled by passing as a man (*Odd Girls* 43). John D'Emilio stresses that passing offered working-class women "an immediate, substantial improvement in their economic status and a protective covering for a lesbian relationship" (97). Lynne Friedli discusses women who cross-dressed in order to marry other women or become soldiers (238).

Although women who cross-dress as men are not the main focus of this chapter, discussing this phenomenon brings to light a few of the benefits women receive from certain forms of passing and suggests that passing might not be as negative as some critics have argued. Passing as a man might cause a woman to lose what many regard as her "authentic" identity, but she can also benefit. For instance, lesbian historian Joan Nestle reflects on Esther, a woman Nestle once knew who passed as a man.[4] Rather than discussing Esther's weaknesses, Nestle writes about her strengths, pointing out that it is Esther's woman's body in men's attire that creates its unique strength: "I looked at her," the narrator comments, "at the woman in a neat white shirt and grey pants, and wondered how her passengers could be so deceived. It was our womanness that rode with us in the car, that filled the night with tense possibilities" (*Restricted* 41). In no way is Esther depicted as a victim.

Passing as a man is one of the more sensational manifestations of passing, but there are other ways to pass as well. The form that most interests me is what Paul Spickard calls discontinuous passing (Haizlip 48). According to him there are two forms of passing in African American communities: continuous and discontinuous. Continuous passing occurs when a person passes herself off as a member of a privileged group, never once returning to the race, sexual orientation, or religious background that she has cast aside. Discontinuous passing occurs when a person passes at some time in her life, perhaps for economic reasons, yet returns periodically to her former identity. I am interested primarily in discontinuous passing because it is a form of passing that, I argue, lesbians cannot avoid.

Another variation on passing is the partial pass; in this case the lesbian does not try to appear as heterosexual as possible but instead provides an opaque surface on which viewers can inscribe lesbianism or heterosexuality. This form of passing is one that I personally experience in my daily life. Though my colleagues know that I am a lesbian, I do not make it obvious to my students. I look around my office, for instance, and there are no open signs of my lesbian identity. I have no photographs on my desk. None of my books are clearly lesbian, except to a knowledgeable reader. Some lesbians might claim that the lack of clear signifiers of my lesbianism in my office means that I seek to pass by nonrecognition, and they would disparage such an activity. Yet one of my central scholarly concerns is lesbian studies, and I have published and presented papers about topics that are unmistakably queer, including butch identities and women's same-sex crushes. This very book is by no means "in the closet." On the weekend, wearing a t-shirt and jeans, I look suspiciously butch. And even during the work week many people might suspect that I am a lesbian, since I adopt few straight signifiers. Though my appearance often results in my being labeled a lesbian, I partially pass when I fail to talk explicitly about my lesbianism in a society that presumes heterosexuality. Judith Butler talks about a similar dynamic in Larsen's *Passing:* "Clare passes not only because she is light-skinned, but because she refuses to introduce her blackness into conversation, and so withholds the conversational marker which would counter the hegemonic presumption that she is white. Irene herself appears to 'pass' insofar as she enters conversations which presume whiteness as the norm without contesting that assumption" (*Bodies* 171). In the same fashion, I pass because I do not mention my sexual orientation in a culture where heterosexuality is the norm, and many people fail to even consider another alternative. Clearly, passing is more complex than an either/or situation. Claudia Card writes: "Successful passing hides one's status as a target of oppression" (198), but is this always true? My office passing experience only partially obscures my lesbianism and does an ineffective job of hiding my status as a lesbian because my passing is discontinuous.

Partial passing occurs in many different environments, including one's place of employment. Due to its centrality in most of our lives, work shapes our lesbianism, requiring us constantly to renegotiate our relationship to passing as we move from our home environment to the potentially dangerous environment of the workplace, where lesbianism is often a taboo subject. Partial passing sometimes becomes intricately intertwined with maintaining one's economic stability.

Reflecting on what it entails to pass by courting nonrecognition, one might assume that this is an easy way to avoid the hatred directed at lesbians who are more visible, but is it, really? The partial passer who refuses to mimic heterosexuals as closely as possible but who passes because her status is not recognized by those who view her does *not* follow the path of least resistance. She often fails to conform to society's notions of acceptable feminine behavior. Even so, she may still be mistakenly perceived as heterosexual. She cannot always influence how others construct her subjectivity.

Partial passing does *not* allow the heterosexual viewing audience the secure sense that the lesbian is "one of them." Quite to the contrary, partial passing actually might accentuate a lesbian's otherness, because of the ways that she fails to adhere to societal gender norms. The lesbian who partially passes is not invisible. She stands out from the crowd in many ways. She does not adopt overt signifiers of heterosexual identification, such as a picture of her husband on her office desk, nor does she speak about a husband or boyfriend, though coworkers may know she is involved in a relationship or has a "roommate"; thus her sexual orientation remains a cipher. This positioning of the partial passer, rather than being a sign of weakness, actually can be a sign of strength, since she does not accept the security offered by full passing. It is important to acknowledge, however, that the partial passer does accept some security by not "flaunting it," allowing others the comfort of not having to face the possibility of her lesbianism.

But, one might argue, doesn't the partial passer present a "false" appearance of who she is and thus deserve only condemnation? The partial passer does present an image that fails to be sharply and clearly demarcated as lesbian, but she is only doing what, as Judith Butler has argued, a woman does every day as she endlessly acts out her life, constantly changing and altering the surface that she presents to the world. In this sense, I view performance as an essential part of one's life experiences, rather than only a negative reaction to oppression.[5] The partial passer presents one form of performance, the full passer another.

Passing the Test: Accessibility Issues

Because passing is less available to some lesbians than to others, we cannot think of passing, whether partial or full, as a monolithic experience. Due to their masculine physical appearance, lesbians such as Stephen Gordon or Jess Goldberg would find it difficult or even impossible to pass as heterosexual. Feminine-appearing lesbians would have an easier time. On the other hand, the situation would be reversed if the goal were to pass as a man. Different women have different levels of accessibility to passing and its many varieties. I began to think about accessibility in relationship to passing after talking to one of my colleagues, Alice, about the difficulties she sometimes encounters when announcing her lesbianism to her students. The problem is not that she wishes to conceal her lesbianism—quite to the contrary, she wants to make sure that her students recognize her sexual orientation—but she struggles with how to bring it up in classes in which lesbianism is not strictly relevant. Even after she announces she is a lesbian, her students often refuse to believe her because she can easily pass as "straight." They force passing on her by refusing to acknowledge her lesbianism, even when she admits it. Thus passing is *not* always of the lesbian's choosing; sometimes it is a choice made partially or entirely by the viewers. Managing to avoid passing is something that Alice has to pursue aggressively and often fails to achieve. Even with a postcard on the door that features two women kissing and a picture of her lover on her desk, she is still apt to be read as straight because many of her students think of lesbians only as mannish women who wear leather jackets covered with chains, roar around on Harleys, and buzz-cut their hair.

For Alice, passing is too easy to accomplish. Other lesbians find it difficult or impossible. For instance, when I enter a public restroom, I can find myself caught up in the dynamics of partial passing. In the women's room, I often look sufficiently like a lesbian to make some heterosexual women uneasy. I am aware of furtive glances, and I have had women tap me on the shoulder and say, "Excuse me, but don't you know this is the women's room?" To these women, I appear as Other; I stand out and in many ways fail to pass as a correctly socialized heterosexual woman. Yet, at the same time, I do not proclaim, as I enter the bathroom, "I am a lesbian," and my physical build is androgynous enough so that it does not necessarily signify lesbianism to heterosexuals, who might read me differently if I were a "diesel dyke." In the bathroom, paradoxically, I both pass and do not pass at the same moment, which is the experience of the partial passer. Other lesbians find passing as heterosexual even more difficult than I do. My girlfriend once went into the women's room at a highway rest area, leaving me standing outside. While I was waiting, I heard one young boy shout to another, "Hey, Mike, come here. A man just went into the women's room." They assumed that she was a man, an identity that she was not attempting to project. Actually, she was just wearing her usual attire of jeans and short-sleeved shirt. She looked like a woman to me, and I coded her that way. To the boys, she was a man. Thus passing is read differently by different viewers. To me, she was not passing. To the boys, she was, and so convincingly that they supposed she was a man.

We can see that physical appearance has a great deal to do with the accessibility of passing, but other factors also come into play, that make partial passing either more or less feasible. Socioeconomic status plays an important role in how passing is formulated by different people. Upper- and middle-class women might find it easier to purchase the accoutrements that signify heterosexuality or merely obscure lesbianism. For instance, a very well-dressed professional woman would be less likely to be categorized by heterosexuals as a lesbian than would a working-class woman who is employed as a carpenter and dresses in jeans, t-shirts, and boots. Age also influences one's ability to pass. Because of the common societal assumption that elderly people are asexual and because lesbianism is often considered a purely sexual act, older women are more likely to be coded as "heterosexual" than younger women.

Clothing also plays an important role in partial passing. The partial passer does not actively strive to look as stereotypically feminine as possible, but she might try to appear androgynous. After a quick trip to the Gap, the partial passer appears, dressed in khakis, a white button-down shirt, a pullover sweater, and loafers. Perhaps she favors pure black and comes to school dressed in a black turtleneck, black leggings, and black sandals. Or she might prefer wool slacks, a silk blouse, and a tweed blazer. Such outfits, which are coded as neither specifically heterosexual nor lesbian, make it feasible for a lesbian to pass as heterosexual; yet she might not be attempting to build up a façade of heterosexuality. If a woman wore clothing that was distinctly categorized as "lesbian"—say, a black leather jacket, jeans, and a boy's shirt—she could still partially pass if her lesbian identity was revealed in no other way. But if she were wearing "dykey" clothing, it is likely that she would raise more heterosexual suspicions about her sexual orientation. Clothing, along with economic status and age, changes how accessible partial passing is to a particular woman. It is clear that there is a broad continuum of passing possibilities, similar to Adrienne Rich's view of the continuum of subject positions available to women who classify themselves as lesbians.

I have discussed at length the factors that make partial passing feasible to different women because I do not believe women should be condemned on the basis of how accessible partial passing is to them. Alice is not trying to conceal her sexual orientation (quite to the contrary), but she finds it is sometimes difficult to avoid passing. Should she be criticized? Gay, lesbian, and queer radical politics tend to privilege the visible, as Lisa M. Walker argues so astutely. But if visibility is privileged, then Alice is judged as "less a lesbian" by some because her appearance, although elegant, fails to signify lesbianism to many viewers, even though she linguistically attempts to avoid passing. On the other hand, if she would shave her head completely, wear a "Queer Nation" t-shirt, and get a tattoo (preferably many) on her biceps, she would be judged "more a lesbian" by some. I believe that such visibility is positive and is an important way to express lesbian identities, but I also believe that the vast majority of lesbians who partially pass deserve equal legitimacy in lesbian and gay communities and should not be considered less queer than more visible members.

Partial passing is not without its shortcomings. The potential to pass, even if only in a partial fashion, in a particular discursive system reveals a degree of power. "The very ability to 'pass' as educated, as white, as heterosexual, even if one chooses not to do so, is to exert a certain . . . power. The different modes of passing available to a woman, even if refused, define her identity through unchosen mobilities in discursive systems" (Dhairyam 27). Partial passers, for example, might more easily find employment and room for advancement than lesbians who are more blatantly queer. Partial passers are also more likely to be accepted by the dominant mainstream society, although this varies greatly from woman to woman. I do not question that partial passing has its weaknesses and can sometimes help to perpetuate the status quo. Yet, at the same time, the partial passer's subversive potential must also be acknowledged. She has the ability to cast into doubt gender stereotypes and notions of what is acceptable femininity in a way that is not identical to that of a very "out" lesbian but that is equally important. She has the opportunity to infiltrate the system at all levels and to help change that system.

Passing Is a Spectator Sport

Because of their ambiguity, partial passers make it clear that it is, at least partially, the spectators who make a pass feasible. As Teresa de Lauretis writes, "the very issue of passing, across any boundary of social division, is related quite closely to the frame of vision and the conditions of representation" (36). Spectators play an important role in "reading" the pass, and their interpretations are often beyond the control of the passing subject. For example, when I was a fellow at the Five Colleges Center for Research on Women, located on the campus where my identical twin, Julie, teaches, people frequently confused us. Students would ask me to sign forms and accept papers. At one point, I was forced to show a colleague of my sister's my driver's license because he would not believe that I was Julie's twin; he thought that I was Julie and did not wish to be recognized because I was on sabbatical. Whether I wanted to or not, I was passing as my twin. Sometimes I could escape passing by informing people that I was not Julie, but sometimes it was not so easy. There were moments when I was inevitably trapped. It was a common experience for people to drive or bicycle by me and wave, yelling "Hi, Julie." It was obviously impossible to stop and enlighten all these people, so I simply nodded, smiled, and let them think I was my sister.

Other people have similar experiences. A light-skinned black, for instance, might be judged by onlookers to be white whether she wishes to be considered white or not. Adrian Piper, an African American who could be easily mistaken for white, describes such an experience when she was growing up in Harlem. She was greeted with suspicion by blacks who were blacker than she was, called "paleface," and made to endure what she calls the "Suffering Test," where she had to prove to darker blacks that she had suffered as much under racism as they had (218). I have already mentioned Alice and her difficulties with spectators. Onlookers have a tremendous amount of power in constructing the identity of a partial or full passer. For instance, a lesbian going grocery shopping might not wish to pass but does so because there is no opportunity to alert the clerk to difference other than announcing to her, "I am a lesbian," or wearing a button that says "dyke." Even if this woman displayed signifiers of lesbian identity, such as a shaved head, multiple ear piercings, and a leather jacket, she still might be interpreted incorrectly by the spectator, who might view the lesbian as nothing more than a punk-influenced dresser, since so many of the signifiers of lesbian identity have become trendy in the avant-garde heterosexual community. These examples show the many ways in which passing is not always volitional for a lesbian. She passes or does not pass as a heterosexual because of how she is viewed by heterosexuals. Moreover, I would argue that probably all lesbians, no matter how obviously butch they might seem—which is the most common stereotype of how lesbians are supposed to appear—are perceived as "not lesbian" at one time or another because lesbianism is something to which many heterosexuals give very little thought, often assuming that everyone is heterosexual. The heterosexual spectator has the power to make a lesbian pass, whether or not she wishes to, and this must be taken into account. The passer should not solely bear the responsibility for passing.

Discussing the dynamic between spectator and passer in her essay "It Takes One to Know One: Passing and Communities of Common Interest" (1994), Amy Robinson argues that there must be a passer, an unwitting dupe, and a person who sees the pass for what it is. I hesitate to think of the spectator as a gullible figure who is fooled by the pass. Is the spectator merely a "dupe"? I would suggest that the spectator might hold a variety of positions. Although some might be duped completely, other spectators are going to have more qualified responses. The pass is interpreted in different ways according to the knowledge base of the spectator and her suspicion or lack of suspicion that she is viewing a pass. The qualified nature of the spectator's gaze is particularly relevant when considering partial passing, which encourages rather than discourages ambivalent feelings from the spectators. Because the partial passer is not clearly marked as either heterosexual or homosexual, she raises doubts in the viewers' minds but provides them with no clear answers. She has not simply abandoned her "true" identity; quite to the contrary, the partial passer is still very much connected to her lesbianism, which is one reason that she does not pass with ease.

The partial passer also raises doubts in the minds of her lesbian spectators, who might suspect but cannot know the partial passer's sexual orientation. Between the partial passer and the lesbian spectator a special relationship exists, a connection, a bond, which has been acknowledged many times before: "Throughout the literature of racial and sexual passing, members of the in-group insist on a distinctive location that allows them to recognize a never truly hidden prepassing identity" (Robinson 715). Although it might not *always* be possible, it is likely that the lesbian spectator will recognize that the partial passer *could* also be a lesbian. The dynamic between passer and knowing spectator is most accurately described by Jill Dolan. Although she is talking specifically about lesbians on the stage, her words are also germane to the operations of passing outside the theater: "[F]or lesbian spectators of passing performances the subcultural subtext is always there to be read. . . . A lesbian required to pass as heterosexual, on the street or on the stage, is placed in the Brechtian position of commenting on her role, editorializing on the trappings of her impersonation for those who can see" (140). The major difference between the lesbian spectator watching a full passer and a partial passer is that the full passer, on one hand, makes it necessary for the viewer to discover what is often deeply hidden and secret. The partial passer, on the other hand, often has a sexual orientation that is easy to discover for the lesbian spectator. Clothing, the lack of a wedding ring, haircuts, carriage—a hundred clues reveal the partial passer's lesbianism to a knowing spectator. Yet all of these signs, no matter how much they might seem to reveal, fail to be a definite acknowledgment that someone is a lesbian. Although she might be suspicious, a lesbian almost never knows for sure that a woman she sees on the street is also a lesbian, no matter how much that woman might "look like a dyke." The partial passer is still passing, if only incompletely.

Another connection between the partial passer and her lesbian spectators is that they have the potential ability to change her status by announcing her "true" status as a lesbian. Outing is, of course, a subject that has appeared frequently in the media of the late 1980s and 1990s, and it is an activity that has been both lauded and disparaged. Claudia Card discusses the ethics of outing: "For those who share a socially stigmatized identity but do not pass, the question arises whether to protect the passing of others, particularly if the stigmatized identity is in truth honorable enough even though public opinion treats it as dishonorable, abnormal, or shameful" (195). The ethics of outing grow even more convoluted when one considers the partial passer. Her lesbianism might not be acknowledged openly in a particular environment—for instance, at work—but she has not abandoned lesbianism. She might appear openly, even blatantly, lesbian at other times in other places; does she deserve lesbian opprobrium because she is not always clearly marked as "lesbian"? I think not.

Passing Thoughts

> The more I pass the shiftier I become, like my children who never played with a toy the way the manufacturers had intended, or played a game according to the "rules." Passing is never unidirectional; it is always a travesty: some days I pass as "straight," others as a lesbian, andro/gynous, Jewish, North American, francophone, a student of signification, of mug shots. (Parker 336)

Alice Parker's words sum up my own thoughts on the dynamics of partial passing, a performance that all lesbians are caught up in at one point or another because we live in a society where heterosexuality is assumed. Lesbians are fated to become partial passers because spectators have the power to read a lesbian as heterosexual even if she does not wish this to happen. Lesbians who do not look stereotypically "butch" are more likely to be forced to pass because they lack the masculine attributes that are assumed by most heterosexuals to reveal lesbianism.

As I have pointed out, it is also a mistake for the radical lesbian/gay/queer society to accept a code of identity construction in which the most admired lesbian or gay man is the one who is most visible. This strategy based on a person's visibility inevitably marginalizes the lesbians and gays for whom radical visibility might not be an option but who are as vital to the gay/lesbian community as are more visible members. Also, privileging a certain style of visibility dramatically limits opportunities to display one's own personal style rather than conforming to the dictates of a few.

In this chapter I hoped to make my readers reflect on the importance of passing in their lives and to create a more complex and diverse portrait of passing and its many varieties. I also wanted to reflect on the constructed silences within lesbian and gay studies, a subject at the heart of the final chapters of this book. Chapter 8 will in some ways come full circle by discussing butch identities, a subject first addressed in chapter 1. Whereas the first chapter argues that depictions of the masculine lesbian can function to maintain heterosexual stereotypes about lesbianism, the final chapter will examine the importance of the butch in lesbian culture and the need for creating a definition of butch that does not presuppose she is one part of the dyadic construction butch-femme. Together, these two chapters show the different ways that heterosexuals and lesbians interpret gay and lesbian cultures, demonstrating the importance of understanding the triangular relationship that exists between heterosexuals, lesbians, and representations of gay and lesbian life.

8

GI Joes in Barbie Land

Recontextualizing the Meaning
of Butch in Twentieth-Century
Lesbian Culture

With Michele E. Lloyd

> High school years are much harder on butches [than on femmes].
> Femmes passed as straight, even to themselves. Butches can't. We
> stick out like G.I. Joes in Barbie Land. (Cordova 276)

> Straight people call me sir and faggots cruise me, but other
> butches say: "Aww, you're not so butch." That's cuz I don't go for
> femmes like I'm supposed to. This confuses people. When I'm out
> with a femme buddy, everyone assumes we're on a date; when I'm
> out with a butch date, everyone assumes we're buddies. That's if I
> can even *get* a date, which isn't easy for someone like me. . . .
>
> To the femmes I'm immediately suspect. They figure if I'm
> butch and I don't go for femmes, it's because I secretly hate
> femmes, because I secretly hate women, because I secretly hate
> myself. Either that or I'm simply a closet femme who's trying to
> weasel in on the already slim supply of eligible butches. Femmes,
> on the other hand[,] are allowed to go for butches—that's normal.
>
> To the butches, I'm the ultimate threat. If you're butch, you
> gotta have a femme under your arm at all times, that's how you
> know you're butch. So, when I hit on another butch, it naturally
> throws her off balance. (Trish Thomas 21)

These quotations from Jeanne Cordova and Trish Thomas leave
us with more questions than answers about butchness: Why might a
butch have conflicting notions of what it means to be butch? Why do
people make the facile assumption that butches must be attracted
to femmes? Can a butch be defined without reference to her "natural" counterpart, the femme? This chapter seeks to address these

and related questions, because I believe that butchness has been inadequately described, explained, and theorized by contemporary scholarship.

Butch is a concept that has long permeated lesbian culture. Nearly every lesbian, regardless of her self-identification, is at least familiar with the term.[1] JoAnn Loulan writes of her experiences giving talks about lesbian sexuality: "I ask the following: How many women here who have been lesbians for longer than two weeks have *not* ever rated [yourselves] or been rated by others on a butch/femme scale? At the most, five percent of the audience raises their hands" (42–43).[2] Current scholarship tends to focus on the butch-femme dyad, usually either emphasizing its historical significance for the lesbian community or decrying it as an outdated imitation of patriarchal gender roles that fails to embody feminist values.[3] Even within these and other related debates, however, the term "butch" remains ill defined. Can anyone be a butch just by saying so, or are there certain criteria a woman must meet before she can be called butch? Does a woman need to self-identify as butch in order to be butch? Is a lesbian butch because of how she looks, whom she is attracted to, who is attracted to her, or because of what she does in bed? How do one's race and class background influence how one perceives butchness? Various writers have answered all of these questions in conflicting fashions, leading to numerous dissenting concepts of what constitutes butchness. By examining the content in which butch and butch-femme occur today and by analyzing current scholarship on the topic, we can unravel some of this confusion.

The agenda for this chapter is to clarify and ultimately radically reorient the prevailing conceptions of butch. I accomplish this by examining the common definitions of butch and showing that the term, despite its flexibility, is not a word with limitless applicability. In this process of redefinition I explode the myth that the butch is characterized by the object of her desire. Examining two common ways butch is perceived—as the aggressor in sexual encounters and as desiring femmes—I demonstrate that neither is a fundamental component of butchness. Most important, I suggest that butch is a singular identity position, not a coupled one—that butches should be viewed independently from any possible relationship to femmes. I believe that scholars largely have ignored butch identity and butch-butch relationships in favor of concentrating on the more culturally predominant butch-femme relations.[4] My premise is that butch and femme are not always interdependent terms, each requiring the other. Rather, butch and femme are two expressions of gender that can, but do not necessarily, intersect. I shall need to focus on butch-femme at times, however, since much of the available material discusses butch only in this manner.[5] My subject position as a butch, and as a butch who is primarily attracted to other butches, provides experiential knowledge that informs my approach to gender theory. My interest in this topic is derived from an awareness of the gaps in current theory that deny and invalidate my personal experience as well as the experiences of other butches.

What Is a Butch?

"A butch is someone no one understands and no one can explain." So says Mike, the main character in Jay Rayn's novel *Butch* (1991).[6] In heterosexual culture, the term "butch" connotes manliness but is not often used as a descriptive term, as in "Jimmy's really butch," nor is it used in reference to women except in a derogatory sense. But in the gay male lexicon "butch" is an important word with multiple meanings. Employed as a campy adjective—"Oh, isn't Brian looking *butch* today!"—the word has a lighthearted tone; on the other end of the spectrum are the gay men who take their butch identity very seriously, laboring endlessly to achieve and maintain the most masculine physique, bearing, and overall presence. How male homosexuals use "butch" deserves a complete chapter, but this issue is beyond the spectrum of this study.

Among lesbians "butch" describes a vast realm of attitudes, behaviors, appearances, and actions. For instance, Cherríe Moraga writes: "To be butch, to me, is not to be a woman. The classic extreme-butch stereotype is the woman who sexually refuses another woman to touch her" (Hollibaugh and Moraga 400). Another woman states: "Part of identifying as butch stems from a desire to defend, protect, and defy the traditional feminine stereotype" (qtd. in Loulan 34). For yet another woman, "being butch is an ethical choice, a choice of resistance. . . . It's more than a preference in clothes, jewelry, shoes; more than a haircut. Butches have a cultural identity that embraces but exceeds mere costumes" ("Femme and Butch" 98). These three descriptions show the wide range of ideas that women have about what constitutes butchness. Some women consider being butch to be primarily a matter of one's sexual behavior, and in particular one's desire to be the dominant subject in sexual activities. Others understand butch primarily as a means of resisting the cultural norms for feminine behavior. Given the large number of ways in which a lesbian can appear butch, it is no wonder that lesbians are confused about what exactly makes a woman a butch. As Susan Ardill and Sue O'Sullivan comment,

> The absence of any precise or agreed definition about what butch and femme are produces endless heated arguments among lesbians. One straightforward and fairly widespread view is that they are merely methods of dress and behaviour—roles, in other words. Another view is that butch/femme are metaphors for subject/object in lesbian relationships: that talking about ourselves or others as butch/femme essentially describes how we negotiate desire. . . . [T]hese two words (and their equivalents in other cultures and contexts) have become dreadfully overburdened. They have to be infinitely elastic terms. (80)

Although few lesbians can agree on the precise definition of butch, most do seem to agree about who is or is not butch;[7] thus there must be some specific, observable characteristics a lesbian needs to display before she will be labeled butch. This section elucidates the fundamental components of the butch image today and argues that there are very real limits placed on butch identity, limits that make it impossible for anyone who so desires to claim to be a butch.[8]

The term "butch" has historic specificity: The meaning of butch in the 1950s is not the same as the meaning of butch in the 1990s. To understand butch today, the concept must be viewed in its proper context. For much of the twentieth century, lesbians as well as nonlesbians have perceived the butch largely, although not entirely, in relationship to the femme, the butch's assumed "natural" partner. In the 1940s and 1950s, participation in the butch-femme lifestyle was de rigueur for many lesbians, especially working-class or young women, but such roles fell out of favor in the 1960s and 1970s, when many lesbian feminists condemned them as replicating patriarchal relationships. Butch was seen as male-identified, and femme was seen as selling out to the traditional feminine stereotypes about women. Androgyny replaced butch-femme as the cultural imperative in the post-Stonewall lesbian feminist movement. Ironically, many aspects of this androgynous ideal were indistinguishable from butchness: wearing comfortable, nonconstrictive clothing such as flannel shirts, jeans, and hiking boots; sporting short, boyish haircuts; and acquiring the skills of male-dominated trades such as carpentry and auto repair. Butch-femme roles never completely died out, particularly in rural or working-class communities, but they became less central. Butch-femme culture saw a resurgence, in altered form, among urban upper- and middle-class lesbians in the 1980s. "Butch" and "femme" had now become broader and more fluid in meaning. More butch styles, such as clothing inspired by the punk movement, were being created and adopted by lesbians. A sense of the theatrical inspired some women to express their butch or femme images in glamorous and highly visible ways. Instead of being the standard of lesbian identity, butch and femme were two options for the expression of lesbian gender. Butch and femme were also a way for lesbians to challenge the lesbian feminist status quo. "Many young women who claimed butch or femme identities in the 1980s saw themselves as taboo-smashers and iconoclasts," writes Lillian Faderman (*Odd Girls* 263–64).

To some women familiar with the butch-femme culture of the 1950s, these neo butches and femmes appeared to be merely playing with roles that were once an integral part of identifying as a lesbian. As Faderman writes about the 1980s, "for most lesbians the roles [were] not the life-or-death identity they often were in the 1950s, but rather an enjoyable erotic statement and an escape from the boring 'vanilla sex' that they associated with lesbian-feminism" ("Return" 593). The apparent lack of seriousness attached to these roles leads some scholars, such as Faderman, to argue that butch and femme have ceased to be terms with discrete meaning: "Butch and femme today can mean whatever one wants those terms to mean. A woman is a butch or a femme simply because she says she is" ("Return" 594). Although there is little doubt that butch and femme roles have become far more flexible today than they were forty years ago, I question Faderman's belief that butch and femme today are entirely subjective terms. I also wonder whether one can state accurately that the contemporary butch is merely making "an enjoyable erotic statement," since butches still suffer harassment and abuse for stepping outside the traditional feminine role. Although butches certainly do not make up the entire lesbian community, they are frequently the ones who bear the brunt of homophobic attacks. As Judith Butler notes in *Gender Trouble* (1990), "we regularly punish those who fail to do their gender right" (140). This punishment takes many forms, ranging from overt violence to covert discrimination. All butches endure such castigation. Even if a particular butch has not fallen victim to physical violence, she has almost certainly experienced verbal harassment. That butches continue to exist in such an inhospitable environment is a testament to the seriousness of butch identity.

Since the butch is such a prominent figure in lesbian culture, I object to claims that the term has become "infinitely elastic" or "totally subjective"—after all, an infinitely elastic term has no meaning at all. Though definitions of butch may appear to be hopelessly divergent, research reveals patterns in how butches are usually described. Studying a broad range of texts, including first-person accounts, lesbian literature, the theoretical statements of writers like Judith Butler, Eve Kosofsky Sedgwick, Sue-Ellen Case, and Judith Roof, and the works of historians like Lillian Faderman, Joan Nestle, Madeline Davis, and Elizabeth Lapovsky Kennedy, I found that definitions of the butch tended to fall into some configuration of the following four categories: She is a masculine woman; she is like a man; she adopts an active sexual role; and she desires femmes. One of the more complex configurations of these categories can be seen in some accounts of the 1950s bar culture:[9] A butch had to be masculine, be attracted to femmes, and be the "top" in her sexual encounters. Yet, must a lesbian fall into *all* of these categories to qualify as butch? Some of these rubrics have been displaced by recent changes in cultural and theoretical conceptions of sex, sexuality, and gender. By examining the meanings and implications of the categories, I hope to distill four core elements of butchness. The fourth category, I believe, deserves special attention since the relationship between butches and femmes, and how that relationship either does or does not constitute butch identity, is radically undertheorized and misunderstood today.

"I just can't relate to that wanting to look like a man trip"

The first category—masculinity—is generally accepted as an essential foundational element of butchness. A woman who usually expresses herself in a traditionally feminine style is rarely, if ever, thought of as a butch by other lesbians.[10] When JoAnn Loulan's audience declares a lesbian to be butch, it is because this lesbian appears visibly masculine in her dress, physical appearance, or carriage. According to Gayle Rubin, butch is "a category of lesbian gender that is constituted through the deployment and manipulation of masculine gender codes and symbols" (467). Rubin writes: "Butch is the lesbian vernacular term for women who are more comfortable with masculine gender codes, styles, or identities than with feminine ones. The term encompasses individuals with a broad range of investments in 'masculinity' " (467). Lesbians have associated masculinity with butchness throughout much of the twentieth century, and masculinity continues to be crucial to a butch's self-presentation today. In sorting out just what makes a butch a butch, placing an emphasis on the role of masculinity in the butch's daily life permits the flexibility needed to account for the "nineties butch" without invoking Ardill and O'Sullivan's "infinite elasticity," since many lesbians are more comfortable with feminine appearances and attributes than with masculine ones.

But "masculinity" is itself an ill-defined term, one that describes a vast variety of appearances, behaviors, and attitudes that society commonly considers to be expressive of maleness: "Forms of masculinity are molded by the experiences and expectations of class, race, ethnicity, religion, occupation, age, subculture, and individual personality. National, racial, and ethnic groups differ widely in what constitutes masculinity, and each has its own system for communicating and conferring 'manhood'" (Rubin 470). Various historical periods have different definitions of masculinity as well. Some traits that are identified as masculine today by the culture at large include physical strength, daring and boldness, emotional nonexpressiveness, and straightforwardness. Also, masculinity is always defined in opposition to femininity and femaleness. "Masculine" attire does not include dresses, purses, or panty hose and is generally lacking in frills and bright colors. "Masculine" jobs either require some "masculine" trait such as physical strength or the ability to think logically or confer "masculine" privilege such as power or leadership.

Masculinity, in short, is a set of signs that connote maleness within a given cultural moment, and masculinity is as fluid and changing as the society defining it. No one universal presentation of masculinity exists in our contemporary culture. A corporate lawyer presents a different image of masculinity than a rodeo bronco rider. A football player presents a different image of masculinity than President Clinton. An English professor presents a different style of masculinity than a punk rocker. Nor will all these men agree about the masculinity of the others. Class, race, ethnicity, and geography all shape how masculinity is perceived. The rodeo rider, who rides bulls and broncos for a living, may think the corporate lawyer, with his endless paper pushing and swank office, a sissy. The lawyer, however, with his wealth, power, and prestige, might consider the bronco rider to be less masculine because he does not wield identical power.

A butch, as I have noted above, is a lesbian who adopts masculine identifiers. Clearly, this fact raises many interesting questions. What does masculinity mean on a female body? How much masculinity does a lesbian need to display to be considered butch? How does masculinity function among lesbians?

Not surprisingly, butches draw much of their style from the culture around them. Clothing is one of the most obvious ways that a butch displays masculinity. Leather jackets, men's shirts, suit jackets, pants, ties, and shoes are all part of the butch sartorial iconography. But the role of butch clothing is complex. The significance of clothing for butches can be understood better in light of Dick Hebdige's study of English punk subcultures, in which he refers to the use of mundane objects to form a distinctive punk style: "On the one hand, they warn the 'straight' world in advance of a sinister presence—the presence of difference—and draw down upon themselves vague suspicions, uneasy laughter, 'white and dumb rages.' On the other hand, for those who erect them into icons, who use them as words or as curses, these objects become signs of forbidden identity, sources of value" (*Subculture* 2–3). Like the English punks, butch lesbians use clothing as a way to indicate membership in a group. Butches are easily recognized as lesbians because both lesbian and heterosexual cultures typically interpret masculine appearance and clothing, particularly when such feminine signifiers as lipstick, makeup, long hair, and jewelry are absent, as indicators of homosexuality. Being butch is thus a way to announce to the world, "I am a lesbian." Since lesbians are, for the most part, invisible as a group, the ability to recognize, and be recognized by, other members of the lesbian subculture is vital to creating a sense of belonging, not only for the butch but also for all lesbians who see and recognize her.

What makes a butch a butch and not just a woman in men's clothing is a combination of factors, including her self-presentation and her self-perception. Lesbians identify many different subcategories of butch, all of which are related to varying degrees of masculinity. The ubiquitous nature of the butch-femme scale in lesbian culture is an example of this awareness of diversity, as it allows for several "levels" of butchness. Some extremely masculine women, such as the proverbial "diesel dyke,"[11] are easily labeled butch. The "soft butch" may look less macho than the diesel dyke, but her personal style leans toward the masculine, and she dresses and wears her hair in ways that are coded as butch.[12] An androgynous woman, such as the musician k. d. lang, is trickier to categorize by appearance alone, but this does not imply that lang cannot be butch, since butchness is dependent on a variety of masculine signifiers.

Being butch is more complicated than merely slipping on a man's suit and tie; it also entails adopting behavioral patterns that are typically perceived as nonfeminine. The butch's carriage and demeanor are as much a part of her masculine image as her clothing. Dressed in a skirt and high heels, the butch might look ill at ease. To the observer, she may even appear somehow "wrong" because her lack of familiarity with the physical bearing that is typically associated with such attire makes her performance of femininity appear awkward. When dressed in a tuxedo or men's jeans and a white t-shirt, however, she frequently looks at ease and "natural." The most famous literary example of the butch is Stephen Gordon in Radclyffe Hall's *Well of Loneliness* (1928). Although she certainly does not represent all butches, Hall's heroine represents an idealized image of how a butch should appear: "[Her] figure was handsome in a flat, broad-shouldered and slim flanked fashion; and her movements were purposeful, having fine poise, she moved with the easy assurance of the athlete" (72). Her face is handsome, but there is "something about it that went ill with the hats on which [her mother] insisted—large hats trimmed with ribbons or roses or daisies, and supposed to be softening to the features" (72). Hall's description of Stephen highlights a key component of what distinguishes a butch: The butch is *comfortable* with masculine identifiers and most likely uncomfortable with feminine ones. She feels attractive and sexual in her pants and boots and silly in lingerie. Her preferred clothing reflects her perception of herself.

Yet individual variations must still be accounted for. A woman who considers herself butch because she prefers and is most comfortable presenting a masculine appearance may be forced by social and economic necessity to wear a skirt, hose, and pumps to work. Is she a "real" butch? Is a woman who presents a feminine appearance, but who has masculine attitudes and behaviors, a butch? What about the otherwise masculine woman who cries easily and is afraid of bugs? Rubin notes that "There are at least as many ways to be butch as there are ways for men to be masculine; actually, there are more ways to be butch, because when women appropriate masculine styles the element of travesty produces new significance and meaning. Butches adopt and transmute the many available codes of masculinity" (469). To complicate matters further, each lesbian is exposed to different ideas about what it means to be butch on the basis of a number of cultural variables. The white Harvard graduate might have a different way of showing her butchness than the Chicano working-class lesbian living in central Los Angeles, although both might be influenced by similar ideologies about what constitutes a butch. Still, the questions remain: Is there some minimum of masculinity required to be a butch? Which combinations of traits distinguish the butch from the femme who can fix cars? How do we tell the difference between the androgyne and the butch, or explain why the masculine straight woman is not a butch?

Obviously, there are no clear-cut answers to these questions, but there are several factors that help to distinguish the butch. First, it is apparent that the butch must repeatedly present and create herself as butch in order to be butch. To borrow Judith Butler's words, "Gender is the repeated stylization of the body, a set of repeated acts within a highly rigid regulatory frame that congeal over time to produce the appearance of substance, of a natural sort of being" (*Gender* 33). Although she is speaking primarily about heterosexuals, her words can also describe the way gender congeals into certain forms for butches and for other nonheterosexual groups. Applying Butler's definition, butchness is a repeated production of the body's image following certain cultural conventions about what it means to be butch. I concur with Butler that butchness, like any other display of gender, is constituted by regular performance; the butch's butchness is dependent on her adopting various masculine signifiers that identify her as "butch" both to herself and to other lesbians, and it is the repetition of this display that distinguishes the butch from the lesbian (or heterosexual woman) who wears a tuxedo to a party one Saturday night. Second, by claiming masculine identifiers for her own use, the butch sets herself apart from the "average" heterosexual woman by failing to present herself as traditionally feminine in order to appeal to the male gaze. Although no woman can control how a man will look at her, a woman whose appearance is designed to gain the sexual attention of men is not butch, even if she is tough or has a masculine occupation. Under this view, the heroine of *La Femme Nikita* (1990; director Luc Besson), an assassin, would not qualify as a butch. Nor would the models crowding the pages of *Vogue, Elle, Essence, Glamour,* and other fashion magazines, even when they are wearing men's clothing.

Such an approach would seem to rule out the possibility of a heterosexual woman being butch. But what about a figure such as Kira

Nerys of the television series "Star Trek: Deep Space Nine"? She's tough, she's in control, she's wearing a uniform just like the men are. But because she is a heterosexual, she cannot be called a butch. As Alisa Solomon notes, butches are "dykes with such objects or attributes as motorcycles, wingtips, money, pronounced biceps, extreme chivalry. Straight women with such objects or attributes are just straight women with motorcycles, cummerbunds, biceps, etcetera. The difference is audience. Butches present their butchness for women. . . . For [the butch], they are not only attributes, but signs" ("Not Just" 37). Earlier I noted the significance of butch clothing, discussing how attire makes the butch visible to other lesbians and helps to engender a sense of community. For butch as a lesbian gender category to exist, its audience must recognize and understand the signs of butchness—out of context, butch has no meaning. This is why heterosexual women, no matter how butch they might act or appear, cannot be butch. Were Kira to say to her shipmates, "I'm a butch," they likely would not know what she was talking about since butch is a concept and an identity that has cultural relevance to lesbians but rarely to heterosexuals. Kira may look butch and act butch, but she is not a butch.

Still, since the masculine heterosexual woman shares with the butch the rejection of feminine gender roles, surely she suffers some of the same harassment. After all, when a woman adopts a masculine identity, she challenges the association between masculinity and maleness. A female body with masculine carriage, in masculine clothing, confounds the meanings of terms such as masculinity, woman, and male. Butler, discussing the butch, argues in *Gender Trouble*: "Within lesbian contexts, the 'identification' with masculinity that appears as butch identity is not a simple assimilation of lesbianism back into the terms of heterosexuality. As one lesbian femme explained, she likes her boys to be girls, meaning that 'being a girl' contextualizes and resignifies 'masculinity' in a butch identity. As a result, that masculinity, if it can be called that, is always brought into relief against a culturally intelligible 'female body'" (123). As Butler points out, within the dominant conception of gender, the butch makes no sense: Her female body ultimately transforms masculinity in a way that makes it nonintelligible to heterosexual society. To the "straight mind," as Monique

Wittig calls it, the butch's masculinity comes as a shock. The butch does not conform to social expectations of what constitutes woman-hood, throwing into question basic assumptions about people and their place in the world. Given this, we would expect the reaction of straight society to all female masculinity, whether the subject is het-erosexual or homosexual, to be hostile. Such is not the case, however. Examining heterosexuals' responses to hyperfeminine women, aver-age feminine women, and hypofeminine women, Mary Laner and Roy Laner found that heterosexual feminine women were the most-liked group and were frequently described as normal, agreeable, and nice (349). The least-liked group were hypofeminine homosexual women, who were categorized as unappealing, disagreeable, and hostile (349). The authors concluded: "Women, it seems, may be either excessively or typically feminine and yet be liked, or at least not disliked, by the majority. Departures toward the masculine end of the continuum of gender-related appearance, interests, or activities are disliked by the heterosexual majority when, and only when, the woman is thought to be a lesbian" (346).[13]

Theorist Judith Roof provides a lucid explanation of the relation-ship between lesbian masculinity and heterosexual hatred: "Perceiving lesbians as masculine reveals the threat to masculine supremacy and to a heterosexual system lesbians potentially pose. The representation of the lesbian as masculine is thus two-edged: a put-down, it also encap-sulates the very instability of gender prerogatives that undermines heterosexuality. For this reason, attributions of masculinity to lesbians are often expression[s] of anger and anxiety about a de-centering of phallic privilege" (248–49). Her words are particularly applicable to the butch, the embodiment of this stereotype, and the anxiety that Roof describes is at the root of the antipathy expressed by heterosexual society toward the butch. The butch's appearance announces that she does not belong or wish to belong in a society that expects or demands femininity in women, and this upsets the status quo and subverts gender norms. Further, by adopting a conspicuously masculine image, the butch also rejects the role of woman-as-commodity, to be ex-changed and bartered by men. As Alisa Solomon explains, the butch refuses "to play a part in the heterosexist binary" ("Not Just" 36). She fails to adopt the feminine appearance and behavior (such as flirting with men) that identify her sexual availability to men. In our society, femininity is frequently "expressed through modes of dress, movement, speech, and action which communicate weakness, dependency, [and] ineffectualness" (Devor 51). The butch rejects this vision of womanhood and in doing so becomes an outcast in a predominantly heterosexual society.

The Laner study is just a reflection of what most butches know from daily experience: The opprobrium of heterosexuals is more likely to be directed at butches than at femmes or lesbians who could be defined as "averagely feminine." Butches are singled out for harassment because their masculine presentation both challenges feminine gender stereotypes and makes them easily identifiable as lesbians. The fact that she is perceived as such a threat demonstrates that the butch is engaged, however unwittingly, in a radical critique of that reality. Butch is more than just a style; it is a political statement.

The Female Man

At first, the second category—that the butch is like a man or wants to be a man—seems to differ little from the first category. The two categories are actually quite distinct, since the desire for masculinity does *not* necessarily entail a desire to be a man. The stereotypical perception of a butch as being "a female man,"[14] a view held by both homo- and heterosexuals, arises from her adoption of masculine signifiers. This perception is a manifestation of the larger cultural discourse that defines "man" as a conflation of "male" and "masculine," when in fact masculinity is a set of attributes that can be adopted by any person, regardless of his or her sex. Therefore, a woman who adopts masculine signifiers is merely adopting a self-presentation that society codes as "male"; she is not necessarily trying to be a man. Still, because the culture assumes that "woman" and "man" are exclusive opposites, the butch's failure to follow prescribed gender norms means that she is disqualified from the category "woman," just as the lesbian is not a woman for Monique Wittig in her essay "One Is Not Born a Woman" (1980). In refusing heterosexuality, the lesbian denies the

binary system that defines "woman." Hence, in the heterosexual reality, the butch—a not-woman—must therefore be like a man, though
she cannot *be* a man because she does not possess the correct anatomy.
As Jacquelyn N. Zita points out, in writing about why males cannot be
lesbians, "This body is not only a thing in the world, subject to
physical gravity, but a thing that carries its own historical gravity, and
this collected weight bears down on the 'sexedness' of the body and
the possibilities of experience" (126). Applied to the butch, Zita's
words suggest that, by virtue of her female body, the butch will have
different life experiences and expectations than will a man. For example, a man does not experience the social pressure to be feminine that a
butch does. A man is less likely to worry about being raped. And,
because she is a woman, a butch may often be considered less intelligent and capable than her male coworkers. Butches are raised to be
women, are treated like women, but suffer the stigma of not looking
and acting the way women are expected to. All these factors and more
shape butches in a way that is radically different from the experiences
that constitute men.

Although heterosexual society sees the butch as "play-acting"
the role of a man and considers her lack of physical maleness to be a
failure, in actuality the butch's transgressive behavior exposes the
artificiality of social constructs about sex and gender. Thus one can
reinterpret a claim such as Moraga's that "a butch is not a woman" as
an extrapolation from Simone de Beauvoir's observation that "woman
is made, not born": For Moraga, the butch, while female, is constituted
differently than is a woman. It could be said that the butch is neither
man nor woman, since she fails to fit into society's conventions about
how men and women should look and act. I do not wish to suggest,
however, that the butch is born "butch"; while there is always the
possibility that biological factors may influence her development, the
butch is very much constructed through her interactions with other
lesbians.

Even so, the butch is raised and lives within a largely heterosexual society and is inevitably affected by it. Not only is she inundated
with images of masculine males and feminine females—and a cultural
obsession with maintaining this congruence—but the butch may occa-

sionally, or even frequently, be mistaken for a man. Even as commonplace an act as going to a public restroom can be a disconcerting experience for the butch, one that is memorialized in many pieces of lesbian writing. In Judy Grahn's poem "Edward the Dyke," Edward has trouble with restrooms, such as the time when three middle-aged housewives mistake her for a man invading a department store's powder room. In Lee Lynch's novel *Toothpick House* (1983), the butch heroine, Annie Heaphy, is sharply admonished by another woman, "This is a ladies' room, sir" (4). The butch, as a result of being frequently mistaken for a man, comes to feel defensive about her right to enter this "women's" space, where gender solidarity is supposedly openly expressed, because though she has the correct anatomy required for entrance, she fails to conform to the social conventions for decorating that anatomy.

The foregoing examples of the butch and the bathroom show how a butch is affected by society's view of the image that she projects. Judith Roof's analysis of how cultural configurations influence lesbian identity can help us better understand how butch identity is similarly constructed.

> The relation of [the] cultural imaginary to individual women is complex, as women internalize imaginary configurations while at the same time producing images that confirm the configurations. Configurations help define the lesbian and help the woman identify herself as a lesbian, though like other kinds of stereotype, they never quite succeed in thoroughly containing her. Depending on cultural variables such as class, education, age, race, ethnic group, geographical location, historical context, and even accidents such as whom they know when, women internalize or accept aspects of these configurations. (244)

It is impossible to imagine the butch constructing her image in a vacuum. She, like any other lesbian, constantly discovers that her butchness is shaped and altered by how both homosexual society and heterosexual society perceives her. Some butches internalize the message that lesbians want to be men, and so for them being butch is about being like a man. Yet not all lesbians are so profoundly affected by stereotypes of lesbians and butches. For them, the myth of butch-as-man fails to explain fully their own experiences and is seen as a cultural misapprehension. Even so, commonly being mistaken for a man because of her masculinity will likely affect the butch's self-perception to one degree or another.

The Butch on Top

The third category—the butch as sexual doer who receives her pleasure from giving pleasure to her partner—must be explored to unlink butch from its connection to desire, a necessary step in altering the perception that butch is only half of a coupled identity. One of the common ways the butch is defined is by her supposed role as the active agent in sexual encounters, a role exemplified in Moraga's discussion about the extreme stereotype of the butch, also known as the stone butch. In the 1950s and 1960s, being the active sexual partner was often considered one of the defining characteristics of butchness— a butch who "rolled over" in bed might be called a femme by her peers and suffer loss of status; the stone butch was the epitome of the 1950s butch, a figure that "became a publicly discussed model for appropriate sexual behavior, and it was a standard that young butches felt they had to achieve to be a 'real' or 'true' butch" (Davis and Kennedy 433).

But the stone butch is no longer the exemplar of butchness, nor are there the same kinds of cultural sanctions against butches who wish to be the recipients of sexual attention. Personal ads in almost any big-city gay newspaper reveal numerous butch "bottoms" (and femme "tops") seeking partners. For these lesbians, the fact that their preferred sexual positioning is an inversion of what was once considered the norm does not affect their sense of gender identification at all. Though "butch" still connotes the active sexual partner to many lesbians, the acceptance of the butch bottom is a noteworthy shift in cultural expectations. The years between the "heyday" of butch-femme and its resurgence in the 1980s saw several changes in gay and lesbian culture—ranging from more numerous mainstream representations of lesbians in films and books to the expanding academic debate about gender in the lesbian community to the growth of a more diverse, radical young lesbian culture influenced by AIDS activism—

changes that plainly affected lesbians' conceptions of butch. Contributing to this shift is the increased visibility of lesbian sadomasochists.

When Second Wave feminism became the dominant ideology of the middle-class lesbian community, as Lillian Faderman and other historians argue, attitudes toward sex changed as well. In the mid 1970s, "feminist sex," many lesbians thought, required equality between partners; butch-femme sex, seen as a replication of unequal heterosexual roles, was thus patriarchal and antifeminist. In the extreme, butches and femmes were perceived as engaging in what Sheila Jeffreys later called "an erotic communication based on sado-masochism, the eroticising of power difference" (179). But in the late 1970s, the real sadomasochists started coming out of the closet, arguing that there was no conflict between feminism and sadomasochism. The ensuing "sex wars," which periodically resurfaced throughout the 1980s and into the 1990s, had a tremendous influence on many lesbians, affecting their perceptions of sadomasochism, butch-femme, and sex in general. The works of Pat Califia, JoAnn Loulan, Gayle Rubin, and Susie Sexpert, among others, and the emergence of such lesbian erotic publications as *Bad Attitude, On Our Backs,* and *Quim* all helped to expand conceptions of what constituted acceptable, healthy sex for lesbians, though S/M sex has never been accepted by the lesbian community at large as "normal" or desirable. These "sex wars" had an impact on the butch in at least one crucial way. Over the years, more material became available that portrayed lesbian sadomasochism in a positive light, the most influential work being the groundbreaking *Coming to Power: Writings and Graphics on Lesbian S/M* (1981) by SAMOIS, a San Francisco–based lesbian-feminist S/M group. Encouraged by such publications, some lesbians, particularly young urban lesbians who felt dissatisfied with "vanilla sex" and who wanted to experiment with sexual power play without necessarily embracing the S/M lifestyle, adopted S/M concepts, such as "top" and "bottom," as positive additions to their sexual repertoire. As the negative impact of at least some of the vocabulary of sadomasochism was reduced, the term "top" came to denote a lesbian who preferred to "run the sex," reducing the burden formerly carried by the word "butch." This transition affected butch sadomasochists as well as their "vanilla" counterparts: Lesbian masochists, as well as lesbians who simply enjoyed being the recipients of lovemaking, could claim the identity "butch" without conflict, thus further blurring cultural conflations of sex, gender, sexuality, and desire. Just as femme lesbians demonstrate the fallacy of theories of inversion, the butch bottom exemplifies the distinction between sexual positioning and gender.

Butch Desire

The fourth category—that to be butch, "You gotta have a femme under your arm at all times" (Trish Thomas 21)—has received the least critical scrutiny in current scholarship on butch identity: It assumes that butch and femme are interdependent opposites, like the yin and yang of Taoist philosophy, bound together, as Ardill and O'Sullivan and Thomas all note, by the energy of sexual desire. Under this view a butch is a butch because she finds femmes erotic and appealing, and a femme is a femme because she is sexually attracted to butches. For example, Loulan writes, "It's impossible for us to get away from the fact that butches and femmes are in opposition. This doesn't mean that they are completely different, only that there is an opposing force in the other that each finds to be an erotic turn-on" (125–26). Amber Hollibaugh concurs: "butch/femme is an erotic system. It's deeply based in an erotic definition" (qtd. in Loulan 26).

But not all butches agree with this assessment: "You're expected to like femmes, if you're butch," one lesbian writes; "it's part of the 'like a man' myth, as far as I see. . . . [but] I'm no more comfortable with most femmes than with straight women" ("Femme and Butch" 97). I suggest that the term "butch" need not inevitably and "naturally" appear along with "femme." The conception of butch-femme interdependence has historical roots dating back to the beginning of the century. When sexologists such as Krafft-Ebing, and Ellis, and Freud believed that masculine women would be attracted to feminine ones. In "Three Essays on the Theory of Sexuality" (1905) Freud wrote that, among women, "active inverts exhibit masculine characteristics, both physical and mental, with peculiar frequency and look for femininity in their sexual objects—though here again a closer knowledge of the facts might reveal greater variety" (145). Even much later in his career, when he was less sure that lesbianism always required physical masculinity, Freud still insisted in "Psychogenesis of a Case of Homosexuality in a Woman" (1920) that his lesbian patient, despite not showing the "bodily traits and mental traits belonging to the opposite sex" (154) that lesbians "normally" possessed, still displayed a "masculine" attitude toward a "feminine" love object.

This idea has been remarkably persistent, and although I recognize and appreciate the importance of butch-femme relationships, I do not believe they are the only way to understand butchness (or femmeness). Rather, I maintain that butch can be interpreted more precisely if it is divorced from the butch-femme bipolarity, which has acted as a stranglehold on theorists who have tried to produce new ideas about what it means to be butch in the 1980s and 1990s. Scholars such as Loulan, Hollibaugh, and Nestle fall into the trap of limiting their discussions to butch and femme as a dyadic system, overlooking that butch can be a signifier that has little to do with femme, or even with sexuality at all. As one butch I know comments, "If I were celibate for the rest of my life, I would still be butch."

The idea that butches and femmes are a matched set is so predominant even today that many lesbians uncritically assume that butches *must* be attracted to femmes. For instance, Loulan, in her lengthy survey of butch-femme identities, asked her respondents, "If you identify as butch, choose three words to describe aspects of femmes you find erotic," which presupposes that butches *will* find aspects of femmes erotic (250). Yet even Loulan admits that, among the respondents to her survey, only 50 percent of the butches expressed an attraction mainly for femmes while a full 25 percent expressed an attraction mainly for other butches. If Loulan's figures are correct, then the theoretical focus on the butch-femme couple presents a skewed view of reality.

Loulan's implicit erasure of the reality of butch-butch desire is only one example of this type of elision. On a more theoretical level, Sue-Ellen Case, in her essay "Towards a Butch-Femme Aesthetic," postulates butch-femme as an ideal feminist subject position, one that provides "agency and self-determination to the historically passive subject" (65) while at the same time positioning her outside dominant ideology. Case writes: "the butch-femme couple inhabit the subject position together—'you can't have one without the other,' as the song says. The two roles never appear as . . . discrete. The butch-femme as subject is reminiscent of Monique Wittig's 'j/e,' or coupled self, in her novel *The Lesbian Body*. These are not split subjects, suffering the torments of dominant ideology. They are coupled ones" (56). Yet, in building her argument, Case begins with the assumption that butch and femme are linguistically indissoluble, thereby overlooking the possibility of even more disruptive and powerful constructs than butch-femme. For while butch-femme gains its subversive strength from its parody of heterosexual couplings, "providing [the subject] with at least two options for gender identification and, with the aid of camp, an irony that allows her perception to be constructed from outside ideology" (Case 65), other constructs, such as butch-butch, go a step farther by also destabilizing constructs of heterogendered desire and homosexuality as well.

Though butch and femme are most certainly linked because they arise in a culture for which gender is a dyadic system, this does not presuppose that the cultural representation of gender encompasses all variations of gender in existence, or that the relationships between genders are limited to those that are culturally sanctioned. Indeed, the very existence of homosexuals, hermaphrodites, butches, and queens is ample evidence of the fallacy of the cultural conflation of sex, gender, and sexuality; to persist in the argument that butch and femme are, or should be, symbiotically intertwined ignores reality and only replicates the dominant ideology.

Case, Loulan, and other critics fall into the trap of upholding the prevailing perception that desire itself is essentially heterosexual; as Eve Kosofsky Sedgwick explains, "desire, in this view, by definition subsists in the current that runs between one male self and one female self, in whatever sex of bodies these selves may be manifested" (86–87). In such a system, the desire of butches for other butches is impossible, a state of affairs that results in an inaccurate view of what it means to be butch in our culture. To borrow Sedgwick's words, "To alienate conclusively, *definitionally,* from anyone on any theoretical ground the authority to describe and name their own sexual desire is a terribly consequential seizure" (26). By assuming that part of what constitutes a butch is her attraction to femmes, we deny butches this authority; we also deny masculine lesbians who are attracted to other masculine lesbians the right to claim butch as an identity.

Although Biddy Martin writes about an erasure of being that lesbians in general must confront, her words are equally applicable to the erasure that butches experience: "We are not always confronted with direct, coercive efforts to control what we do in bed, but we are constantly threatened with erasure from discursive fields where the naturalization of sexual and gender norms works to obliterate actual pluralities" (95). We must be aware of how sexual and gender norms work within society at large and within the many diverse lesbian communities that marginalize lesbians who differ from subcultural norms. For instance, the very existence of butches who are passionately attracted to other butches is frequently ignored, if not denied outright. When such butches do become visible, they are often seen as abnormal, as in the novel *Cass and the Stone Butch,* where Jacko thinks that Cass, a butch, is "perverted to like [those] butch types" (Azolakov 46). There is little difference between this sentiment and the notion that says that lesbianism is perverse; both attitudes are designed to maintain the status quo. The denial of butch-butch desire and eroticism is symptomatic of a society that can recognize sexual desire only between a self that is gendered masculine and one that is gendered feminine. Butch-butch desire negates the binary oppositions female/male, self/other on which Western culture is based, and hence it is tremendously threatening.

The elision of butch-butch desire is apparent in lesbian films targeting a mass audience. *Lianna, Personal Best, Desert Hearts*—all of these movies star at least one, if not two, stunningly attractive and very feminine women. None of the films feature two butches, and two of them focus exclusively on the relationship between two feminine women who could easily pass as straight. As I have argued in the first chapter, sexuality between two feminine women is a threat to the dominant social order, but it can be contained through representational conventions. For instance, supposed feminine lesbians are often featured in heterosexual male pornography, but there is always the illusion that a man will suddenly appear. If two butches appeared, a man might seem superfluous, perhaps even endangered. Butches fail to fulfill heterosexual ideas about what is attractive and sexually appealing in women, and therefore, at least up to the present, mass-market lesbian films have been carefully crafted to include lesbians who could be as desirable to heterosexuals as to homosexuals. In addition, butch-butch eroticism raises the specter of male homosexuality, which might offend and confound the audience.

Given the slim representation of lesbianism in the mass media, it is hardly surprising that butch-butch desire has been largely invisible. More curious is how rarely the lesbian media represent butch-butch eroticism. In films, newspapers, magazines, and novels, one sees countless images of the butch-femme couple, but the butch-butch couple is rarely depicted. Even in erotic videos produced for the lesbian market, such as those created by Fatale Video, one constantly sees femme with femme or femme with butch in such videos as *Hungry Hearts* (1989; directors Debi Sundahl and Nan Kinney) and *Suburban Dykes* (1990; directors Debi Sundahl and Nan Kinney), but only rarely butch with butch. This erasure denies that butch-butch relationships are as significant a part of the lesbian community as butch-femme relationships.

A few critics have nonetheless given attention to erotic relationships between butches. Gayle Rubin provides the most thoughtful commentary in her article, "Of Catamites and Kings: Reflections on Butch, Gender, and Boundaries":

> Butches are often identified in relation to femmes. Within this framework, butch and femme are considered an indissoluble unity, each defined with reference to the other; butches are invariably the partners of femmes. Defining "butch" as the object of femme desire, or "femme" as the object of butch desire presupposes that butches do not desire or partner with other butches, and that femmes do not desire or go with other femmes.
>
> Butch-butch eroticism is much less documented than butch-femme sexuality and lesbians do not always recognize or understand it. Although it is not uncommon, lesbian culture contains few models for it. Many butches who lust after other butches

have looked to gay male literature and behavior as sources of
imagery and language. The erotic dynamics of butch-butch sex
sometimes resemble those of gay men, who have developed many
patterns for sexual relations between different kinds of men. Gay
men also have role models for men who are passive or subordinate in sexual encounters yet retain their masculinity. Many
butch-butch couples think of themselves as women doing male
homosexual sex with one another. (472–73)

An even more singular view of butch-butch sexuality than Rubin's is
Jan Brown's opinion that when two butches "hook up . . . sexually"
they are "faggots" (414). Both Rubin and Brown are attempting to
accomplish something worthwhile, to show that butch-butch sexuality *does* exist and must be accounted for in a different fashion than
butch-femme sexuality. They seem stymied, however, when it comes
to defining butch sexuality in a way that exemplifies the butches'
lesbian identities. By suggesting that butches who are erotically interested in other butches are modeling their behavior on that of homosexual men or are actually "faggots" themselves, Rubin and Brown
distance butches from "normal" lesbians who engage in "normal"
lesbian sex. More insidiously, Rubin and Brown are classifying butches
who are sexually attracted to other butches as not even lesbians but
something else completely; though some butches might find this
attitude appealing, others might find that such a theory positions them
as outsiders in the lesbian community. I am critical of such an approach to butch sexuality and argue that when two butches engage in
sex, no matter what the practice, they need to be seen as two women
engaged in lesbian sexuality, not gay male sexuality.

The numerous social restrictions on acceptable forms of desire
make it hard for writers like Rubin and Brown to come to grips with
something as transgressive as the butch who desires other butches.
Two female bodies having sex violates the myth of "natural" heterosexuality; female bodies in (or out of) men's clothing violate gender
restrictions; and female bodies in men's clothing having sex with each
other constitutes a triple whammy. The butch-butch couple confounds all of these conventions, which is why this form of relationship
makes even some lesbians uncomfortable. Trish Thomas describes

what can happen when a butch pursues another butch: "She wonders if I've mistaken her for femme. . . . She becomes concerned that she's throwing off femme vibes without even knowing it. . . . And suddenly she gets this overwhelming urge to arm wrestle" (22). There is a constant effort to assimilate butch-butch sexuality into familiar categories, as with the butch who worries that Thomas must be picking up "femme vibes" or in Brown's description of butches who have sex with other butches as "faggots."

Despite such overwhelming conceptual resistance, butches, unconcerned with theoretical disputes, continue to desire other butches. Stand on Castro Street any Saturday evening, and you are likely to notice a number of butch couples strolling by. Visit a chic lesbian bar in San Francisco, and you are apt to see two leather-jacketed, buzz-cut young women clinging to each other on the dance floor—and they will be far from alone. Might butch-butch even be getting *trendy*? The increasingly apparent presence of butch-butch couples points out the curious location of butch desire today in lesbian communities across the United States. On the one hand, the existence of butch-butch relationships still tends to be ignored or minimized. On the other hand, butches involved with other butches appear to be moving increasingly into the spotlight. As media overexposure causes other forms of lesbian relationships to become more accepted, women who wish to transgress social expectations, whether lesbian or nonlesbian, seek new avenues for sexual expression. Butch-butch relationships are one means of so doing. But I do not mean to suggest that butch-butch sexuality is merely the trend of the season and will quickly disappear when a newer trend surfaces. Quite to the contrary, I believe that the butch-butch couples, like other sexual radicals, are altering our conceptions of lesbian identity and desire.

Butch and Beyond

Being butch, as I have shown, affects every moment of the butch lesbian's life because she lives in a culture dominated by the myth that gender is a biologically determined behavioral manifestation of anatomical sex. The butch who refuses to pass as nonbutch—a "GI Joe in Barbie Land"—is, in many situations, a social outcast who might be denied jobs, professional advancement, or social acceptance because of her appearance and actions. It is this very real persecution that provided the incentive for me to write about the butch.

This chapter has shown that it is masculinity, not sexual desire and choice of sexual object, that should be the chief identifying trait of the butch. Associating the butch with her masculine display rather than with her choice of sexual partner frees the butch to have sex with whomever she wants in whatever way she desires but avoids the trap of "infinite elasticity."

I hope this chapter has exploded the "natural" assumption that butches almost always belong with femmes. This false claim works to negate the experiences of many butches (and femmes). Recognizing that butch-femme is only one of a myriad of different relationships that function in lesbian communities brings into question the all-too-common linkage of the terms "butch" and "femme" and ensures that femme-femme or butch-butch relationships can also be regarded as "normal." A butch like Trish Thomas should not be considered "suspect" and "the ultimate threat" because she prefers sexual involvement with other butches. Her sexual expression should not be regarded any differently than that of a butch who finds femmes more sexually appealing. As lesbians, we need to make sure that we do not create definitions that function to delineate who is a "proper" lesbian and who is not. Articulating the elements that make up various queer identities, from the butch to the femme to the pansy boy to the "clone," is vitally important in order to understand how gender is produced and performed among lesbians and gay men. Exploring the many facets of such images also helps to elucidate the virulent homophobia that some of these individuals experience.

Breaking the linkage between "butch" and "femme" brings to light new thoughts about how gender operates among lesbians. Butch-butch or femme-femme relationships might also tell us much about how sexuality functions in the lesbian world, and these relationships deserve more scholarly attention than they have yet received. Studying such "marginal" relationships will help us better understand the multiplicity of ways lesbianism is defined and constructed by both homosexuals and heterosexuals.

I would like to end this chapter with a quotation from Ralph Ellison's *Invisible Man* (1952) that aptly describes the experiences of the butch, especially the butch who is sexually attracted to other butches: "I am invisible, understand, simply because people refuse to see me. Like the bodiless heads you see sometimes in circus sideshows, it is as though I have been surrounded by mirrors of hard, distorting glass. When they approach me they see only my surroundings, themselves, or figments of their imagination—indeed, everything and anything except me" (3). Like Ellison's invisible man, the butch is simultaneously the most visible and least visible member of society. She is visible because she stands out as an "abnormal" woman who does not adhere to society's dictates about "correct" femininity. She is invisible for exactly the same reason: Twisted by attempts to fit her into sanctioned conceptual categories, she becomes a distorted figure, the Other, the nonperson. It is the transgressive nature of butch that produces this double vision, and I hope that this chapter has helped to bring her into better focus.

Notes

Introduction

1. Information about the treatments offered to gay women and men was taken from historian John D'Emilio's description in his book *Sexual Politics, Sexual Communities: The Making of a Homosexual Minority in the United States, 1940–1970* (1983). He writes: "In their search for a cure, doctors experimented on their wards with procedures ranging from the relatively benign, such as psychotherapy and hypnosis, to castration, hysterectomy, lobotomy, electroshock, aversion therapy, and the administration of untested drugs" (18).

2. The terminology in this book varies. Frequently, I use "lesbian," but I also use "queer," "gay," or "homosexual." I have chosen not to rely entirely on the word "queer" because I feel that this word elides the specificity of lesbian lives. At the same time, however, I believe "queer" is a word that appropriately describes some of my agenda, such as in my chapter on queer geography. "Homosexual" is a word that I use rarely, since it conjures up images of old-fashioned medical books describing sexual "perversions." It also brings up the image of the homosexual as a primarily sexual creature. Still, this word is sometimes appropriate, such as when I juxtapose "homosexual" with "heterosexual" or discuss how

homosexuals were perceived in the twenties, a time when "homosexual" would have been far more likely to be used than "queer."

3.   See Paul Burston and Colin Richardson, eds., *A Queer Romance: Lesbians, Gay Men, and Popular Culture;* Corey K. Creekmur and Alexander Doty, eds., *Out in Culture: Gay, Lesbian, and Queer Essays on Popular Culture;* Gabriele Griffin, ed., *Outwrite: Lesbianism and Popular Culture,* Diane Hamer and Belinda Budge, eds., *The Good, the Bad, and the Gorgeous: Popular Culture's Romance with Lesbianism;* and Erica Rand, *Barbie's Queer Accessories.*

1. Who's Afraid of Stephen Gordon?

1.   Ruehl argues for the importance of *The Well* as a starting point for a wide discussion of lesbianism: "The trial and surrounding publicity about [*The Well*] put lesbianism on the map. . . . for the first time, the idea of 'the lesbian' as a specific identity and image was given wide public currency" (15); and Smith-Rosenberg, in "The Female World of Love and Ritual: Relationships between Women in Nineteenth-Century America," describes the mannish lesbian as a figure used by sexologists and the general public from the 1880s to the 1920s. See also Cott (178) and Ernst and Seagle (259–60).

2.   I recognize that my argument is at odds with the common assumption that only the masculine lesbian poses a threat to society because she impersonates a man and adopts male prerogatives (Faderman, *Surpassing* 52–54). I believe, however, that the threat posed by the feminine lesbian has been too frequently overlooked. As I shall show, she poses even more of a danger to heterosexual society because she, unlike the masculine lesbian, is difficult or impossible to distinguish from heterosexual women.

3.   After first being produced in Paris in March of 1926, *The Captive* opened in New York on September 29, 1926. *The Well* was first published in the United States on December 15, 1928.

4.   Contemporary reviewers of *The Captive* include John Mason Brown, Carb, and Freeman.

5.   Katz provides an excellent collection of documents about the censorship of these works (82–92, 397–405).

6.   It is easy to assume that *The Well* was censored to remove a lesbian representation from heterosexual society. Instead, I suggest that censor-

ship actually encouraged the novel's circulation among heterosexuals. A similar case of how censorship of homosexuality in art can increase its consumption by a mass audience is the Robert Mapplethorpe trial.

7. This famous raid even appeared on the front page of the *New York Times*. Both producers and actors were arrested and charged with corrupting public morals. Although the charges were dropped, the play was discontinued. It was also closed by police in Los Angeles and Detroit.

8. Some critics might suggest that *The Well*'s greater popularity can be explained by the fact that it is a novel, not a play. Although this argument is partially true—a play does not gain as large an audience as a mass-market novel—it does not adequately explain *The Captive*'s obscurity, since other plays about lesbianism have gained widespread attention. For instance, Lillian Hellman's *The Children's Hour* went through 691 performances in its first run and continues to be read and produced.

9. Even today, *The Well* is one of the books most likely to be purchased by a lesbian or a heterosexual wanting to know more about lesbianism. O'Rourke's reader survey suggests the dominance of Hall's novel in the present lesbian literary market; 37 percent of the women questioned had read *The Well* as their first lesbian novel (124). See also Newton, "Mythic" 559.

10. Hall herself intended her book for both homosexual and heterosexual readers (Faderman, *Surpassing* 467 n.).

11. Unfortunately, no record is available of the sexual orientation of purchasers of *The Well* either in the 1920s or in any other period. The assumption, however, that many heterosexuals were also purchasing this well-known scandalous work seems unquestionable.

12. For another essay that examines the message of *The Well* to its heterosexual readers, see Barale's "Below the Belt: (Un)covering *The Well of Loneliness*." In particular, Barale examines the changing cover art of *The Well* through several different editions.

13. It is revealing to compare West's article to one published in a popular medical periodical in 1938—Ralph Hay's "Mannish Women or Old Maids?"—in which the author assumes that society will perceive the woman wearing mannish clothing to be a lesbian.

14. In the 1920s, the general public was much more likely to receive its ideas about lesbianism from such popular accounts as that of Collins rather than directly from Ellis's weighty, many-volume work. Thus, popular

accounts of the lesbian character may provide a more accurate representation of the mass perceptions of the lesbian than more scholarly works.

15. For support for this claim, see Faderman, *Surpassing* 361; Collins 67;
Weeks 116–17; and Simmons 56.

16. Chideckel goes on to say that "Rhyming . . . is a favorite method of
communication among most homosexuals, especially among those who
practice tribadism" (121). One is at a loss to understand how the doctor
reached his conclusions.

17. In the United States, membership in the Masonic order increased from
1,317,000 in 1910 to 3,303,000 in 1930 (Dumenil 225).

18. In his case studies on lesbians, Krafft-Ebing discusses case 159 who has
planned suicide, case 156 who suffers from anxiety and severe depression, and case 157 who has attacks of melancholia (400–39). Ellis and
Freud also depict lesbians with depressive disorders. Although one can
argue that these men were treating only a small group of depressed and
distraught women, not a representative body of lesbians, what I emphasize is that the unhappy lesbian was the image most frequently described
to heterosexual readers from the 1880s through the 1930s (and even up
to the present). When *The Well* was published, it fit neatly into this
preestablished discourse about the angst-ridden lesbian.

19. I recognize that Bourdet—a male—and Radclyffe Hall—a lesbian—confronted different problems and encountered different audience reactions.
Because of his gender, Bourdet was less open to public censure than Hall.
I must emphasize, however, that my main interest is not in how the
public viewed the authors but in how heterosexuals perceived the images
of the lesbian within these texts.

20. For a contrasting novel in this tradition, read Adolphe Belot's *Mademoiselle Giraud, My Wife*. In this novel, the narrator drowns Berthe, a stereotypical evil lesbian, on the pretext of saving her. Rather than being upset,
her husband sends the murderer a note, thanking him for getting rid of a
"reptile." It is not so easy to get rid of the more durable lesbians of *The
Captive*.

2. "Malevolent, neurotic, and tainted"

1. Peter Rose, a professor at Smith College, commented that racism is rarely
discussed when he talks to the school's alumnae, but they frequently wish
to know about the status of lesbians on campus (Roche 32).

2. The best-known studies of lesbianism in the nineteenth century are Faderman, *Surpassing,* and Smith-Rosenberg, "Female World."

3. For a longer discussion of the changing views of crushes at women's colleges and their fictional depiction at the turn of the century, see my essay "Mashes, Smashes, Crushes, & Raves: Woman-to-Woman Relationships in Popular Women's College Fiction, 1895–1915."

4. In 1926, Dr. Joseph Collins remarked with evident alarm that "Ulrichs, Krafft-Ebing, Freud, Stekel and dozens of their countrymen have flooded the Western world. . . . One might readily gather from reading the latest from Vienna that there were no normal people left in the world" (67). Albeit hyperbolic, Collins's language does reveal the cultural uneasiness about homosexuality that existed in the 1920s.

5. Similarly, Nathan Hale understands the language of popular psychoanalysis as developing between 1909 and 1918 and becoming firmly entrenched by the 1920s, see Hale 397–433.

6. Faderman also points out the linkage made between women's colleges and lesbianism in the 1920s, see *Surpassing* 338–39.

7. When Lapsley's novel was first published, the reviewer for the *New York Times* approved of the book because its author did not pretend "half of her virgins are abnormal and the other half are gin-guzzling flappers" as did other college novelists ("*Parable*" 6). This view seems to be off target; the inescapable conclusion one draws from the novel is that the vast majority of the school's members *are* lesbians or gin-guzzling flappers or, in some cases, both.

8. Crosby is only one of many heroines in women's college novels who turn to Ellis and Freud for ideas about sexuality. For instance, Rebecca in *Against the Wall* reads the work of Havelock Ellis not for a class but for her own personal enlightenment. The first-person narrator of Carol Denny Hill's novel *Wild* reads both Ellis and Freud and considers them "knockout stuff" (75).

9. For an even earlier criticism of crushes, see "Your Daughter: What Are Her Friendships?"—an article from a popular magazine that tells mothers to watch their daughters for signs of "crushitis," warning readers that 10 percent of the women who have crushes on other women are "moral degenerates" (16).

10. Lesbianism was not the only perceived danger to women's college students in the 1920s; they also had to beware of the communist threat. In an influential article by Calvin Coolidge, "Enemies of the Republic: Are

the 'Reds' Stalking Our College Women?" (1921), the author warned that the northeastern women's colleges harbored socialism, bolshevism, and internationalism. Though Coolidge stated that "Smith [seemed] sane," he was less sure about Barnard, Wellesley, and, most of all, Radcliffe, which he condemned as a "hotbed of Bolshevism" (67). Far from showing that the Seven Sisters colleges were in danger of being overrun by hordes of lesbian bolsheviks, Coolidge's fears reveal that society was concerned about the prominence of educated women and their increasing societal power. Such exaggerated fears have operated and continue to operate as an effective way to control the growth of women's colleges.

11. Floyd Dell is typical of writers from the interwar years who perceived single-sex institutions as breeding homosexuality. In his book *Love in the Machine Age: A Psychological Study of the Transition from Patriarchal Society* (1930), he wrote that a "segregated woman's institution" produced a "quasi-homosexual atmosphere" that resulted in graduates adopting "life-long homosexuality" (305). A longer discussion of the presumed prevalence of homosexuality among college women from this period can be found in Bromley and Britten 117–30.

12. Similar language is found in Tess Slesinger's short story about a girls' boarding school. In "The Answer on the Magnolia Tree" there are strong hints that a single-sex environment breeds lesbianism, and Miss Laurel, one of the teachers, writes in a letter to her fiancé: "If you could see, and feel, and *smell* this great woman-filled dormitory. On a night like this . . . it positively reeks of suppressed desires" (367–68). Slesinger's work depicts overheated sexuality as a prime problem of the single-sex school.

3. "They're here, they're flouncy"

1. Studies of women's magazines include Kalia Doner, "Women's Magazines: Slouching towards Feminism;" Marjorie Ferguson, *Forever Feminine: Women's Magazines and the Cult of Femininity;* Janet Lee, "Care to Join Me in an Upwardly Mobile Tango? Postmodernism and the 'New Woman'"; Ellen McCracken, "Demystifying *Cosmopolitan:* Five Critical Methods" and *Decoding Women's Magazines from "Mademoiselle" to "Ms.";* Kathryn McMahon, "The *Cosmopolitan* Ideology and the Management of Desire," and Janice Winship, *Inside Women's Magazines.* Two works that specifically discuss images of lesbians in popular women's magazines are Erica Rand's intelligent and well-written essay "Lesbian Sightings:

Scoping for Dykes in Boucher and *Cosmo*," and Alisa Solomon's "That *Cosmo* Dyke."

2.   Articles about bisexuality or male homosexuality in popular women's magazines include Peg Corning, "The Hardest Hurt to Heal: Losing Your Husband to a Man," *Glamour*; Susan Gerrard and James Halpin, "The Risky Business of Bisexual Love," *Cosmopolitan*; Vincent T. Lathbury, "Mothers and Sons: An Intimate Discussion," *Ladies' Home Journal*; Merle Miller, "Homosexual Husbands: What Wives Must Know," *Redbook*; Gloria Naylor, "A Message to Winston," *Essence*; Peter Rainer, "Why Heterosexual Males Feel Threatened by Gays," *Mademoiselle*; Patricia Elam Ruff, "Cover Girls," *Essence*; "Story of a Tragic Marriage," *Good Housekeeping*; and Linda Villarosa, ed., "Straight Women/Gay Men: A Talk between Friends," *Essence*.

3.   This theme of the heterosexual woman discovering her husband is a homosexual—or, less commonly, vice versa—became popular in women's magazines of the 1960s and 1970s. Another example is Kitty Kelley's article "I Married a Homosexual" (1977), a sensationalistic account in which the author gives her readers a description of her "disastrous entry into the bizarre world of homosexual men" (192). In 1968, *Good House-keeping* published a first-person account of a "tragic marriage" in which a women is horrified to discover that her husband is a "sexual pervert" ("Story" 40). The author hopes that her "sordid, unhappy story" can lead to further research about homosexuality so that "some day we can safe-guard our sons against the crippling illness of homosexuality just as we now routinely inoculate our children against diseases that maim and kill" (46). Also see Corning, "The Hardest Hurt to Heal."

4.   *Cosmopolitan's* interest in lesbianism comes as no surprise; among wom-en's magazines, it has long been one of the most explicit in discussions about sexuality, although this was not always true. First published in 1886, *Cosmo* was fairly staid and conventional until Helen Gurley Brown spiced it up when she became the editor of the Hearst Corporation publication in 1964. Her combination of frank discussions about sex-uality and advice about how a woman should find and keep her man made *Cosmo* a hit in the 1960s and 1970s. In the 1980s and 1990s *Cosmo* has grown even more adventurous in discussing sexuality, a reflection of society's increasing openness.

5.   After this steamy beginning, it is interesting that the writer is later careful to defuse the threat of lesbian sexuality: "Lesbians describe sex with other women as the most emotionally satisfying sex they've ever experienced, a

natural outgrowth of the emotional empathy they share. Ironically, it's this emotional bonding—mostly a blessing—that can be a bane, sexually, for some lesbian couples: According to researchers, women's yearning for intimacy—untempered by the traditional male urge for autonomy and distance—can lead some lesbian couples to fuse so closely that after several years the sexual spark (which hetero couples use to overcome distance between them) goes out entirely" (231). In other words, the sex might start out great, but do not expect it to last. Since heterosexuality is one of the underlying premises that support their production, women's magazines must be wary that they do not depict lesbianism as more appealing than heterosexuality.

6.   We see a very different style of photography of supposed lesbians in many recent high-fashion magazine advertisements where the photographer focuses on androgynous women who come equipped with such lesbian signifiers as leather jackets, motorcycles, or men's clothing. Clark describes the pleasure that lesbians take in these advertisements: "part of the pleasure . . . might be what Elizabeth Ellsworth calls 'lesbian verisimilitude,' or the representation of body language, facial expression, and general appearance that can be claimed and coded as 'lesbian' according to current standards of style within lesbian communities" (187). The photographs I examine in *Cosmopolitan* strive for no such lesbian verisimilitude but openly reveal that they are nothing more than staged theatrical performances of lesbianism. A simulacrum is created that fools no one, and lesbians are far more likely to read the *Cosmopolitan* women as heterosexual than as homosexual. The lesbian, even when she seems most central, is still peripheral.

7.   When talking about lesbianism, women's magazines commonly use personal narratives, but most frequently these women are heterosexual or have merely dallied with lesbianism. The heterosexual subject position thus retains its centrality. When a lesbian does speak, as in Alice Taylor's "Women in Love: Straight Talk from a Gay Woman," she is depicted as a sophisticated urbanite, typically from New York City, whose lesbianism fits into her generally avant-garde image and style. In this situation, the lesbian's voice serves the purpose of confirming her exotic nature and assuring readers that such a lifestyle is not the norm.

8.   Articles about contemporary lesbian fashions include Inge Blackman and Kathryn Perry, "Skirting the Issue: Lesbian Fashion for the 1990s"; Lisa Duggan, "The Anguished Cry of an 80s Fem: 'I Want to Be a Drag Queen'"; Arlene Stein, "All Dressed Up, but No Place to Go? Style Wars and the New Lesbianism"; and Elizabeth Wilson, "Deviant Dress."

4. Is Nancy Drew Queer?

1. Yet another television show about Nancy's exploits sprung up in the 1990s. In the fall of 1995, Nancy returned to television in a series that took the suburban sleuth into the big city.

2. The popularity of Maney's work has led her to write two sequels, *The Case of the Good-for-Nothing Girlfriend* (1994) and *Nancy Clue and the Hardly Boys in a Ghost in the Closet* (1995).

3. See "Barbie: Vengeance Is Mine!" For more information about Barbie's potential for subversion, see Michele Lloyd, "Barbie," and Erica Rand, *Barbie's Queer Accessories.*

4. For a thought-provoking feminist study of Nancy Drew, read Ellen Brown, "In Search of Nancy Drew, the Snow Queen, and Room Nineteen: Cruising for Feminine Discourse." Another feminist approach to Drew is found in Jackie Vivelo, "The Mystery of Nancy Drew." A feminist fictional retelling of Nancy Drew's life is Zana's "Nancy Drew and the Serial Rapist."

5. Some of the best-known essays about lesbian reading are Marilyn Farwell, "Heterosexual Plots and Lesbian Subtexts: Toward a Theory of Lesbian Narrative Space"; Jean E. Kennard, "Ourself behind Ourself: A Theory for Lesbian Readers"; and Catharine R. Stimpson, "Zero Degree Deviancy: The Lesbian Novel in English." Also see Terry Castle's related work in *The Apparitional Lesbian: Female Homosexuality and Modern Culture.*

6. For more information about the Stratemeyer syndicate, see Carol Billman, *The Secret of the Stratemeyer Syndicate: Nancy Drew, the Hardy Boys, and the Million Dollar Fiction Factory;* Deidre Johnson, *Edward Stratemeyer and the Stratemeyer Syndicate;* Russel Nye, *The Unembarrassed Muse: The Popular Arts in America;* Karen Plunkett-Powell, *The Nancy Drew Scrapbook;* Catherine Sheldrick Ross, " 'If They Read Nancy Drew, So What?': Series Book Readers Talk Back"; Peter A. Soderbergh, "The Stratemeyer Strain: Educators and the Juvenile Series Book, 1900–1973"; and Bruce Watson, "Tom Swift, Nancy Drew, and Pals All Had the Same Dad."

7. The Nancy Drew series was not unique in focusing on a girl sleuth. Dozens of other series about girl detectives exist including the Beverly Gray College Mystery Series (Grosset, 1934–55), the Blythe Girls (Grosset, 1925–32); the Connie Blair Mystery Series (Grosset, 1948–58), the Dana Girls Mystery Stories (Grosset, 1934–76), the Judy Bolton books (Gros-

set, 1932–67), the Kay Tracey Mystery Stories (Cupples, 1934–42), and the Penny Parker Mystery Stories (Cupples, 1941–58). These series, however, never achieved the same huge sales as did Nancy Drew. For an article on the success (or lack of success) of some of these series, see Anne Scott MacLeod, "Nancy Drew and Her Rivals: No Contest."

8. For more information on the difficulties of assigning authorship to the Nancy Drew books, see Geoffrey S. Lapin, "The Ghost of Nancy Drew," in which the author argues that Mildred Wirt Benson is Nancy Drew's true mother.

9. Background information about Nancy can be found in Billman 99–120; Betsy Caprio, *The Mystery of Nancy Drew: Girl Sleuth on the Couch;* Patricia Craig and Mary Cadogan, "A Sweet Girl Sleuth: The Teenage Detective in America"; Arthur Daigon, "The Strange Case of Nancy Drew"; Carolyn Stewart Dyer and Nancy Tillman Romalov, eds., *Rediscovering Nancy Drew;* John M. Enright, "Harriet Adams: The Secret of the Old Clock"; Deborah Felder, "Nancy Drew: Then and Now"; James P. Jones, "Nancy Drew, WASP Super Girl of the 1930's"; Bobbie Ann Mason, *The Girl Sleuth: A Feminist Guide* 48–75; Plunkett-Powell; Jackie Vivelo, "The Mystery of Nancy Drew"; and Lee Zacharias, "Nancy Drew, Ballbuster." The children's literature journal *The Lion and the Unicorn* also devoted an entire issue to Nancy (Nancy Drew Issue, June 1994).

10. The Nancy Drew series is not the first girls' series to focus on cars. The automobile had an important role in earlier series like the Motor Girls (1910–17), the Automobile Girls (1910–13), and the Motor Maids (1911–17) (See *Girls Series Books*). In numerous juvenile series during the first half of the century, the automobile offered characters "mobility, speed, protection, and often the opportunity to demonstrate exceptional physical coordination" (Vaughn 78). It is Nancy Drew, however, who has been most identified with the car that she drives. For more information on cars in early series novels, see my essay "On the Road and in the Air: Gender and Technology in Girls' Automobile and Airplane Serials, 1909–1932"; Nancy Tillman Romalov, "Mobile Heroines: Early Twentieth-Century Girls' Automobile Series"; and David K. Vaughn, "On the Road to Adventure: The Automobile and American Juvenile Series Fiction, 1900–1940."

11. Penelope J. Engelbrecht, for instance, writes: "Like many budding lesbians, I was once perplexed at clever Nancy Drew's retention of that tag-along boyfriend" (85).

12. Further accounts of the role of the butch-femme couple can be found in

Vern Bullough and Bonnie Bullough, "Lesbianism in the 1920s and 1930s: A Newfound Study"; Sheila Jeffreys, "Butch & Femme: Now and Then"; Elizabeth Lapovsky Kennedy and Madeline Davis, "The Reproduction of Butch-Fem Roles: A Social Constructionist Approach"; and Joan Nestle, ed., *The Persistent Desire: A Femme-Butch Reader.*

13. Studies that address the new image of Nancy Drew include Kathleen Chamberlain, "The Secrets of Nancy Drew: Having Their Cake and Eating It Too"; Frances Fitzgerald, "Women, Success, and Nancy Drew"; James Hirsch, "Nancy Drew Gets Real"; Connie Richards, "Nancy Drew: Gothic or Romance?"; and Nancy Wartik, "Nancy Drew, Yuppie Detective."

14. I would like to thank all the lesbian readers who talked to me about their youthful experiences with the Nancy Drew books.

5. "Candy-coated cyanide"

1. For more information about Louise Fitzhugh's sexual orientation, see Virginia L. Wolf, *Louise Fitzhugh.*

2. A number of bibliographical sources are available on gay and lesbian images in children's literature. See, for instance, Laurel A. Clyde and Marjorie Lobban, *Out of the Closet and into the Classroom: Homosexuality in Books for Young People*; Nancy Garden, "Dick and Jane Grow Up Gay: The Importance of (Gay) Young Adult Fiction"; Frances Hanckel and John Cunningham, "Can Young Gays Find Happiness in YA Books?"; Christine Jenkins, "Heartthrobs & Heartbreaks: A Guide to Young Adult Books with Gay Themes"; and D. E. Wilson, "The Open Library: YA Books for Gay Teens."

3. Children's books and young adult novels about gay men include Clayton Bess, *Big Man and the Burn-Out*; Francesca Lia Block, *Weetzie Bat* and *Witch Baby*; Forman Brown, *The Generous Jefferson Bartleby Jones*; Scott Bunn, *Just Hold On*; Aidan Chambers, *Dance on My Grave*; B. A. Ecker, *Independence Day*; Paula Fox, *The Eagle Kite*; Bette Greene, *The Drowning of Stephan Jones*; Lynn Hall, *Sticks and Stones*; Ann Heron and Meredith Maran, *How Would You Feel If Your Dad Was Gay?*; MaryKate Jordan, *Losing Uncle Tim*; M. E. Kerr, *Nightkites*; Ron Koertge, *The Arizona Kid*; Liza K. Murrow, *Twelve Days in August*; Sandra Scoppettone, *Trying Hard to Hear You*; Marilyn Singer, *The Course of True Love Never Did Run Smooth*; Judith Vigna, *My Two Uncles*; and Michael Willhoite, *Uncle What-Is-It Is Coming to Visit.*

4. See, for instance, Kirk Fuoss's essay "A Portrait of the Adolescent as a Young Gay: The Politics of Male Homosexuality in Young Adult Fiction" (1994).

5. Many different, sometimes conflicting, definitions of "children's literature" exist. In this chapter, I use it as an umbrella term with which to refer to both books written for small children and novels targeted at teenage readers. Children's literature is distinct from adult literature in that many of its themes are specifically related to children's concerns (i.e., maturation, sibling relationships, education). Also, children's books often, although not always, have more limited vocabularies than books for adults. Inevitably, "children's literature" is a term that escapes a narrow definition since, after all, children read many books written for adults and adults read many books written for children (think about *Anne of Green Gables, Gulliver's Travels, Little Women, The Adventures of Huckleberry Finn, Robinson Crusoe,* and *The Adventures of Tom Sawyer*).

6. A few of the many fine children's books from the 1990s that represent culturally diverse populations include Margaree King Mitchell, *Uncle Jed's Barbershop;* Gloria Jean Pinkney, *The Sunday Outing;* Patricia Polacco, *Chicken Sunday;* Faith Ringgold, *Tar Beach;* Allen Say, *Grandfather's Journey;* Gary Soto, *Too Many Tamales;* Joyce Carol Thomas, *Brown Honey in Broomwheat Tea;* and Sherley Anne Williams, *Working Cotton.*

7. Kirk Fuoss describes the complex web of relationships that surrounds children's books, making censorship possible on several different levels. Although Fuoss is talking particularly about young adult novels with gay male themes, his words apply to all children's literature: "YA novels that address homosexuality are embedded in a complex network of power relations, including, among other agents of power, authors, readers, editors, reviewers, and library acquisition staffs" (169). This Foucauldian web of power makes it difficult, often impossible, for children's books with gay or lesbian themes ever to get published. Market forces even act as a form of censorship, since many publishing companies worry about the commercial viability of gay and lesbian children's books.

8. Literature is not the only media form where images of gays and lesbians are censored for a young audience. Anything can be censored. One parent complained about a school showing the television show "Sesame Street" to youngsters because Bert and Ernie, two puppets, are male and live together; thus they might encourage homosexuality (Weiser A5). For more information on how depictions of gay and lesbian youth are censored on television, see Alfred P. Kielwasser and Michelle A. Wolf's arti-

cle "Mainstream Television, Adolescent Homosexuality, and Significant Silence."

9. For information about the legal debate surrounding lesbian parents and their children, see Nancy D. Polikoff, "Lesbian Mothers, Lesbian Families: Legal Obstacles, Legal Challenges."

10. Works that address censorship and gay or lesbian children's literature include Michael Cart, "Annie . . . Still on Our Minds"; Michael Thomas Ford, "Gay Books for Young Readers: When Caution Calls the Shots"; Nancy Garden, "Banned: Lesbian and Gay Kids' Books under Fire"; Mary Jo Godwin, "Conservative Groups Continue Their Fight to Ban *Daddy's Roommate*"; Susan Podrygula, "Censorship in an Academic Library"; and Michael J. Sadowski, "In Biggest School Challenge, *Daddy's Roommate* Is Staying."

11. Accounts that address what it means to be a gay or lesbian youth today include Linnea Due, *Joining the Tribe: Growing Up Gay & Lesbian in the '90s*; Tony Grima, ed., *Not the Only One: Lesbian and Gay Fiction for Teens*; Gilbert Herdt and Andrew Boxer, *Children of Horizons: How Gay and Lesbian Teens Are Leading a New Way Out of the Closet*; Ann Heron, ed., *Two Teenagers in Twenty: Writings by Gay and Lesbian Youth*; Rachel Pollack and Cheryl Schwartz, *The Journey Out: A Guide for and about Lesbian, Gay, and Bisexual Teens*; Bennet L. Singer, ed., *Growing Up Gay: A Literary Anthology*; Roger Sutton, *Hearing Us Out: Voices from the Gay and Lesbian Community*; and Gerald Unks, ed., *The Gay Teen: Educational Practice and Theory for Lesbian, Gay, and Bisexual Adolescents*.

12. For another example of a juvenile novel that focuses on a lesbian crush, see Catherine Brett, *S. P. Likes A. D.*

13. The fact that *Heather Has Two Mommies* tied for the title of second-most-challenged book on the American Library Association's list stands in glaring contrast to the book's syrupy content ("*Daddy's*" 368).

6. Lost in Space

1. Recent geography studies shaped by postmodernism and feminism have influenced my thinking about queer geography. See, e.g., John A. Agnew and James S. Duncan, eds., *The Power of Place: Bringing Together Geographical and Sociological Imaginations*; James Duncan and David Ley, eds., *Place/Culture/Representation*; J. Nicholas Entrikin, *The Betweenness*

of Place: Towards a Geography of Modernity; Derek Gregory, *Geographical Imaginations;* Susan Hanson and Geraldine Pratt, *Gender, Work, and Space;* Michael Keith and Steve Pile, eds., *Place and the Politics of Identity;* Gillian Rose's feminist critique of traditional geography studies, *Feminism and Geography: The Limits of Geographical Knowledge;* Edward H. Soja, *Postmodern Geographies: The Reassertion of Space in Critical Social Theory;* and Women and Geography Study Group of the IBG, *Geography and Gender: An Introduction to Feminist Geography.*

For information specifically about lesbians and gay men and their relationship to space, see Sy Adler and Johanna Brenner, "Gender and Space: Lesbians and Gay Men in the City"; many of the essays in the outstanding collection edited by David Bell and Gill Valentine, *Mapping Desire: Geographies of Sexualities;* Gill Valentine, "Toward a Geography of the Lesbian Community"; Barbara Weightman, "Commentary: Towards a Geography of the Gay Community"; and Maxine Wolfe, "Invisible Women in Invisible Places: Lesbians, Lesbian Bars, and the Social Production of People/Environment Relationships."

2. I decided to vary terminology in this chapter to show that many of the topics addressed are applicable to *all* queers, however they might define that term. In some places, I refer to "queers"; in other places, my preferred terminology is "lesbians and gays." Sometimes, I use "gays" to refer to both gay men and lesbians. Elsewhere "gay" or "lesbian" is used when the issues discussed apply specifically to one group or the other. In yet other places I speak from a subject position that is particularly coded as "lesbian" to ensure that lesbians are not subsumed by the generic word "gay." These variations in terminology, I believe, are important in order to understand the slippage and confusion of identities that constitute queer communities.

3. A text that analyzes the cultural focus on the East and West Coasts and the reasons behind it is Patrick Douglas, *East Coast/West Coast.*

4. Studies of lesbian/gay experiences outside of New York, San Francisco, and Los Angeles include Martha Barron Barrett, *Invisible Lives: The Truth about Millions of Women-Loving-Women;* Frank Browning, *The Culture of Desire: Paradox and Perversity in Gay Lives Today,* and *A Queer Geography: Journeys toward a Sexual Self;* Joseph P. Goodwin, *More Man Than You'll Ever Be: Gay Folklore and Acculturation in Middle America;* Elizabeth Lapovsky Kennedy and Madeline Davis, *Boots of Leather, Slippers of Gold: The History of a Lesbian Community;* Susan Krieger, *The Mirror Dance: Identity in a Women's Community;* Neil Miller, *In Search of Gay America: Women and Men in a Time of Change;* James T. Sears, "The Impact of

Gender and Race on Growing Up Lesbian and Gay in the South"; and Edmund White, *States of Desire: Travels in Gay America*. A number of these works, however, including those by Barrett, Browning, Miller, and White, devote significant space to life in New York, San Francisco, and Los Angeles.

5. There have been numerous studies of the influence of environment on people's sense of well-being and feeling of belonging. See Barbara Allen and Thomas J. Schlereth, eds., *Sense of Place: American Regional Cultures*; Winifred Gallagher, *The Power of Place: How Our Surroundings Shape Our Thoughts, Emotions, and Actions*; John Brinckerhoff Jackson, *A Sense of Place, a Sense of Time*; and Simon Schama, *Landscape and Memory*.

6. Studies that focus on different forms of lesbian community include Marilyn Frye, "The Possibility of Lesbian Community"; Denyse Lockard, "The Lesbian Community: An Anthropological Approach"; Barbara Ponse, *Identities in the Lesbian World: The Social Construction of Self*; Kath Weston, *Families We Choose: Lesbians, Gays, Kinship*; and Deborah Goleman Wolf, *The Lesbian Community*.

7. My thanks to Michele Lloyd for suggesting this idea.

8. Similarly, in her essay, "Do Clothes Make the Woman? Gender, Performance Theory, and Lesbian Eroticism," Kath Weston concentrates solely on the lesbian fashions found in San Francisco at a lesbian prom night sponsored by a local women's center. Some of the articles that emphasize the high-fashion lesbian styles found in such urban centers as New York or San Francisco include Lisa Duggan, "The Anguished Cry of an 80s Fem: 'I Want to Be a Drag Queen'"; Esther Kaplan, "All Dressed Up, No Place to Go?"; and Arlene Stein, "All Dressed Up, but No Place to Go? Style Wars and the New Lesbianism."

9. In Cincinnati, I do not have the same access to lesbian friends that I had in San Francisco, and therefore I make a different political statement, whether I wish to or not. Queer friends make one visible; they provide support and a sense of community. Peter M. Nardi writes about how friendship functions in gay communities: "[G]ay friendship can be seen as a political statement, since at the core of the concept of friendship is the idea of 'being oneself' in a cultural context that may not approve of that self. For many people, the need to belong with others in dissent and out of the mainstream is central to the maintenance of self and identity" (115).

10. María Lugones calls such movement between different cultures and communities "world traveling": "I think that most of us who are outside

the mainstream of, for example, the U.S. dominant construction or organization of life, are 'world travelers' as a matter of necessity and of survival. It seems to me that inhabiting more than one 'world' at the same time and 'traveling' between 'worlds' is part and parcel of our experience and our situation" (282).

11. Numerous sources are available on the distinct regional identities of the United States. Geographical studies include Michael Bradshaw, *Regions and Regionalism in the United States*; and Raymond D. Gastil, "Cultural Regions of America." For an economic study, see Ann Markusen, *Regions: The Economics and Politics of Territory.*

12. For a collection that addresses rural lesbians and their perception of the importance of place, see Joyce Cheney, ed., *Lesbian Land.*

7. To Pass or Not to Pass

1. Shirlee Haizlip also creates a flexible definition of passing. She talks about blacks who pass as whites, but her words also apply to homosexuals who pass as heterosexuals: "[I]f you look white, marry white, live in a white community, attend a white church and a white school, join white associations, have white-looking children and grandchildren, you are 'white,' as defined by the majority in this country" (47–48). In a similar fashion, lesbians can pass as heterosexual by adopting signifiers of straight identity. Having a child, marrying a man, wearing a wedding band, having a picture of a man on one's desk—these are just a few of the many ways that lesbians can masquerade as heterosexual.

2. Interestingly enough, not passing fails to offer a woman a more satisfying life in Larsen's fictional universe. In her novel *Quicksand* (1928), the protagonist, Helga Crane, a mulatto, finds only misery because she can fit into neither white nor black society, even though she attempts to fit into both.

3. Sources that include information about women who have passed as men in the past include Rudolf Dekker and Lotte C. van de Pol, *The Tradition of Female Transvestism in Early Modern Europe*; Lillian Faderman, *Surpassing the Love of Men: Romantic Friendship and Love between Women from the Renaissance to the Present*, and *Odd Girls and Twilight Lovers: A History of Lesbian Life in Twentieth-Century America*; San Francisco Lesbian and Gay History Project, "'She Even Chewed Tobacco': A Pictorial Narrative of Passing Women in America"; Marian West, "Women Who

Have Passed as Men"; and Julie Wheelwright, *Amazons and Military Maids: Women Who Dressed as Men in the Pursuit of Life, Liberty, and Happiness.* Other studies of women and cross-dressing include Vern L. Bullough and Bonnie Bullough, *Cross Dressing, Sex, and Gender;* Anne Herrmann, "Travesty and Transgression: Transvestism in Shakespeare, Brecht, and Churchill"; Sherrie A. Inness, "Girls Will Be Boys and Boys Will Be Girls: Cross-Dressing in Popular Turn-of-the-Century College Fiction"; and Kristina Straub, "The Guilty Pleasures of Female Theatrical Cross-Dressing and the Autobiography of Charlotte Charke."

4. Other narrative descriptions of what it means for a woman to pass as a man include Alisa Solomon's "Rites of Passing" and Leslie Feinberg's novel *Stone Butch Blues.*

5. In her essay "Passing in *Europa, Europa:* Escape into Estrangement" (1995), Julie Inness writes: "Oppression produces superb actors. Jews take on gentile roles. Homosexuals learn to play the part of heterosexuals. African-Americans mask themselves as whites. All learn to live life as a masquerade, donning costume after costume in order to survive in a hostile world" (218).

8. GI Joes in Barbie Land

1. A complete history of butch is beyond the scope of this chapter, but a brief explanation is useful. It is impossible to state exactly when butch became a clear identity. The historian Martha Vicinus argues that the "mannish lesbian," a forerunner to the butch, appeared in the early 1800s (480) and points out that in the nineteenth century women such as George Sand, Rosa Bonheur, and Harriet Hosmer dressed and acted in a mannish fashion. Some of these women, if not all of them, were undoubtedly precursors of the twentieth-century butch, but they lacked the politicized notion of themselves as both butches and lesbians. By the late nineteenth century, Richard von Krafft-Ebing and Havelock Ellis were stressing the masculine appearance of the typical female invert. Some historians, such as Faderman, have suggested that cross-dressed "inverts" in the 1890s were the first "conscious 'butches' and 'femmes'" (*Odd Girls* 59), but these women may not have perceived themselves as such.

    Butch and femme roles were commonly found in the white, working-class, urban lesbian subculture of the 1920s (Faderman, *Odd Girls* 80). Butches and femmes also existed in the middle and upper classes of the time, two of the most famous being Gertrude Stein and

Radclyffe Hall. As the century progressed, butch-femme roles became even more prominent in the lesbian communities of the United States. By the 1940s and 1950s, butch-femme roles were essential for many lesbians, particularly working-class or young women. As Elizabeth L. Kennedy and Madeline Davis write about the mid-twentieth-century working-class lesbian culture in Buffalo, New York, "butch-fem roles were what we call a social imperative. They were the organizing principle for this community's relation to the outside world and for its members' relationships with one another" (*Boots* 244). Some women did resist butch-femme roles, but they were often made to feel uncomfortable and marginalized by those who did adopt roles. Audre Lorde, for instance, felt uneasy with the strict roles adopted by many black lesbians in the 1950s: "Their need for power and control seemed a much-too-open piece of myself, dressed in enemy clothing. They were tough in a way I felt I could never be" (224).

2. The butch-femme scale is similar to (and possibly derived from) the Kinsey sexuality scale. The scale ranges from 1 to 10, where 1 represents an extreme expression of femininity and 10 represents extreme masculinity (in some parts of the country the poles are reversed). A rating of 5.5 is perfect androgyny.

3. Some exceptions are Lily Burana and Roxxie Linnea, eds., *Dagger: On Butch Women*; Colleen Lamos, "The Postmodern Lesbian Position: *On Our Backs*"; Gayle Rubin, "Of Catamites and Kings: Reflections on Butch, Gender, and Boundaries"; and Alisa Solomon, "Not Just a Passing Fancy: Notes on Butch."

4. Many scholars have focused almost exclusively on butch-femme relationships. For histories of butches and butch-femme relationships, see Vern Bullough and Bonnie Bullough, "Lesbianism in the 1920s and 1930s: A Newfound Study"; Madeline Davis and Elizabeth Lapovsky Kennedy, "Oral History and the Study of Sexuality in the Lesbian Community: Buffalo, New York, 1940–1960"; Kennedy and Davis, *Boots of Leather, Slippers of Gold: The History of a Lesbian Community*, "The Reproduction of Butch-Fem Roles: A Social Constructionist Approach," and "'They Was No One to Mess With': The Construction of the Butch Role in the Lesbian Community of the 1940s and 1950s"; Lillian Faderman, *Odd Girls and Twilight Lovers*, and "The Return of Butch and Femme: A Phenomenon in Lesbian Sexuality of the 1980s and 1990s"; Sheila Jeffreys, "Butch & Femme: Now and Then"; Joan Nestle, "Butch-Fem Relationships: Sexual Courage in the 1950's," and many of the articles in Nestle, ed., *The Persistent Desire: A Femme-Butch Reader*. George Chauncey, Jr., in

"From Sexual Inversion," and Martha Vicinus both provide excellent summaries of how "wife" and "husband" roles were associated with lesbian behavior before the twentieth century. In addition, Esther Newton describes the importance of the 1920s masculine lesbian in her essay "The Mythic Mannish Lesbian: Radclyffe Hall and the New Woman." For a contemporary analysis of butch-femme roles, see Michele Fisher, "Butch Nouveau," or Kath Weston's thoughtful essay "Do Clothes Make the Woman?: Gender, Performance Theory, and Lesbian Eroticism."

5. Though this chapter's focus is primarily on the butch, I recognize and appreciate the importance of femmes in lesbian culture, and conclusions similar to those I shall draw could probably be arrived at by studying the femme. A number of scholars have produced important accounts of femme identity. The best-known is Joan Nestle; see her essay "The Fem Question." Also see Paula Mariedaughter, "Too Butch for Straights, Too Femme for Dykes"; Lesléa Newman, ed., *The Femme Mystique;* and Tracy Morgan, "Butch-Femme and the Politics of Identity." Christine Holmlund discusses femme identity in the context of mainstream films in "When Is a Lesbian Not a Lesbian? The Lesbian Continuum and the Mainstream Femme Film."

6. Other fictional accounts about what it means to be a butch include Antoinette Azolakov, *Cass and the Stone Butch;* Leslie Feinberg, *Stone Butch Blues;* Lee Lynch, *Toothpick House;* and Jay Rayn, *Butch II.*

7. Loulan describes an exercise in which she asks a random member of the audience to come to the front of the room and then has audience members, most of whom do not know the volunteer, rate the position of this woman on the butch-femme scale. "The fact that the audience is for the most part in agreement indicates to me that there is a collective opinion about where a woman fits on the butch/femme scale" (44).

8. I recognize the difficulties of discussing what constitutes a butch—as is any lesbian, she is an entity that does not and cannot exist according to the dominant heterosexual reality. As Sarah Hoagland points out, "In the conceptual schemes of phallocracies there is no category of woman-identified-woman, woman-loving-woman or woman-centered-woman; that is, there is no such thing as a lesbian" (qtd. in Frye, "To See" 77), and Marilyn Frye concurs that "Lesbians are outside the [phallocratic] conceptual scheme, and this is something done, not just the way things are" ("To See" 92). Nevertheless, I attempt to use what words and concepts are available to describe the phenomenon of the butch rather than enter into an epistemological discussion that could only replicate the work of Frye.

9. See Kennedy and Davis's excellent study, *Boots of Leather, Slippers of Gold: The History of a Lesbian Community.*

10. The subhead to this section is a quotation from Loulan 113.

11. "Diesel dyke" is a term used by both homosexuals and heterosexuals to define a lesbian who is domineering, aggressive, brash, hypermasculine, and frequently working class. Stereotypically, she is depicted driving a Harley-Davidson motorcycle and spending too much time in lesbian bars, drinking beer and playing pool: "we see her in the image of the 50s and 60s, dressed in her jeans with the pegged legs, motorcycle boots, worn workshirt open at the neck, short hair slicked down, swaggering across the barroom floor with her arm around a sweet young thing" ("Femme and Butch" 100).

12. At different points, popular boys' haircuts, such as the D.A., the crewcut, and the flattop, have all been adopted by lesbians. Actually, any short "boy's haircut," which makes no attempt to camouflage itself as a pixie cut or any other girl's hair style, is a butch look. Butch haircuts are influenced by age, class, ethnicity, and race and are constantly evolving. A lesbian who came out in the 1950s might still wear her hair in a D.A., whereas a young 1990s butch might shave the sides of her head.

13. Whether heterosexuals perceive a masculine woman as a lesbian or not is a complicated process, which works in a variety of ways. Though her masculine appearance alone makes her suspect, other factors are involved, such as her profession, marital status, friends, and hobbies. A masculine physical education teacher is more likely to be thought a lesbian than a masculine home economics teacher. And a single, masculine woman who rides a Harley and goes on camping trips with groups of other women is more apt to be categorized as a lesbian than is a masculine woman who lives with a boyfriend and goes on hiking trips with a mixed group of men and women.

14. With thanks to Joanna Russ, *The Female Man.* Marilyn Frye makes the following observation: "The term 'female man' has a tension of logical impossibility about it that is absent from parallel terms like 'female cat' and 'female terrier'" (86).

Works Cited

Adams, Jane. "When Your Friend Tells You She's Gay." *Glamour* 80 (Apr. 1982): 264–65; 291.

Adler, Sy, and Johanna Brenner. "Gender and Space: Lesbians and Gay Men in the City." *International Journal of Urban and Regional Research* 16.1 (1992): 24–34.

"Against the Wall." New York Times, 25 Aug. 1929: 14.

Agnew, John A., and James S. Duncan, eds. *The Power of Place: Bringing Together Geographical and Sociological Imaginations.* Boston: Unwin Hyman, 1989.

Allen, Barbara, and Thomas J. Schlereth, eds. *Sense of Place: American Regional Cultures.* Lexington: UP of Kentucky, 1990.

Allen, Frederick Lewis. *Only Yesterday: An Informal History of the Nineteen-Twenties.* New York: Harper, 1931.

Anzaldúa, Gloria. *Borderlands/La Frontera: The New Mestiza.* San Francisco: Spinsters, 1987.

Ardill, Susan, and Sue O'Sullivan. "Butch/Femme Obsessions." *Feminist Review* 34 (Spring 1990): 79–85.

Azolakov, Antoinette. *Cass and the Stone Butch.* Austin: Banned Books, 1987.

Barale, Michèle Aina. "Below the Belt: (Un)covering *The Well of Loneliness.*" *Inside/Out: Lesbian Theories, Gay Theories.* Ed. Diana Fuss. New York: Routledge, 1991. 235–57.

"Barbie: Vengeance Is Mine!" *Off Our Backs* 24.2 (Feb. 1994): 4.

Barrett, Martha Barron. "Double Lives: What It's Like to Be Lesbian Today." *Glamour* 87.9 (Sept. 1989): 316–17; 352; 356; 358–59.

——. *Invisible Lives: The Truth about Millions of Women-Loving-Women.* New York: Morrow, 1989.

Bartocci, Barbara. "'Mom, I'm Gay': Coping with the News No Parent Wants to Hear." *Woman's Day* 55.17 (3 Nov. 1992): 76–81.

Bauer, Marion Dane, ed. *Am I Blue? Coming Out from the Silence.* New York: HarperCollins, 1994.

Baum, L. Frank. *The Marvelous Land of Oz. Classics of Children's Literature.* Ed. John W. Griffith and Charles H. Frey. New York: Macmillan, 1992. 771–856.

Bell, David, and Gill Valentine, eds. *Mapping Desire: Geographies of Sexualities.* New York: Routledge, 1995.

Belot, Adolphe. *Mademoiselle Giraud, My Wife.* 1870. Chicago: Laird and Lee, 1892.

Bess, Clayton. *Big Man and the Burn-Out.* Boston: Houghton Mifflin, 1985.

Billman, Carol. *The Secret of the Stratemeyer Syndicate: Nancy Drew, the Hardy Boys, and the Million Dollar Fiction Factory.* New York: Ungar, 1986.

Black, Pam. "When a Friend Tells You She's Gay." *Mademoiselle* 89 (Mar. 1983): 248; 250.

Blackman, Inge, and Kathryn Perry. "Skirting the Issue: Lesbian Fashion for the 1990s." *Feminist Review* 34 (1990): 67–78.

Blanchard, Phyllis. *The Adolescent Girl: A Study from the Psychoanalytic Viewpoint.* New York: Dodd, Mead, 1924.

Blasius, Mark. "An Ethos of Lesbian and Gay Existence." *Political Theory* 20.4 (1992): 642–71.

Block, Francesca Lia. *Weetzie Bat.* New York: Harper, 1989.

——. *Witch Baby.* New York: HarperCollins, 1991.

Blunt, Alison, and Gillian Rose. Introduction. *Writing Women and Space: Colonial and Postcolonial Geographies.* Ed. Alison Blunt and Gillian Rose. New York: Guilford, 1994. 1–25.

"Board Tells Reason for Banning Book." *Kansas City Star,* 5 Oct. 1995: C-4.

Bourdet, Edouard. *The Captive.* New York: Brentano's, 1926.

Bradshaw, Michael. *Regions and Regionalism in the United States.* Jackson: UP of Mississippi, 1988.

Brett, Catherine. *S. P. Likes A. D.* Toronto: Women's P, 1989.

Brittain, Vera. *Radclyffe Hall: A Case of Obscenity?* London: Femina, 1968.

Bromley, Dorothy, and Florence Britten. *Youth and Sex: A Study of 1300 College Students.* New York: Harper, 1938.

Brown, Ellen. "In Search of Nancy Drew, the Snow Queen, and Room Nineteen: Cruising for Feminine Discourse." *Frontiers* 13.2 (1992): 1–25.

Brown, Forman. *The Generous Jefferson Bartleby Jones*. Boston: Alyson Won-derland, 1991.

Brown, Jan. "Sex, Lies, and Penetration: A Butch Finally 'Fesses Up." *The Persistent Desire: A Femme-Butch Reader.* Ed. Joan Nestle. Boston: Alyson, 1992. 410–15.

Brown, John Mason. "Diadems of Paste." *Theatre Arts Monthly* 10 (1926): 809–22.

Brown, Patricia Leigh. "Nancy Drew: 30's Sleuth, 90's Role Model." *New York Times,* 19 Apr. 1993: A1; B12.

Browning, Frank. *The Culture of Desire: Paradox and Perversity in Gay Lives Today.* New York: Crown, 1993.

——. *A Queer Geography: Journeys toward a Sexual Self.* New York: Crown, 1996.

Bullough, Vern L., and Bonnie Bullough. *Cross Dressing, Sex, and Gender.* Philadelphia: U of Pennsylvania P, 1993.

——. "Lesbianism in the 1920s and 1930s: A Newfound Study." *Signs* 2 (1977): 895–904.

Bunn, Scott. *Just Hold On.* New York: Delacorte, 1982.

Burana, Lily, and Roxxie Linnea, eds. *Dagger: On Butch Women.* San Francisco: Cleis, 1994.

Burston, Paul, and Colin Richardson, eds. *A Queer Romance: Lesbians, Gay Men, and Popular Culture.* New York: Routledge, 1995.

Butler, Judith. *Bodies that Matter: On the Discursive Limits of 'Sex.'* New York: Routledge, 1993.

——. *Gender Trouble: Feminism and the Subversion of Identity.* New York: Routledge, 1990.

——. "Imitation and Gender Insubordination." *Inside/Out: Lesbian Theories, Gay Theories.* Ed. Diana Fuss. New York: Routledge, 1991. 13–31.

Calverton, V. F. *Sex Expression in Literature.* New York: Boni and Liveright, 1926.

Caprio, Betsy. *The Mystery of Nancy Drew: Girl Sleuth on the Couch.* Trabuco Canyon, Calif.: Source Books, 1992.

Carb, David. "The Captive." *Vogue* 68 (1926): 82–83.

Card, Claudia. *Lesbian Choices.* New York: Columbia UP, 1995.

Cart, Michael. "Annie . . . Still on Our Minds." *Booklist* 91.2 (15 Sept. 1994): 127.

Case, Sue-Ellen. "Towards a Butch-Femme Aesthetic." *Discourse* 11 (Winter 1988–89): 55–73.

Castle, Terry. *The Apparitional Lesbian: Female Homosexuality and Modern Culture.* New York: Columbia UP, 1993.

Caughie, Pamela L. "Passing as Pedagogy: Feminism in(to) Cultural Studies." *English Studies/Culture Studies: Institutionalizing Dissent.* Ed. Isaiah Smithson and Nancy Ruff. Urbana: U of Illinois P, 1994. 76–93.

Chamberlain, Kathleen. "The Secrets of Nancy Drew: Having Their Cake and Eating It Too." *The Lion and the Unicorn* 18.1 (1994): 1–12.

Chambers, Aidan. *Dance on My Grave.* New York: Harper and Row, 1982.

Chapman, Bernadine. "The Quest for Nancy Drew." *Antiques & Collecting Hobbies* 98.6 (Aug. 1993): 29–31.

Chauncey, George, Jr. "From Sexual Inversion to Homosexuality: The Changing Medical Conceptualization of Female 'Deviance.'" *Passion and Power: Sexuality in History.* Ed. Kathy Peiss and Christina Simmons. Philadelphia: Temple UP, 1989. 87–117.

———. *Gay New York: Gender, Urban Culture, and the Making of the Gay Male World, 1890–1940.* New York: Basic, 1994.

Cheney, Anne. *Millay in Greenwich Village.* University: U of Alabama P, 1975.

Cheney, Joyce, ed. *Lesbian Land.* Minneapolis: Word Weavers, 1985.

Chideckel, Maurice. *Female Sex Perversion.* New York: Eugenics, 1935.

Clark, Danae. "Commodity Lesbianism." *Camera Obscura* 25–26 (1991): 181–201.

Cliff, Michelle. *The Land of Look Behind.* Ithaca: Firebrand, 1985.

Clyde, Laurel A., and Marjorie Lobban. *Out of the Closet and into the Classroom: Homosexuality in Books for Young People.* Port Melbourne: ALIA Thorpe, 1992.

Collins, Joseph. *The Doctor Looks at Love and Life.* Garden City, N.Y.: Doran, 1926.

Coolidge, Calvin. "Enemies of the Republic: Are the 'Reds' Stalking Our College Women?" *Delineator* (June 1921): 4–5; 66–67.

Cordova, Jeanne. "Butches, Lies, and Feminism." *The Persistent Desire: A Femme-Butch Reader.* Ed. Joan Nestle. Boston: Alyson, 1992. 272–92.

Corning, Peg. "The Hardest Hurt to Heal: Losing Your Husband to a Man." *Glamour* 76 (Apr. 1978): 140; 145–46.

Cott, Nancy F. *The Grounding of Modern Feminism.* New Haven: Yale UP, 1987.

Craig, Patricia, and Mary Cadogan. "A Sweet Girl Sleuth: The Teenage Detective in America." *The Lady Investigates: Women Detectives and Spies in Fiction.* New York: St. Martin's, 1981. 149–63.

Creekmur, Corey K., and Alexander Doty, eds. *Out in Culture: Gay, Lesbian, and Queer Essays on Popular Culture.* Durham: Duke UP, 1995.

Cunningham, Amy. "Not Just Another Prom Night." *Glamour* 90 (June 1992): 222–25; 259–62.

"*Daddy's Roommate* Year's 'Most Challenged' Book." *American Libraries* 26.4 (Apr. 1995): 368.

Daigon, Arthur. "The Strange Case of Nancy Drew." *English Journal* 53 (1964): 666–69.

"Dance on the Tortoise." *New York Times,* 6 Sept. 1930: 6.

Dane, Clemence. *Regiment of Women*. 1917. New York: Macmillan, 1932.

Davis, Katharine Bement. "Why They Failed to Marry." *Harper's Magazine* 156 (Mar. 1928): 460–69.

Davis, Madeline, and Elizabeth Lapovsky Kennedy. "Oral History and the Study of Sexuality in the Lesbian Community: Buffalo, New York, 1940–1960." *Hidden from History: Reclaiming the Gay and Lesbian Past.* Ed. Martin Duberman, Martha Vicinus, and George Chauncey, Jr. New York: New American Library, 1989. 426–40.

Dekker, Rudolf, and Lotte C. van de Pol. *The Tradition of Female Transvestism in Early Modern Europe.* New York: St. Martin's, 1989.

de Lauretis, Teresa. "Sexual Indifference and Lesbian Representation." *Performing Feminisms: Feminist Critical Theory and Theatre.* Ed. Sue-Ellen Case. Baltimore: Johns Hopkins UP, 1990. 17–39.

Dell, Floyd. *Love in the Machine Age: A Psychological Study of the Transition from Patriarchal Society.* New York: Farrar and Rinehart, 1930.

D'Emilio, John. *Sexual Politics, Sexual Communities: The Making of a Homosexual Minority in the United States, 1940–1970.* Chicago: U of Chicago P, 1983.

Devor, Holly. *Gender Blending: Confronting the Limits of Duality.* Bloomington: Indiana UP, 1989.

Dhairyam, Sagri. "Racing the Lesbian, Dodging White Critics." *The Lesbian Postmodern.* Ed. Laura Doan. New York: Columbia UP, 1994. 25–46.

Disney, Dorothy Cameron. "Alma Hid from the Truth." *Ladies' Home Journal* 85.10 (Oct. 1968): 30–33.

Dolan, Jill. *Presence and Desire: Essays on Gender, Sexuality, and Performance.* Ann Arbor: U of Michigan P, 1993.

Doner, Kalia. "Women's Magazines: Slouching towards Feminism." *Social Policy* 23 (1993): 37–43.

Donovan, John. *I'll Get There: It Better Be Worth the Trip.* New York: Harper and Row, 1969.

Donovan, Stacey. *Dive.* New York: Dutton, 1994.

Douglas, Patrick. *East Coast/West Coast.* New York: D. I. Fine, 1989.

Duberman, Martin. *Stonewall.* New York: Dutton, 1993.

Due, Linnea. *Joining the Tribe: Growing Up Gay & Lesbian in the '90s.* New York: Anchor, 1995.

Duggan, Lisa. "The Anguished Cry of an 80s Fem: 'I Want to Be a Drag Queen.'" *Out/Look* 1.1 (1988): 62–65.

Dumenil, Lynn. *Freemasonry and American Culture, 1880–1930.* Princeton: Princeton UP, 1984.

Duncan, James, and David Ley, eds. *Place/Culture/Representation.* New York: Routledge, 1993.

Durbin, Karen. "The Intelligent Woman's Guide to Sex." *Mademoiselle* 82 (June 1976): 46; 54.

Dyer, Carolyn Stewart, and Nancy Tillman Romalov, eds. *Rediscovering Nancy Drew.* Iowa City: U of Iowa P, 1995.

Eaton, S. Catherine. "A Matter of Pride: Being a Gay Woman in the Nineties." *Cosmopolitan* 215.5 (Nov. 1993): 226–29.

Ebert, Alan. "Lea Hopkins: Just Different." *Essence* 10 (Apr. 1980): 88–89; 124; 127–36.

Ecker, B. A. *Independence Day.* New York: Avon Flare, 1983.

Ellis, Havelock. "The School-Friendships of Girls." *Studies in the Psychology of Sex.* 1897. New York: Random House, 1942. 368–84.

——. *Studies in the Psychology of Sex.* 1897. Vol 1. New York: Random House, 1936.

Ellison, Ralph. *Invisible Man.* 1952. New York: Random House, 1982.

Elwin, Rosamund, and Michele Paulse. *Asha's Mums.* Toronto: Women's P, 1990.

Engelbrecht, Penelope E. "'Lifting Belly Is a Language': The Postmodern Lesbian Subject." *Feminist Studies* 16.1 (1990): 85–114.

Enright, John M. "Harriet Adams: The Secret of the Old Clock." *Dime Novel Roundup* 58.4 (Aug. 1989): 52.

Entrikin, J. Nicholas. *The Betweenness of Place: Towards a Geography of Modernity.* Baltimore: Johns Hopkins UP, 1991.

Ernst, Morris L., and William Seagle. *To the Pure . . . : A Study of Obscenity and the Censor.* New York: Viking, 1928.

Ewen, Stuart. *All Consuming Images: The Politics of Style in Contemporary Culture.* New York: Basic, 1988.

Fabian, Warner. *Unforbidden Fruit.* New York: Boni and Liveright, 1928.

Faderman, Lillian. *Odd Girls and Twilight Lovers: A History of Lesbian Life in Twentieth-Century America.* New York: Columbia UP, 1991.

——. "The Return of Butch and Femme: A Phenomenon in Lesbian Sexuality of the 1980s and 1990s." *Journal of the History of Sexuality* 2 (1992): 578–96.

——. *Surpassing the Love of Men: Romantic Friendship and Love between Women from the Renaissance to the Present.* New York: Morrow, 1981.

Farwell, Marilyn. "Heterosexual Plots and Lesbian Subtexts: Toward a Theory of Lesbian Narrative Space." *Lesbian Texts and Contexts: Radical Revisions.* Ed. Karla Jay and Joanne Glasgow. New York: New York UP, 1990. 91–103.

Feinberg, Leslie. *Stone Butch Blues.* Ithaca: Firebrand, 1993.

Felder, Deborah. "Nancy Drew: Then and Now." *Publishers Weekly* 229.22 (30 May 1986): 30–34.

"Femme and Butch: A Readers' Forum." *Lesbian Ethics* 2 (Fall 1986): 86–104.

Ferguson, Marjorie. *Forever Feminine: Women's Magazines and the Cult of Femininity.* London: Heinemann, 1983.

Fetterley, Judith F. "Writes of Passing." *Gossip* 5 (1991): 21–28.

Fisher, Michele. "Butch Nouveau." *Utne Reader,* Aug. 1996: 27–28.

Fiske, John. *Understanding Popular Culture.* New York: Routledge, 1989.

Fitzgerald, Frances. "Women, Success, and Nancy Drew." *Vogue,* May 1980: 323–24.

"The Flap over Gay Literature for Children." *CQ Researcher* 3.7 (19 Feb. 1993): 151–52; 54.

Ford, Michael Thomas. "Gay Books for Young Readers: When Caution Calls the Shots." *Publishers Weekly* 241.8 (21 Feb. 1994): 24–27.

Foucault, Michel. "Of Other Spaces." *Diacritics* 16 (1986): 22–27.

——. "Questions on Geography." *Power/Knowledge: Selected Interviews and Other Writings, 1972–1977.* Ed. Colin Gordon. New York: Pantheon, 1980. 63–77.

Fox, Paula. *The Eagle Kite.* New York: Orchard, 1995.

Freeman, Donald. "La Prisonnière: An Account of Bourdet's Sensational Drama, Known to America as 'The Captive.'" *Vanity Fair* 27 (1926): 69; 154.

Freud, Sigmund. *Standard Edition of the Complete Psychological Works.* Ed. and trans. James Strachey. London: Hogarth, 1953–74; New York: Macmillan.

——. "Psychogenesis of a Case of Homosexuality in a Woman." 1920–22. In *Standard Edition* 18: 143–170.

——. "The Sexual Aberrations." *Three Essays on the Theory of Sexuality.* Ed. James Strachey. New York: Basic, 1962. 1–38.

——. "Three Essays on the Theory of Sexuality." 1905. In *Standard Edition* 7: 125–246.

——. "The Transformations of Puberty." 1916. *Three Essays on the Theory of Sexuality.* Ed. James Strachey. New York: Basic, 1962. 73–96.

Friedli, Lynne. "'Passing Women': A Study of Gender Boundaries in the Eighteenth Century." *Sexual Underworlds of the Enlightenment.* Ed. G. S. Rousseau and Roy Porter. Chapel Hill: U of North Carolina P, 1988. 234–60.

Frye, Marilyn. "The Possibility of Lesbian Community." *Lesbian Ethics* 4.1 (1990): 84–87.

——. "To See and Be Seen: The Politics of Reality." *Women, Knowledge, and Reality: Explorations in Feminist Philosophy.* Ed. Ann Garry and Marilyn Pearsall. Boston: Unwin Hyman, 1989. 77–92.

Fuoss, Kirk. "A Portrait of the Adolescent as a Young Gay: The Politics of Male

Homosexuality in Young Adult Fiction. *Queer Words, Queer Images: Communication and the Construction of Homosexuality.* Ed. R. Jeffrey Ringer. New York: New York UP, 1994. 159–74.

Furtak, Joanne. "Of Clues, Kisses, and Childhood Memories: Nancy Drew Revisited." *Seventeen,* May 1984: 90.

Futcher, Jane. *Crush.* Boston: Little, Brown, 1981.

Gallagher, Winifred. *The Power of Place: How Our Surroundings Shape Our Thoughts, Emotions, and Actions.* New York: Poseidon, 1993.

Garber, Marjorie. *Vested Interests: Cross-Dressing & Cultural Anxiety.* New York: Routledge, 1992.

Garden, Nancy. *Annie on My Mind.* New York: Farrar, Straus and Giroux, 1982.

——. "Banned: Lesbian and Gay Kids' Books under Fire." *Lambda Book Report* 4.7 (Nov. 1994): 11–13.

——. "Dick and Jane Grow Up Gay: The Importance of (Gay) Young Adult Fiction." *Lambda Book Report* 3.7 (Nov. 1992): 7–10.

——. *Lark in the Morning.* New York: Farrar, Straus and Giroux, 1991.

Gastil, Raymond D. "Cultural Regions of America." *Making America: The Society and Culture of the United States.* Ed. Luther S. Luedtke. Chapel Hill: U of North Carolina P, 1992. 129–43.

Gerrard, Susan, and James Halpin. "The Risky Business of Bisexual Love." *Cosmopolitan,* Oct. 1989: 203–5.

Girls Series Books: A Checklist of Hardback Books Published 1900–1975. Minneapolis: U of Minnesota, Children's Literature Research Collections, 1978.

Godwin, Mary Jo. "Conservative Groups Continue Their Fight to Ban *Daddy's Roommate.*" *American Libraries* 23.11 (Dec. 1992): 917; 968.

Goodsell, Willystine. *The Education of Women: Its Social Background and Its Problems.* New York: Macmillan, 1923.

Goodwin, Joseph P. *More Man Than You'll Ever Be: Gay Folklore and Acculturation in Middle America.* Bloomington: Indiana UP, 1989.

Gould, Robert E. "Understanding Homosexuality." *Seventeen* 28 (July 1969): 90–91; 128.

Grahn, Judy. *"Edward the Dyke" and Other Poems.* Oakland: Women's P Collective, 1971.

Greene, Bette. *The Drowning of Stephan Jones.* New York: Bantam, 1991.

Gregory, Derek. *Geographical Imaginations.* Cambridge: Blackwell, 1994.

Griffin, Gabriele. *Heavenly Love? Lesbian Images in Twentieth-Century Women's Writing.* Manchester: Manchester UP, 1993.

——, ed. *Outwrite: Lesbianism and Popular Culture.* London: Pluto, 1993.

Griggers, Cathy. "Lesbian Bodies in the Age of (Post)mechanical Reproduction." *Fear of a Queer Planet: Queer Politics and Social Theory.* Ed. Michael Warner. Minneapolis: U of Minnesota P, 1993. 178–92.

Grima, Tony, ed. *Not the Only One: Lesbian and Gay Fiction for Teens.* Boston: Alyson, 1994.

Groocock, Veronica. "Lesbian Journalism: Mainstream and Alternative Press." *Daring to Dissent: Lesbian Culture from Margin to Mainstream.* Ed. Liz Gibbs. New York: Cassell, 1994. 91–119.

Gross, Amy. "If Lesbians Make You Nervous . . ." *Mademoiselle* 84 (Feb. 1978): 126–27; 183–84.

Gubar, Susan. " 'The Blank Page' and Issues of Female Creativity." *Critical Inquiry* 8 (1981): 243–63.

Guy, Rosa. *Ruby.* New York: Viking, 1976.

Gwynne, H. A. *The Cause of World Unrest.* New York: Putnam's, 1920.

Haizlip, Shirlee Taylor. "Passing." *American Heritage* 46.1 (1995): 46–54.

Hale, Nathan. *Freud and the Americans: The Beginnings of Psychoanalysis in the United States, 1876–1917.* New York: Oxford UP, 1971.

Hall, Lynn. *Sticks and Stones.* Chicago: Follett, 1972.

Hall, Radclyffe. *The Well of Loneliness.* 1928. New York: Avon, 1981.

Hamer, Diana, and Belinda Budge, eds. *The Good, the Bad and the Gorgeous: Popular Culture's Romance with Lesbianism.* San Francisco: Pandora, 1994.

Hanckel, Frances, and John Cunningham. "Can Young Gays Find Happiness in YA Books?" *Wilson Library Bulletin* 50 (Mar. 1976): 528–34.

Hanson, Susan, and Geraldine Pratt. *Gender, Work, and Space.* New York, Routledge, 1995.

Harrington, Linda. "What a Woman Taught Me about Love." *Cosmopolitan* 194.3 (Apr. 1983): 98; 104; 108–9; 112.

Harris, Elise. "Women in Love." *Mademoiselle* 99 (Mar. 1993): 180–83; 208.

Hart, Lynda. *Fatal Women: Lesbian Sexuality and the Mark of Aggression.* Princeton: Princeton UP, 1994.

Hatfield, Sarah. "Why Is Grandma Different?" *Ladies' Home Journal* 102 (Jan. 1985): 18; 20; 140.

Hautzig, Deborah. *Hey, Dollface.* New York: Greenwillow, 1978.

Hay, Ralph. "Mannish Women or Old Maids?" *Know Yourself* 1 (July 1938): 75–81.

Hayden, Dolores. *Redesigning the American Dream: The Future of Housing, Work, and Family Life.* New York: Norton, 1984.

Hebdige, Dick. *Subculture: The Meaning of Style.* New York: Methuen, 1979.

——. "Subjects in Space." *New Formations* 11 (1990): v–x.

Hellman, Lillian. *The Children's Hour.* New York: Knopf, 1934.

Herdt, Gilbert, and Andrew Boxer. *Children of Horizons: How Gay and Lesbian Teens Are Leading a New Way out of the Closet.* Boston: Beacon, 1996.

Heron, Ann, ed. *Two Teenagers in Twenty: Writings by Gay and Lesbian Youth.* Boston: Alyson, 1994.

Heron, Ann, and Meredith Maran. *How Would You Feel If Your Dad Was Gay?* Boston: Alyson Wonderland, 1991.

Herrmann, Anne. "'Passing' Women, Performing Men." *Michigan Quarterly Review* 30.1 (1991): 60–71.

——. "Travesty and Transgression: Transvestism in Shakespeare, Brecht, and Churchill." *Performing Feminisms: Feminist Critical Theory and Theatre.* Ed. Sue-Ellen Case. Baltimore: Johns Hopkins UP, 1990. 294–315.

Hill, Carol Denny. *Wild.* New York: Day, 1927.

Hirsch, James. "Nancy Drew Gets Real." *New York Times Book Review,* 9 Oct. 1988: 47.

Hobson, Sarah. *Through Persia in Disguise.* London: Murray, 1973.

Holland, Isabelle. *The Man without a Face.* New York: Lippincott, 1972.

Hollibaugh, Amber, and Cherríe Moraga. "What We're Rollin' Around in Bed With: Sexual Silences in Feminism." *Powers of Desire: The Politics of Sexuality.* Ed. Ann Snitow, Christine Stansell, and Sharon Thompson. New York: Monthly Review P, 1983. 394–405.

Hollindale, Peter. "Ideology and the Children's Book." *Signal* 55 (Jan. 1988): 3–22.

Holmlund, Christine. "When Is a Lesbian Not a Lesbian? The Lesbian Continuum and the Mainstream Femme Film" *Camera Obscura* 25 (1991): 145–79.

Horowitz, Helen Lefkowitz. *Alma Mater: Design and Experience in the Women's Colleges from Their Nineteenth-Century Beginnings to the 1930s.* New York: Knopf, 1984.

Hunt, Peter. *Criticism, Theory, and Children's Literature.* Cambridge: Blackwell, 1991.

——. *An Introduction to Children's Literature.* New York: Oxford UP, 1994.

Inness, Julie. "Passing in *Europa, Europa:* Escape into Estrangement." *Philosophy and Film.* Ed. Cynthia A. Freeland and Thomas E. Wartenberg. New York: Routledge, 1995. 218–32.

Inness, Sherrie A. "Girls Will Be Boys and Boys Will Be Girls: Cross-Dressing in Popular Turn-of-the-Century College Fiction." *Journal of American Culture* 18.2 (1995): 15–23.

——. *Intimate Communities: Representation and Social Transformation in Women's College Fiction, 1895–1910.* Bowling Green: Bowling Green Popular P, 1995.

——. "Mashes, Smashes, Crushes, & Raves: Woman-to-Woman Relationships in Popular Women's College Fiction, 1895–1915." *NWSA Journal* 6.1 (1994): 46–68.

——. "On the Road and in the Air: Gender and Technology in Girls' Automobile and Airplane Serials, 1909–1932." *Journal of Popular Culture* 30.2 (1996): 47–60.

Jackson, John Brinckerhoff. *A Sense of Place, a Sense of Time.* New Haven: Yale UP, 1994.

Jagose, Annamarie. *Lesbian Utopics.* New York: Routledge, 1994.

Jakobson, Cathryn. "Standing Up, Speaking Out, Fighting Back." *Seventeen* 52 (Oct. 1993): 134–37; 153.

Jeffreys, Sheila. "Butch & Femme: Now and Then." *Not a Passing Phase: Reclaiming Lesbians in History, 1840–1985.* Ed. Lesbian History Group. London: Women's P, 1989. 158–87.

Jenkins, Christine. "Heartthrobs and Heartbreaks: A Guide to Young Adult Books with Gay Themes." *Out/Look* 1 (Fall 1988): 82–92.

Johnson, Deidre. *Edward Stratemeyer and the Stratemeyer Syndicate.* New York: Twayne, 1993.

Johnston, Jill. *Lesbian Nation: The Feminist Solution.* New York: Simon and Schuster, 1973.

Jones, James P. "Nancy Drew, WASP Super Girl of the 1930's." *Journal of Popular Culture* 6.4 (1973): 707–17.

Jordan, MaryKate. *Losing Uncle Tim.* Morton Grove, Ill.: Whitman, 1989.

Jung, C. G. "The Love Problem in the Student." *The Sex Problem in Modern Society.* Ed. John Francis McDermott. New York: Modern Library, 1931. 327–47.

Kaplan, Esther. "All Dressed Up, No Place to Go?" *Village Voice* 34.26 (27 June 1989): 29; 36.

Katz, Jonathan. *Gay American History: Lesbians and Gay Men in the U.S.A.* New York: Crowell, 1976.

Keene, Carolyn [pseud.]. *The Secret of the Old Clock.* 1930. New York: Grosset, 1959.

——. *The Bungalow Mystery.* 1930. New York: Grosset, 1960.

——. *The Mystery at Lilac Inn.* 1930. New York: Grosset, 1961.

——. *The Secret of Shadow Ranch.* 1930. New York: Grosset, 1965.

——. *The Secret of Red Gate Farm.* New York: Grosset, 1931.

——. *The Clue in the Diary.* New York: Grosset, 1932.

——. *Nancy's Mysterious Letter.* New York: Grosset, 1932.

——. *The Sign of the Twisted Candles.* 1932. New York: Grosset, 1933.

——. *The Password to Larkspur Lane.* 1932. New York: Grosset, 1966.

——. *The Mystery of the Ivory Charm.* 1936. New York: Grosset, 1974.

——. *The Clue of the Tapping Heels.* New York: Grosset, 1939.

——. *The Quest of the Missing Map.* 1942. New York: Grosset, 1943.

——. *The Secret in the Old Attic.* New York: Grosset, 1944.

——. *The Clue of the Leaning Chimney.* 1949. New York: Grosset, 1967.

——. *The Secret of the Wooden Lady.* 1950. New York: Grosset, 1967.

——. *The Clue of the Black Keys.* 1951. New York: Grosset, 1968.

——. *The Clue of the Velvet Mask.* 1953. New York: Grosset, 1969.

——. *The Ringmaster's Secret*. New York: Grosset, 1953.

——. *The Witch Tree Symbol*. 1955. New York: Grosset, 1975.

——. *The Hidden Window Mystery*. 1956. New York: Grosset, 1975.

——. *The Haunted Showboat*. New York: Grosset, 1957.

——. *The Mystery of the Fire Dragon*. New York: Grosset, 1961.

——. *The Clue of the Dancing Puppet*. New York: Grosset, 1962.

——. *The Moonstone Castle Mystery*. New York: Grosset, 1963.

——. *The Clue of the Whistling Bagpipes*. New York: Grosset, 1964.

——. *The Clue in the Crossword Cipher*. New York: Grosset, 1967.

——. *The Spider Sapphire Mystery*. New York: Grosset, 1968.

——. *The Case of the Disappearing Diamonds*. New York: Simon and Schuster, 1987.

——. *The Ghost of Craven Cove*. New York: Simon and Schuster, 1989.

——. *The Mystery of the Missing Millionairess*. New York: Simon and Schuster, 1991.

——. *The Legend of Miner's Creek*. New York: Simon and Schuster, 1992.

Keith, Michael, and Steve Pile, eds. *Place and the Politics of Identity*. New York: Routledge, 1993.

Kelley, Kitty. "I Married a Homosexual." *Cosmopolitan* 183 (Nov. 1977): 190; 192; 194–96.

Kennard, Jean E. "Ourself behind Ourself: A Theory for Lesbian Readers." *Signs* 9.4 (1984): 647–62.

Kennedy, Elizabeth Lapovsky, and Madeline Davis. *Boots of Leather, Slippers of Gold: The History of a Lesbian Community*. New York: Routledge, 1993.

——. "The Reproduction of Butch-Fem Roles: A Social Constructionist Approach." *Passion and Power: Sexuality in History*. Ed. Kathy Peiss and Christina Simmons. Philadelphia: Temple UP, 1989. 241–56.

——. "'They Was No One to Mess With': The Construction of the Butch Role in the Lesbian Community of the 1940s and 1950s." *The Persistent Desire: A Femme-Butch Reader*. Ed. Joan Nestle. Boston: Alyson, 1992. 62–79.

Kerr, M. E. *Deliver Us from Evie*. New York: HarperCollins, 1994.

——. *I'll Love You When You're More like Me*. New York: Harper and Row, 1977.

——. *Nightkites*. New York: Harper, 1986.

Kielwasser, Alfred P., and Michelle A. Wolf. "Mainstream Television, Adolescent Homosexuality, and Significant Silence." *Critical Studies in Mass Communication* 9.4 (1992): 350–73.

Kimmelman, Marsha. "I Had a Lesbian Lover." *Cosmopolitan* 191 (July 1981): 84; 86.

Klein, Norma. *Breaking Up*. New York: Pantheon, 1980.

——. *My Life as a Body*. New York: Knopf, 1987.

Knopf, Olga. *Women on Their Own*. Boston: Little, 1935.

Koertge, Ron. *The Arizona Kid*. Boston: Little, Brown, 1988.

Krafft-Ebing, Richard von. *Psychopathia Sexualis: A Medico-Forensic Study*. 1886. New York: Stein and Day, 1965.

Krieger, Susan. *The Mirror Dance: Identity in a Woman's Community*. Philadelphia: Temple UP, 1983.

Lamos, Colleen. "The Postmodern Lesbian Position: *On Our Backs*." *The Lesbian Postmodern*. Ed. Laura Doan. New York: Columbia UP, 1994. 85–103.

Laner, Mary Riege, and Roy H. Laner. "Sexual Preference or Personal Style? Why Lesbians Are Disliked." *Journal of Homosexuality* 5 (1980): 339–56.

Lapin, Geoffrey S. "The Ghost of Nancy Drew." *Books at Iowa* 50 (Apr. 1989): 8–27.

Lapsley, Mary. *The Parable of the Virgins*. New York: Smith, 1931.

Larsen, Nella. *Passing*. 1929. New Brunswick: Rutgers, UP, 1986.

——. *Quicksand*. 1928. New Brunswick: Rutgers UP, 1986.

Lathbury, Vincent T. "Mothers and Sons: An Intimate Discussion." *Ladies' Home Journal* 82 (Feb. 1965): 43–45.

Lee, Janet. "Care to Join Me in an Upwardly Mobile Tango? Postmodernism and the 'New Woman.'" *The Female Gaze: Women as Viewers of Popular Culture*. Ed. Lorraine Gamman and Margaret Marshment. Seattle: Real Comet, 1989. 166–72.

L'Engle, Madeleine. *A House like a Lotus*. New York: Farrar, Straus and Giroux, 1984.

Lesselier, Claudie. "Social Categorizations and Construction of a Lesbian Subject." Trans. Mary Jo Lakeland. *Feminist Issues* 7 (Spring 1987): 89–94.

Levy, Elizabeth. *Come Out Smiling*. New York: Delacorte, 1981.

Lloyd, Michele. "Barbie." *Decline of Civilization* 10 (Dec. 1994): n.p.

Lockard, Denyse. "The Lesbian Community: An Anthropological Approach." *Journal of Homosexuality* 11.3–4 (1985): 83–95.

Lorde, Audre. *Zami, a New Spelling of My Name*. Freedom, Calif.: Crossing, 1982.

Louis, Valerie. "What It's Like to Be a Gay Woman Now." *Cosmopolitan* 206.3 (Mar. 1989): 228–31.

Loulan, JoAnn. *The Lesbian Erotic Dance: Butch, Femme, Androgyny, and Other Rhythms*. San Francisco: Spinsters, 1990.

Lugones, María. "Playfulness, 'World'-Traveling, and Loving Perception." *Women, Knowledge, and Reality: Explorations in Feminist Philosophy*. Ed. Ann Garry and Marilyn Pearsall. Boston: Unwin Hyman, 1989. 275–90.

Lyle, Candace. "Lesbian Life Style." *Cosmopolitan* 193.4 (Oct. 1982): 232–35; 281–83.

Lynch, Lee. *Toothpick House.* Tallahassee: Naiad, 1983.

Macdougall, Allan Ross, ed. *Letters of Edna St. Vincent Millay.* Westport, Conn.: Greenwood, 1972.

MacLeod, Anne Scott. "Nancy Drew and Her Rivals: No Contest." *Horn Book* 63 (May–June 1987): 314–22.

Maney, Mabel. *The Case of the Not-So-Nice Nurse.* San Francisco: Cleis, 1993.

———. *The Case of the Good-for-Nothing Girlfriend.* San Francisco: Cleis, 1994.

———. *Nancy Clue and the Hardly Boys in a Ghost in the Closet.* San Francisco: Cleis, 1995.

Mariedaughter, Paula. "Too Butch for Straights, Too Femme for Dykes." *Lesbian Ethics* 2 (Spring 1986): 96–100.

Markusen, Ann. *Regions: The Economics and Politics of Territory.* Totowa, N.J.: Rowman and Littlefield, 1987.

Marshment, Margaret, and Julia Hallam. "From String of Knots to Orange Box: Lesbianism on Prime Time." *The Good, the Bad and the Gorgeous: Popular Culture's Romance with Lesbianism.* Ed. Diana Hamer and Belinda Budge. San Francisco: Pandora, 1994. 142–65.

Martin, Biddy. "Sexual Practice and Changing Lesbian Identities." *Destabilizing Theory: Contemporary Feminist Debates.* Ed. Michèle Barrett and Anne Phillips. Oxford: Polity, 1992. 93–119.

Mason, Bobbie Ann. *The Girl Sleuth: A Feminist Guide.* Old Westbury, N.Y.: Feminist, 1975.

McCarthy, Mary. *The Group.* 1954. New York: Harcourt, 1963.

McCracken, Ellen. *Decoding Women's Magazines from "Mademoiselle" to "Ms."* New York: St. Martin's, 1993.

———. "Demystifying *Cosmopolitan:* Five Critical Methods." *Journal of Popular Culture* 16.2 (1982): 30–42.

McMahon, Kathryn. "The *Cosmopolitan* Ideology and the Management of Desire." *Journal of Sex Research* 27.3 (1990): 381–96.

Mehren, Elizabeth. "Smith Faces Up to Its Reputation on Sexuality." *Los Angeles Times,* 19 Dec. 1991: E14.

Millay, Edna St. Vincent. *Collected Poems.* Ed. Norma Millay. New York: Harper, 1956.

Millay, Kathleen. *Against the Wall.* New York: Macaulay, 1929.

Miller, Isabel. *Patience and Sarah.* Originally titled *A Place for Us.* 1969. New York: Fawcett, 1976.

Miller, Merle. "Homosexual Husbands: What Wives Must Know." *Redbook* 144 (Apr. 1975): 74; 76–77; 178; 180; 182.

Miller, Neil. *In Search of Gay America: Women and Men in a Time of Change.* New York: Atlantic Monthly P, 1989.

Mitchell, Margaree King. *Uncle Jed's Barbershop*. New York: Simon and Schuster, 1993.

Modleski, Tania. *Loving with a Vengeance: Mass-Produced Fantasies for Women*. New York: Archon, 1982.

Morgan, Tracy. "Butch-Femme and the Politics of Identity." *Sisters, Sexperts, Queers: Beyond the Lesbian Nation*. Ed. Arlene Stein. New York: Plume, 1993. 35–46.

Mullins, Hilary. *The Cat Came Back*. Tallahassee: Naiad, 1993.

Murrow, Liza K. *Twelve Days in August*. New York: Holiday House, 1993.

Nancy Drew Issue. *The Lion and the Unicorn* 18.1 (June 1994).

Nardi, Peter M. "That's What Friends Are For: Friends as Family in the Gay and Lesbian Community." *Modern Homosexualities: Fragments of Lesbian and Gay Experience*. Ed. Ken Plummer. New York: Routledge, 1992. 108–20.

Naylor, Gloria. "A Message to Winston." *Essence* 13 (Nov. 1982): 78–85.

Neff, Wanda Fraiken. *We Sing Diana*. Boston: Houghton, 1928.

Nestle, Joan. "Butch-Fem Relationships. Sexual Courage in the 1950's." *Heresies: Sex Issue* 12 (1981): 21–24.

———. "The Fem Question." *Pleasure and Danger: Exploring Female Sexuality*. Ed. Carole S. Vance. Boston: Routledge, 1984. 232–41.

———. *A Restricted Country*. Ithaca: Firebrand, 1987.

———, ed. *The Persistent Desire: A Femme-Butch Reader*. Boston: Alyson, 1992.

Newman, Lesléa. *Gloria Goes to Gay Pride*. Boston: Alyson Wonderland, 1991.

———. *Heather Has Two Mommies*. Boston: Alyson Wonderland, 1989.

———, ed. *The Femme Mystique*. Boston: Alyson, 1995.

Newton, Esther. *Cherry Grove, Fire Island: Sixty Years in America's First Gay and Lesbian Town*. Boston: Beacon, 1993.

———. "The Mythic Mannish Lesbian: Radclyffe Hall and the New Woman." *Signs* 9.4 (1984): 557–75.

Nye, Russel. *The Unembarrassed Muse: The Popular Arts in America*. New York: Dial, 1970.

Olson, Kiki. "Women Who Have Lesbian Affairs." *Cosmopolitan*, May 1986: 192; 194; 196.

O'Rourke, Rebecca. *Reflecting on "The Well of Loneliness."* London: Routledge, 1989.

"The Parable of the Virgins." *New York Times*, 19 Apr. 1931: 6.

Parker, Alice. "Under the Covers: A Synesthesia of Desire (Lesbian Translations)." *Sexual Practice, Textual Theory: Lesbian Culture Criticism*. Ed. Susan J. Wolfe and Julia Penelope. Cambridge: Blackwell, 1993. 322–39.

Patton, Cindy. "Tremble, Hetero Swine!" *Fear of a Queer Planet: Queer Politics and Social Theory*. Ed. Michael Warner. Minneapolis: U of Minnesota P, 1993. 143–77.

Patton, Marion. *Dance on the Tortoise.* New York: Lincoln, 1930.

Paul, Lissa. "Enigma Variations: What Feminist Theory Knows about Children's Literature." *Children's Literature: The Development of Criticism.* Ed. Peter Hunt. New York: Routledge, 1990. 148–65.

Penelope, Julia. *Call Me Lesbian: Lesbian Lives, Lesbian Theory.* Freedom, Calif.: Crossing, 1992.

——. "The Lesbian Perspective." *Lesbian Philosophies and Cultures.* Ed. Jeffner Allen. New York: State U of New York P, 1990. 89–108.

Phelan, Shane. "(Be)coming Out: Lesbian Identity and Politics." *Signs* 18.4 (1993): 765–90.

——. *Getting Specific: Postmodern Lesbian Politics.* Minneapolis: U of Minnesota P, 1994.

Pinkney, Gloria Jean. *The Sunday Outing.* New York: Dial, 1994.

Piper, Adrian. "Passing for White, Passing for Black." *New Feminist Criticism: Art, Identity, Action.* Ed. Joanna Freuh, Cassandra L. Langer, and Arlene Raven. New York: IconEditions, 1994. 216–47.

Plath, Sylvia. *The Bell Jar.* New York: Bantam, 1971.

Plunkett-Powell, Karen. *The Nancy Drew Scrapbook.* New York: St. Martin's, 1993.

Podolsky, Edward. "'Homosexual Love' in Women." *Popular Medicine* 1 (1935): 373–76.

Podrygula, Susan. "Censorship in an Academic Library." *College & Research Libraries News* 55.2 (1994): 76–78; 83.

Polacco, Patricia. *Chicken Sunday.* New York: Philomel, 1992.

Polikoff, Nancy D. "Lesbian Mothers, Lesbian Families: Legal Obstacles, Legal Challenges." *Lesbians and Child Custody: A Casebook.* Ed. Dolores J. Maggiore. New York: Garland, 1992. 229–37.

Pollack, Rachel, and Cheryl Schwartz. *The Journey Out: A Guide for and about Lesbian, Gay, and Bisexual Teens.* New York: Puffin, 1995.

Ponse, Barbara. *Identities in the Lesbian World: The Social Construction of Self.* Westport, Conn.: Greenwood, 1978.

Potter, La Forest. "Strange Loves: A Study in Sexual Abnormalities." 1933. *Gay American History.* Ed. Jonathan Katz. New York: Crowell, 1976. 162–64.

"Public Opinion." *Smith College Weekly* 2.11 (6 Dec. 1911): 4.

Rainer, Peter. "Why Heterosexual Males Feel Threatened by Gays." *Mademoiselle* 86 (Jan. 1980): 16; 18.

Rand, Erica. *Barbie's Queer Accessories.* Durham: Duke UP, 1995.

——. "Lesbian Sightings: Scoping for Dykes in Boucher and *Cosmo.*" *Journal of Homosexuality* 27.1–2 (1994): 123–39.

——. "We Girls Can Do Anything, Right Barbie? Lesbian Consumption in

Postmodern Circulation." *The Lesbian Postmodern*. Ed. Laura Doan. New York: Columbia UP, 1994. 189–209.

Rayn, Jay. *Butch*. Boston: Free Women P, 1991.

———. *Butch II*. Boston: Alyson, 1993.

Reading, J. P. *Bouquets for Brimbal*. New York: Harper, 1980.

"Regiment of Women." *New York Times*, 4 Feb. 1917: 33.

Rich, Adrienne. "Compulsory Heterosexuality and Lesbian Existence." *Adrienne Rich's Poetry and Prose*. Ed. Barbara C. Gelpi and Albert Gelpi. New York: Norton, 1993. 203–24.

Richards, Connie. "Nancy Drew: Gothic or Romance?" *Feminisms* 3.5 (1 Sept. 1990): 18–21.

Ringgold, Faith. *Tar Beach*. New York: Crown, 1991.

Robinson, Amy. "It Takes One to Know One: Passing and Communities of Common Interest." *Critical Inquiry* 20.4 (1994): 715–36.

Roche, B. J. "Making History." *Boston Globe Magazine*, 3 Sept. 1995: 18; 27–33.

Roiphe, Anne. "Who's Afraid of Lesbian Sex?" *Vogue*, Aug. 1977: 150–51; 196; 198.

Romalov, Nancy Tillman. "Mobile Heroines: Early Twentieth-Century Girls' Automobile Series." *Journal of Popular Culture* 28.4 (1995): 231–43.

Roof, Judith. *A Lure of Knowledge: Lesbian Sexuality and Theory*. New York: Columbia UP, 1991.

Rose, Gillian. *Feminism and Geography: The Limits of Geographical Knowledge*. Minneapolis: U of Minnesota P, 1993.

Ross, Catherine Sheldrick: " 'If They Read Nancy Drew, So What?': Series Book Readers Talk Back." *Library and Information Science Research* 17.3 (1995): 201–36.

Rubin, Gayle. "Of Catamites and Kings: Reflections on Butch, Gender, and Boundaries." *The Persistent Desire: A Femme-Butch Reader*. Ed. Joan Nestle. Boston: Alyson, 1992. 466–82.

Ruehl, Sonja. "Inverts and Experts: Radclyffe Hall and the Lesbian Identity." *Feminism, Culture, and Politics*. Ed. Rosalind Brunt and Caroline Rowan. London: Lawrence, 1982. 15–36.

Ruff, Patricia Elam. "Cover Girls." *Essence* 22.11 (1992): 68–69; 106; 109.

Russ, Joanna. *The Female Man*. Boston: Beacon, 1975.

Sadowski, Michael J. "In Biggest School Challenge, *Daddy's Roommate* Is Staying." *School Library Journal* 40.1 (1994): 11–12.

St. George, Judith. *Call Me Margo*. New York: Putnam's, 1981.

Salat, Christina. *Living in Secret*. New York: Yearling, 1993.

Salter, Stephanie. "My Two Moms." *Redbook* 179.1 (May 1992): 64; 66; 70.

SAMOIS, ed. *Coming to Power: Writings and Graphics on Lesbian S/M*. San Francisco: SAMOIS, 1981.

San Francisco Lesbian and Gay History Project. " 'She Even Chewed Tobacco':
    A Pictorial Narrative of Passing Women in America." *Hidden from
    History: Reclaiming the Gay and Lesbian Past.* Ed. Martin Duberman,
    Martha Vicinus, and George Chauncey, Jr. New York: New American
    Library, 1989. 183–94.

Savin-Williams, Ritch C. *Gay and Lesbian Youth: Expressions of Identity.* New
    York: Hemisphere, 1990.

Say, Allen. *Grandfather's Journey.* Boston: Houghton Mifflin, 1993.

Schama, Simon. *Landscape and Memory.* New York: Knopf, 1995.

Schmalhausen, S. D. "The Freudian Emphasis on Sex." 1928. *The Sex Problem
    in Modern Society.* Ed. John Francis McDermott. New York: Modern
    Library, 1931. 50–70.

Scoppettone, Sandra. *Happy Endings Are All Alike.* New York: Harper and Row,
    1978.

———. *Trying Hard to Hear You.* 1974. New York: Harper and Row, 1981.

Sears, James T. "The Impact of Gender and Race on Growing Up Lesbian and
    Gay in the South." *NWSA Journal* 1.3 (1989): 422–57.

Sedgwick, Eve Kosofsky. *Epistemology of the Closet.* Berkeley: U of California
    P, 1990.

Seidman, Steven. "Identity and Politics in a 'Postmodern' Gay Culture: Some
    Historical and Conceptual Notes." *Fear of a Queer Planet: Queer Politics
    and Social Theory.* Ed. Michael Warner. Minneapolis: U of Minnesota P,
    1993. 105–42.

Simmons, Christina. "Companionate Marriage and the Lesbian Threat." *Fron-
    tiers* 4 (1979): 54–59.

Singer, Bennett L., ed. *Growing Up Gay: A Literary Anthology.* New York: New
    P, 1993.

Singer, Marilyn. *The Course of True Love Never Did Run Smooth.* New York:
    Harper and Row, 1983.

Slesinger, Tess. "The Answer on the Magnolia Tree." *On Being Told That Her
    Second Husband Has Taken His First Love and Other Stories.* 1935.
    Chicago: Quadrangle, 1971.

Sloan, Louise. "Do Ask, Do Tell: Lesbians Come Out at Work." *Glamour* 92.5
    (May 1994): 242–43; 291–95.

Smith, Nadine. "Homophobia: Will It Divide Us?" *Essence,* 25.2 (1994): 128.

Smith-Rosenberg, Carroll. "The Female World of Love and Ritual: Rela-
    tionships between Women in Nineteenth-Century America." *Signs* 1
    (1975): 19–27.

———. "The New Woman as Androgyne." *Disorderly Conduct: Visions of Gender
    in Victorian America.* New York: Knopf, 1985. 245–96.

Soderbergh, Peter A. "The Stratemeyer Strain: Educators and the Juvenile Series Book, 1900–1973." *Journal of Popular Culture* 7 (1974): 864–72.

Soja, Edward H. *Postmodern Geographies: The Reassertion of Space in Critical Social Theory.* New York: Verso, 1989.

Solomon, Alisa. "Not Just a Passing Fancy: Notes on Butch." *Theater* 24.2 (1993): 35–46.

———. "Rites of Passing." *Village Voice* 36.45 (5 Nov. 1991): 46.

———. "That *Cosmo* Dyke." *Village Voice* 38.51 (21 Dec. 1993): 24.

Solomon, Barbara Miller. *In the Company of Educated Women.* New Haven: Yale UP, 1985.

Soto, Gary. *Too Many Tamales.* New York: Putnam's, 1993.

Stein, Arlene. "All Dressed Up, but No Place to Go? Style Wars and the New Lesbianism." *Out/Look* 1.4 (1989): 34–42.

Stekel, Wilhelm. *The Homosexual Neurosis.* 1922. New York: Emerson, 1944.

Stimpson, Catharine R. "Zero Degree Deviancy: The Lesbian Novel in English." *Critical Inquiry* 8.2 (1981): 363–79.

"Story of a Tragic Marriage." *Good Housekeeping* 167 (July 1968): 36; 38; 40; 42; 44; 46.

Straub, Kristina. "The Guilty Pleasures of Female Theatrical Cross-Dressing and the Autobiography of Charlotte Charke." *Body Guards: The Cultural Politics of Gender Ambiguity.* Ed. Julia Epstein and Kristina Straub. New York: Routledge, 1991. 142–66.

Sullivan, Mary W. *What's This about Pete?* Nashville: Nelson, 1976.

Sutherland, Robert D. "Hidden Persuaders: Political Ideologies in Literature for Children." *Children's Literature in Education* 16.3 (1985): 143–57.

Sutton, Roger. *Hearing Us Out: Voices from the Gay and Lesbian Community.* Boston: Little, Brown, 1994.

Taylor, Alice. "Women in Love: Straight Talk from a Gay Woman." *Mademoiselle* 84 (Feb. 1987): 124–26; 181–83.

Thomas, Joyce Carol. *Brown Honey in Broomwheat Tea.* New York: HarperCollins, 1993.

Thomas, Trish. "Straight People Call Me Sir." *Quim* 3 (Winter 1991): 21–25.

Trebilcot, Joyce. *Dyke Ideas: Process, Politics, Daily Life.* Albany: State U of New York P, 1994.

Unks, Gerald, ed. *The Gay Teen: Educational Practice and Theory for Lesbian, Gay, and Bisexual Adolescents.* New York: Routledge, 1995.

Valentine, Gill. "Toward a Geography of the Lesbian Community." *Women and Environments* 14.1 (1994): 8–10.

Valentine, Johnny. *The Daddy Machine.* Boston: Alyson Wonderland, 1992.

Vaughan, David K. "On the Road to Adventure: The Automobile and American Juvenile Series Fiction, 1900–1940." *Roadside America: The Automobile in Design and Culture.* Ed. Jan Jennings. Ames: Iowa State UP, 1990. 74–81.

Vicinus, Martha. " 'They Wonder to Which Sex I Belong': The Historical Roots of the Modern Lesbian Identity." *Feminist Studies* 18.3 (1992): 467–97.

Vigna, Judith. *My Two Uncles.* Morton Grove, Ill.: Whitman, 1995.

Villarosa, Linda. "Coming Out." *Essence* 22.1 (1991): 82–84; 125.

——, ed. "Straight Women/Gay Men: A Talk between Friends." *Essence* 24.4 (1993): 62–63; 111–13.

Vivelo, Jackie. "The Mystery of Nancy Drew." *Ms.* 3.3 (1992): 76–77.

Walker, Lisa M. "How to Recognize a Lesbian: The Cultural Politics of Looking like What You Are." *Signs* 18.4 (1993): 866–90.

Wall, Cheryl A. "Passing for What? Aspects of Identity in Nella Larsen's Novels." *Black American Literature Forum* 20.1–2 (1986): 97–111.

Wartik, Nancy. "Nancy Drew, Yuppie Detective." *Ms.*, Sept. 1986: 29.

Watson, Bruce. "Tom Swift, Nancy Drew, and Pals All Had the Same Dad." *Smithsonian* 22.7 (Oct. 1991): 50–61.

Weeks, Jeffrey. *Sex, Politics, and Society: The Regulation of Sexuality since 1800.* London: Longman, 1981.

Weems, Renita J. "Just Friends." *Essence* 20.1 (May 1989): 60–62; 136–37.

Weightman, Barbara. "Commentary: Towards a Geography of the Gay Community." *Journal of Cultural Geography* 1 (1981): 106–12.

Weiser, Carl. "Schools Censor More, Study Finds." *Cincinnati Enquirer,* 31 Aug. 1995, final ed.: A5.

"We Sing Diana." Times Lit. Sup., 11 Oct. 1928: 738.

West, Marian. "Women Who Have Passed as Men." *Munsey's Magazine* 25 (May 1901): 273–81.

Weston, Kath. "Do Clothes Make the Woman?: Gender Performance, Theory, and Lesbian Eroticism." *Genders* 17 (Fall 1993): 1–21.

——. *Families We Choose: Lesbians, Gays, Kinship.* New York: Columbia UP, 1991.

Wheelwright, Julie. *Amazons and Military Maids: Women Who Dressed as Men in the Pursuit of Life, Liberty, and Happiness.* London: Pandora, 1989.

"When Women Love Other Women: A Frank Discussion of Female Homosexuality." *Redbook* 138 (Nov. 1971): 84–85; 186; 188; 190–92; 194–95.

White, Edmund. *States of Desire: Travels in Gay America.* 1980. New York: Plume, 1991.

Whitlock, Gillian. " 'Everything Is out of Place': Radclyffe Hall and the Lesbian Literary Tradition." *Feminist Studies* 13 (1987): 555–82.

Wickens, Elaine. *Anna Day and the O-ring.* Boston: Alyson Wonderland, 1994.

Willhoite, Michael. *Daddy's Roommate.* Boston: Alyson Wonderland, 1990.

———. *Uncle What-Is-It Is Coming to Visit*. Boston: Alyson Wonderland, 1993.

Williams, Sherley Anne. *Working Cotton*. San Diego: Harcourt Brace Jovanovich, 1992.

Wilson, D. E. "The Open Library: YA Books for Gay Teens." *English Journal* 73 (Nov. 1984): 60–63.

Wilson, Elizabeth. "Deviant Dress." *Feminist Review* 35 (1990): 67–74.

Winship, Janice. *Inside Women's Magazines*. London: Pandora, 1987.

Winsloe, Christa. *Girls in Uniform*. Boston: Little, 1933.

Wittig, Monique. "One Is Not Born a Woman." *Feminist Issues* 1.1 (1980): 447–54.

Wolf, Deborah Goleman. *The Lesbian Community*. Berkeley: U of California P, 1979.

Wolf, Naomi. *The Beauty Myth: How Images of Beauty Are Used against Women*. New York: Morrow, 1991.

Wolf, Virginia L., ed. *Louise Fitzhugh*. New York: Twayne, 1991.

Wolfe, Maxine. "Invisible Women in Invisible Places: Lesbians, Lesbian Bars, and the Social Production of People/Environment Relationships." *Architecture and Behaviour* 8 (1992): 137–58.

Women and Geography Study Group of the Institute of British Geographers. *Geography and Gender: An Introduction to Feminist Geography*. London: Hutchinson, 1984.

Wood, Abigail. "Feminine Attractions." *Seventeen* 27 (Aug. 1968): 284; 322.

Woodson, Jacqueline. *The Dear One*. New York: Delacorte, 1991.

———. *From the Notebooks of Melanin Sun*. New York: Blue Sky, 1995.

Woolf, Virginia. *Orlando: A Biography*. New York: Harcourt, 1928.

Young, Francis Brett. *White Ladies*. London: Heinemann, 1935.

"Your Daughter: What Are Her Friendships?" *Harper's Bazaar* 47 (Oct. 1913): 16; 78.

Zacharias, Lee. "Nancy Drew, Ballbuster." *Journal of Popular Culture* 9 (1976): 1027–38.

Zana. "Nancy Drew and the Serial Rapist." *Common Lives/Lesbian Lives* 24 (Fall 1987): 4–19.

Zita, Jacquelyn N. "Male Lesbians and the Postmodernist Body." *Hypatia* 7.4 (1992): 106–27.

Zuckerman, Eileen Goudge. "Nancy Drew vs. Serious Fiction." *Publishers Weekly* 229.22 (30 May 1986): 74.

Index

Kraft-Ebing, Richard von, 16, 17,
18, 21–22, 35, 41, 97, 196,
208n. 18, 221n. 1

L'Engle, Madeleine, 116
Land of Look Behind, The (Cliff),
161
Laner, Mary, 190, 191
Laner, Roy, 190, 191
Lapsley, Mary, 38
Lark in the Morning (Garden), 122
Larsen, Nella, 163, 220n. 2
Lee, Janet, 53
Legend of Miner's Creek, The
(Keene), 98
"Lesbian Bodies in the Age of
(Post)mechanical Reproduc-
tion" (Griggers), 57
Lesbian body, 57–58
Lesbian Body, The (Wittig), 198
Lesbian Choices (Card), 162
"Lesbian Journalism: Mainstream
and Alternative Press"
(Groocock), 55
Lesbian Nation (Johnston), 155
Lesbian Perspective, 84
Lesbian reading strategies, 75, 81,
83, 207n. 9, 213n. 5
Lesbian Utopics (Jagose), 57
Lesbian, 224n. 11
appeal of Nancy Drew books,
88–89
categorizing the lesbian, 17
communal living, 139–40
construction of, 19
depiction in 1920s, 17–19, 21–
24, 36–37
description as unhappy women,
24, 208n. 18
identifying the, 22–23
lesbian/gay reading strategies, 83

"the look," 141
mannish lesbian, 32, 224n. 13
marginalization of, 8–9
medical description in the 1920s,
20
perspective, 6
pre-World War II beliefs about,
21
readings of Nancy Drew, 80
"reality" of, 3
representation of, 19, 31, 56–57
representation of, in children's
literature, 103–4
shaping lesbian identities, 75–76
stereotypical image, 32
textual representation, 6
Lesbianism
in children's novels, 111–15
connection between image of lesbian in magazines and in society, 59–60, 212n. 7
fear of, 36, 209–10n. 10
as popular topic in magazines,
60–61, 211n. 4, 211–12n. 5
perceived increase in 1920s and
1930s, 36
as signifier in the 1920s, 36–37
Lesbians
as consumers, 67
"lipstick" lesbians, 73–74
Lesselier, Claudie, 149
Levy, Elizabeth, 113
Living in Secret (Salat), 122
Lloyd, Michele, 138–39
Long Secret, The (Fitzhugh), 102
Lorde, Audre, 222n. 1
Loulan, JoAnn, 179, 197, 223n. 7
*Love in the Machine Age: A Psycho-
logical Study of the Transition
from Patriarchal Society* (Dell),
210n. 11